Solitary Song

Solitary Song

PAULINE KONER

Duke University Press   Durham and London   1989

Portions of "With Doris Humphrey" appeared as "Working with Doris Humphrey" in *Dance Chronicle*, vol. 7, no. 3, 1984–85, and "The Truth About *The Moor's Pavane*," in *Ballet Review*, vol. 5, no. 4, 1980. Permission to reprint from the following sources is gratefully acknowledged. *The New York Times*: Reviews by John Martin. Copyright © 1930/47/48/51/53/55/62 by The New York Times Company. Reprinted by permission. The *New York Post*: Reviews by Earl Wilson and Clive Barnes. Copyright 1939/79. *Dance Magazine*: Reviews by Doris Hering. Copyright 1952/76. *The Juilliard Review*: Norman Lloyd, "Composing for Dance." Reprinted with permission from *The Juilliard Review*, Spring 1961. *Saturday Review*: Review by Norma Stahl, 1955. Reprinted by permission. *The New York Herald Tribune*: Review by Walter Terry, 1953. I.H.T. Corporation. Reprinted by permission. *The Providence Sunday Journal*: Review by Walter Sorrell, 1963. Reprinted by permission. *The Village Voice*: Review by Deborah Jowitt, 1981. Reprinted by permission. Letters of José Limón by permission of the José Limón Dance Foundation. Letters of John Martin by permission of Zachary Solov. Letter of Thomas Skelton by permission. Letter of Doris Humphrey by permission of Charles Woodford. Every effort has been made to trace ownership of copyrighted material. If errors or omissions have occurred, they will be corrected in subsequent editions upon notification in writing to the publisher.
Library of Congress Cataloging-in-Publication Data appear on the last printed page.

For my family

IDA KONER   SAMUEL KONER   MARVIN KONER

Standing at the edge of Nowhere
I look into the Somewhere
And wonder

Standing at the edge of Somewhere
I look into the Nowhere
And wonder

P.K.

Contents

Acknowledgments

Writing this book meant searching to revive old memories. I am deeply grateful to the many who helped me in that search.

I am grateful to Doris Hering for her critical advice and encouragement, and for listening to my stories, which became vividly alive as I verbalized them.

I am grateful to Barbara Palfy for her sensitivity in the final editing, to Monica Moseley for her preliminary editing, and to Andrew Wentink who typed eight hundred pages of handwritten manuscript.

I am grateful to Phyllis Fokine, Kohana Wiles, Lisan Kay, Saeko Ichinohe, Satoru Shimazaki, Charles H. Woodford, and Helen Caldwell for their help in tracing details and contributing pictures and translations.

I am grateful to Al Pischl for initially commissioning me to write this book.

I am grateful to my sister-in-law, Silvia Koner, and my friend Anna Shenderoff for being objective when I needed an outside eye.

Prologue

There was always music in our home. In the early years of their marriage, when money was very scarce, my parents still managed to have an old upright piano in the dining room of their apartment. Mother played children's songs for me, and we sang them together. She had a lovely voice.

My parents, Samuel Koner and Ida Ginsberg, were born in Russia. My father came from Odessa, the son of a poor tailor, and my mother from Byelorussia. Dad often regaled us with hair-raising stories of how he stole out of his barricaded home to shoot at the cossacks during their wild raids on Jews. But he managed to achieve a *gymnazia* education (an academic curriculum that finishes slightly higher than our high school), subsidized by a wealthy Gentile family whose children he tutored. Mother, whose father was an innkeeper, had the limited education allotted to all girls at that time.

In 1905 the pogroms rose to a peak of violence, forcing mass emigration. My parents' families were among those who left for America. As for all immigrants, things were hard. Dad, whose heart was set on law school, took any job he could find. Mother sewed in a sweatshop.

They met by chance one evening at an amateur theater club and were married in 1910. I was born on June 26, 1912.

Mom said I danced from the moment I could walk. I made my "debut" at the ripe old age of four to the accompaniment of an organ grinder on a New York street. He was playing a tarantella. I stamped and twirled my full skirt for a ring of people who seemed to enjoy it so much that they applauded and threw pennies, much to the delight of the organ grinder. I was not interested in the audience. I was dancing simply because I loved it.

Dad worked all day, went to law school in the evening, and studied at night. One of my earliest memories is of waking up late at night and seeing him bent over his heavy law books spread out on our oak dining table. Usually he had fallen asleep, and the light from the stained-glass shade above shone on his balding head. What a proud little girl I was as I watched him receive his degree from New York University. Mom had helped by renting a room in our tiny Bronx apartment to a friend and taking in sewing. She, too, went to night school to further her education.

Although we were Jewish, I received no formal religious training. My parents were "liberated Americans"—socialists. I loved visiting my grandparents on New York's Lower East Side. Grandpa took me to synagogue on Simchas Torah (a celebration of the cycle of reading and rereading the scrolls of Jewish law). I remember a radiant ritual of men marching with Torahs covered in silver- and gold-embroidered velvet. The children carried brightly colored paper flags topped by apples with lighted candles. To me it was all wondrous theater. I never knew the religious significance, but I did (and still do) identify with being Jewish.

In 1918, Dad was completing his apprenticeship as a law clerk. Finances became so difficult that we had to move. We took an apartment in Coney Island, shared with two cousins and their families, where we had only one small bedroom to ourselves. I had to sleep on top of a trunk.

About that time the Workmen's Circle, a Jewish socialist and benevolent organization, approached Dad to create a medical plan for its members. At first he hesitated because practicing law meant so much to him. After discussing it with Mom, Dad decided to accept only if they would allow him to continue to practice law. They agreed. Dad pioneered a group medical plan that was the first socialized medicine in the United States.

With a secure income Dad bought a brick row house, with a small back garden, in Bensonhurst, Brooklyn, then a pleasant residential area. I grew up in that house. On rainy days my favorite pastime was to contrive costumes from whatever I could find and improvise stories that I danced and acted out with two girl friends. Sometimes we improvised an opera, singing away at the top of our voices all afternoon.

Most of all it was the dancing. When I was alone I danced for hours in front of our hall mirror. The sound of any music was enough to start me dancing. Family friends who saw my improvised performances said I had talent and should be trained. My mother took me to a local dancing teacher and then to the Alviene School, way up on West 72nd Street in Manhattan. It was a well-established school, with a small theater for recitals. I studied there for about a year.

I was eight-and-a-half years old when my brother was born. Times had changed. While I had been born at home on East 22nd Street, Marvin made his debut in a hospital and was brought home in our new automobile. What luxury! A new baby and a new car.

Our household, European in flavor, was warm and loving. Although Dad had a violent temper and was the man of the house, he could also be gentle and compassionate. As time went on, I depended on him more and more. Mom was more controlled. She listened to our problems and in her subtle way got Dad to follow her suggestions. Within, she was a strong woman, very progressive. She was one of the first to bob her hair, to the consternation of my grandparents.

Dad was the intellectual, Mom the artist. She was a vivacious, beautiful woman, with sparkling brown eyes. Her instinct for color and line was enormously helpful later on when she planned my dancing costumes. She loved to entertain and was famous for her New Year's Eve parties. Friends, mostly Russian intelligentsia—painters, singers, and writers—gathered to celebrate. After a few shots of whiskey Dad would break into a hilarious *kazatsky*, one hand behind his head, the other outstretched. He wheeled about full of the joy of living. Others sang gypsy songs. Of course, I always danced. These parties lasted until early morning, with some guests sleeping over, sometimes on the floor. For me it was a special event.

My brother was too young for the parties. When he was old enough, the parties had become too wearing on Mom. Now she was active in politics, and in developing our musical taste. I was paid five cents an hour to practice on our newly acquired grand piano. Marvin was taken to the New York Philharmonic Children's Concerts. These excursions helped to instill in him a lifelong passion for music. His last excursion before his death in 1983 was a musical cruise, which we shared.

Professionally, Marvin became an outstanding photo-journalist. He also did advertising photography, for which he won many awards. Each of us was proud of the other's accomplishments, but perhaps the gap in our ages or the fact that we were temperamentally very different (he gregarious, I somewhat a loner) kept us from being really close. Both of us, however, remained close to our parents. Even after we had well-established careers we continued to turn to them and always found them a haven of help, encouragement, and belief.

The Early Years

With Fokine

I always cried when I saw dance. I sat there, my eyes glued to the stage, tears trickling down my face. For me it was a mixture of ecstasy and frustration. My family were opera buffs, and I cried myself through the ballets of *Aïda*, *Carmen*, and especially *La Gioconda*, with its *Dance of the Hours*. I also saw Anna Pavlova do Michel Fokine's *The Swan*, and of course I cried.

But this time the crying was not for myself. The swan had died and I cried. It was on Saturday evening, October 20, 1923, at the Manhattan Opera House on West 34th Street in New York City, that I saw Pavlova. Aside from opera ballets I had seen nothing of dance, but I ate, slept, and drank it. To see a whole evening of dance at the age of eleven was an overwhelming experience. This was entirely different from the opera ballets which, though I did not realize it at the time, were rather shabby, neglected bits of mediocre dance. Pavlova was another world, a world of exquisite artistry.

Bathed in a pale, blue-green light, a fragile figure in a white-winged tutu, head framed in feathers, she slowly rose to her toes. I did not need to see the blood-red jewel at her heart to know that she was wounded. Every moment of her tremulous *bourrées*, every move of her arms breathed helplessness, her whole body seemed to tremble anguish. It was the waxing and waning of a life as her toes beat the rhythms of her will to go on, one long flow of movement never stopping, but adding drama to the inner flow of emotion. The simplicity of the *bourrées*, the sweep of her arms in winglike movement, the flutter of her hands and tilt of her head constantly changed the palette of emotional color. And then there was that final moment as Pavlova dropped to her knee, folding to the ground over an extended leg; there was a lift of the arms, the last breath, a small body shudder and a final droop of the hands—all life gone.

Though only a child, I was acutely aware of a difference—a difference between just dancing and *being*. Pavlova did not dance *The Swan*. She was that swan. I had died with her, the tears streaming down my face.

On February 27, 1926, I was seeing my second full evening of dance. This was Vera Fokina, wife of Michel Fokine, in a solo concert at Carnegie Hall. She, too, did *The Swan*. I remember nothing.

I often wonder what my life would have been like if my mother had not taken me to Fokina's performance. At intermission, when the lights went up, the woman sitting in front of us turned her head and my mother recognized an old acquaintance. Her daughter took lessons with Michel Fokine. Mom asked for the address. Four Riverside Drive. The lights went out for the second half of the performance.

At home there was much discussion, and finally my parents decided to investigate. We made an appointment to see Mr. Fokine. A butler showed us into a wood-paneled drawing room on the main floor. The room was overpowering with its heavy, carved mahogany armchairs upholstered in red plush. Mahogany tables with porcelain and sculpted objects reflected in an enormous gold-framed mirror on one wall. A beautiful oriental rug was spread in all its splendor on the parquet floor. Shafts of light from tall windows facing the river helped to soften the room, which was hardly what one would call cozy. I was terribly nervous, filled with awe, not knowing what to expect.

Mr. Fokine walked into the room. Suddenly, it seemed luminous. He wore his teaching clothes—gray trousers and a white, open-collared shirt. He smiled and ushered us into his library on the floor above. I think he must have felt my excitement, how desperately I wanted to study with him. I sat at the edge of my seat, tense, my feet twisting (a habit I have never been able to shake).

Mother talked to him in English (her Russian was not too good). "My daughter wants very much to study with you. We think she has a natural talent. She has some training, but not very much." He looked at me and said, "Yes, well, she can join the afternoon class. My fee is five dollars a lesson." My heart stopped. Five dollars a lesson in 1926 was unbelievable. I knew it was impossible. I suddenly felt numb, empty. I pressed my lips together, hard, trying to keep the tears back, and knew my feet were twisting worse than ever. Mother took one look at me, turned to Mr. Fokine and said, "Would it be possible for her to take four lessons, and then you can tell us if you think she has talent?" So it was decided I would take one lesson a week for a month, and then a big question mark. I lived for those classes.

I was in high school. Mother would meet me, bring my practice clothes, and take my books home, while I dashed to the subway to make the trip from Brooklyn to New York in time for the four-thirty class. That first trial month was sheer agony. I spent all my free time between lessons practicing at home in front of our tall hall mirror, trying to relive every moment of the class. How had I done? I knew I was trying too hard; would I look artificial? I came home after each class bursting with excitement, only to worry myself sick wondering what Mr. Fokine would say. What might happen if I could not continue? Dance to me was life itself.

I was in a state of panic and the weeks were like years. The time was here. Dad went with me. Again we were in the library. They spoke Russian. I sat in a corner, wincing at what might happen. My father was a young lawyer, not yet with the kind of income to pay five dollars a lesson for his daughter, no matter how much he believed in her. I could not understand a word. As the conversation went on I sank lower and lower in my corner. I wanted to disappear altogether. Once Fokine looked at me with a warm glance and for a moment I felt a glimmer of hope, but Dad shook his head from side to side. My stomach twisted into a pretzel. The conversation went on and on.

Then, as I sat there shaking, shrunken into my dark corner, I suddenly saw a change. Dad had a talent for rising to an emergency. He became animated, spoke faster, his voice had a positive ring, and Fokine began to smile. Suddenly I found myself gasping for air. An agreement was made. Mr. Fokine said, "Yes, by all means she must continue. In her, the soul dances." Father had offered his legal services in return for classes. I would be able to take lessons whenever I wished, though because of school it could only be twice a week. I was delirious.

The Fokine home and studio was a white stone mansion on Riverside Drive and 73rd Street. In the winter a permanent tornado swings around the corner of 72nd Street and sweeps up the street. Coming down that street in the winter I had to lean with all my weight against the wind. The interior of the house was elegant in European fashion with an entrance foyer, marble staircase, iron balustrade spiraling to the second floor. At the base of the staircase hung a life-size portrait of Fokine in the costume for *Panaderos* and, farther up, hung a smaller portrait of his wife, both painted by Fokine. To the left of the staircase was a carved armchair flanked by a marble-topped table which held the class book we signed as we entered.

When I arrived for class, cold and breathless—sometimes with frost clinging to my eyelashes and the wind still whistling in my ears—I often heard Fokine playing the piano. He was a sensitive musician. I took the tiny elevator to the fifth-floor attic, a bare dressing room with a few plain chairs. If you were lucky to find a free chair, you could hang your clothes on it. If not, the floor would have to do. In a terror about being late, I struggled into my pink tunic with underpants to match (leotard and tights in class were unheard of at that time), taped my blistered toes and heels, slipped into ballet shoes, and rushed to the fourth-floor studio, a small room equipped with a barre.

Fokine entered class with a brisk bouncy step, trim and vibrant. "Good afternoon, ladies," in a heavy Russian accent. At forty-six he was strikingly handsome, his baldness, revealing a finely sculpted head, enhanced rather than detracted from his appearance. The side hair brushed forward softened his face with its high forehead, arrow-straight nose, and piercing gray eyes shadowed by bushy eyebrows. His strong chin was mellowed by a sensitive mouth that curled in the corners. This balance of strength and softness was evident in other aspects. He had a sly sense of humor which could be droll or bitingly sarcastic. At times those gray eyes could take on a steely look and I was sure there was a temper I would rather not see unleashed and a stubborness that could harbor a grudge. Although he was only five feet eight inches in height, I always thought of him as tall. He had a way of holding his body that projected height. He had a lightness and buoyancy, tempered by a strength and sharpness, that made everything he did unique. I could easily imagine how his young students at the St. Petersburg Imperial Theatre School must have worshiped him and vied for his attention. He admitted to having had an entourage and loving it.

In class Fokine was adamant about the details of his style. He never permitted a flexed foot in beats. His *grand rond de jambe* was with a slightly arc-shaped leg, rather than the straight leg, with the knee well turned out. To test the line of the leg, he would put a straight-backed wooden chair at the side of the body where the knee would be in space. The *rond de jambe* had to be executed without the slightly bent knee touching the top of the chair. He showed us that if the knee turned in at the side or if the leg dropped too soon as it moved to the back, it would touch the chair. He insisted on an arm shape that today has completely disappeared in ballet technique. When the arm was held to the side, the palm faced down with a slight arching of the wrist. The fingers were never very separated but reached into space in a rippling curve with the thumb long and tucked under the palm. Fokine always talked about tapering the hand and the need for it to continue the flowing line of the arm, a profile shape that was far more interesting as a design than simply seeing the flat of the palm. Furthermore, to emphasize flow, he wanted the hand to move in slight opposition to the arm. This kept the wrist and fingers alive to the very last movement.

For me, the most important element of the Fokine style and technique was the total awareness of the body. The spirit of the movement was as important as the mechanics.

"I want you to use entire body, always," he said. "If you keep torso stiff, you are not dancer. You look like broomstick." He loved the diagonal line and asymmetry. The reason so much of ballet movement faced front, he claimed, was that in early days it was forbidden to turn your back on royalty.

When barre was finished, I crammed my feet into my toe shoes, which I hated, and trooped with the others down a dark, back spiral staircase to the third floor, then down the marble staircase to the second floor, where the Ampico grand piano stood on the landing. The main studio on the second floor was a magnificent room, running the width of the house. Floor-to-ceiling French windows faced the Hudson River, allowing the sunset to pour in. A crystal chandelier hung in the center of the room, and wall sconces framed by gold paneled molding hung on the walls. At one end was an elegant marble fireplace. Centered on the opposite wall was a gold-framed mirror, the only mirror we had to check our positions.

In this studio we did center floorwork: the adagio, allegro, and finally

Mr. Fokine gave us combinations, sometimes whole excerpts from his ballets. For me this was the most interesting. I could let loose and dance. My class was intermediate-advanced. There was a young stringbeany girl whose legs I envied. Her name was Nora Koreff (we later knew her as the famous ballerina Nora Kaye). I would look at her and think, "My body is all wrong; I'm too short. I hate my legs, but, thank God, I have a long neck and long arms." Nora was one of the most determined hard workers in the group, taking two or three classes a week. I always wondered why, when it was the fashion to change your name from American to Russian, she did the reverse. Of the others, Esther Rosen, who was my friend, danced for years in the Radio City Music Hall Ballet. Betty Eisner, renamed Betty Bruce, was a headliner in Broadway shows. Annabelle Lyon, an exquisite, delicate dancer was in Ballet Theatre for years. She and Nora were in the original cast of Antony Tudor's *Pillar of Fire*. The miniature Leda Anchutina, a brilliant technician, married André Eglevsky and later helped create his school. Orest Sergievsky and William Dollar came to some classes. At times we caught a glimpse of Patricia Bowman, star of the Roxy, Radio City, and Broadway, or Paul Haakon who, at the age of sixteen, was already a professional dancer with an established career.

I never took class with a sense of routine. I was bubbling with excitement. The anticipation, the thinking, the taking, was a special event. My whole life revolved around it. Exposure to Fokine was less a technical development than an artistic experience. Whatever technique I had, I got from him, but more important in Fokine's classes I learned to *dance*. Technique was acquired by the need to perform as classroom exercises excerpts from *Petrouchka*, *Carnaval*, *Les Sylphides*, *Firebird*, and *Les Elfes*.

Fokine always sang for our classes, never at a loss for a melody from Tchaikovsky, Chopin, Schumann, or music remembered from his own student days. We had no regular accompanist, but the Ampico piano was a very special instrument. It was a grand piano of excellent quality, yet its special feature was that it was equipped to play, electrically, piano rolls recorded for it by the leading pianists of the time. After learning a dance to Anton Rubinstein's *Romance* or a section of Fokine's *Les Sylphides*, Fokine would turn on the Ampico. Imagine dancing in class to the world's greatest pianists! Since I was sensitive to sound, it was ecstasy for me, and it helped, I am sure, my musical phrasing and dynamic response.

From the start, I hung onto every word Fokine said and watched every move he made. The depth of his emotional color, the passion with which he attacked a phrase, taught me more than just doing an *entrechat-six*. Fokine hated the use of virtuosity for display; every movement had to fulfill its purpose, his vision of the dance as a whole. I worked hard on my technique and learned to do *entrechat-six* with great ease, but only as a means to an end. It was not the *doing*, it was the *dancing* I craved. He rarely complimented us, but his eyes and his smile were enough for us to know. He often stopped to explain in detail why he had developed his stylistic changes. For him, all his movement had "motivation." He was the first person I ever heard talk about the "harmony of line." For him, *arabesque* meant a sense of flow in space, a crescent shape parallel to the floor, extending from fingertip to toe without any break in the line, a sense of reaching, a need to go forward, a sense of floating or soaring in space. An *attitude* was the vertical opposite, a reaching up to the sky, but again the ever-present flow of line from fingertip through body to the arc-shaped leg tapering toward the earth. Fokine's use of the head was special; its elegance in repose, with its slight tilt up, the lift from chest through throat to chin to complete a movement. He insisted that the flow of movement be continued through the head and through the hands into space: "Reach into the space. Don't stop movement at neck or wrists. I want whole body alive, be involved with smallest movement—expression of whole being."

Fokine gave us long phrases so we could sense the shape of the movement as a whole. When he demonstrated an excerpt from one of his ballets, there would be a sudden transformation. The years dropped away as he swept through the studio with a light, fleet urgency of movement to evoke a sense of delicacy, of fragility that covered the gamut of dynamics. He could convince us that he was Petrouchka, or the Moor, or the Ballerina through an instantaneous change. He could be a diaphanous sylph, then a Greek shepherd, or an oriental slave. His body seemed to take on a different shape and proportion for each role; even his face changed. Sometimes he stopped for a moment and looked out the window, and there was a distant look in his eyes of a long-remembered time: the time of his greatness when these works were first danced by Pavlova, Nijinsky, Karsavina. I could feel his wistfulness. How frustrating it must have been to watch us, a bunch of adolescents, all shapes and sizes, struggling through his masterpieces. I can see him

showing us the moment from *Carnaval* when Pierrot tears out his heart
—his twinge became visible as he said, "I cry." To watch him offer his
heart as a gift to Columbine was to realize what he meant by dance
characterization. It was not pantomine; it was real.

Fokine's sense of period and historic style was of utmost importance.
He talked about the Greek line and was the first one to make me aware
that the true Greek line is not the obvious profile. "The Greeks not
walk around in frieze positions," he said, showing us a hilarious satire.
"The essence of Greek style is opposition of shoulder to weight in
hip." And there he stood, looking like Michelangelo's *David.*

At times Madame, as everyone called Fokina, watched our class. She
made a grand entrance, elegantly dressed in a long gray velvet gown
trimmed with fur. All of us curtsied and greeted her with, "Good afternoon, Madame." She was a stunning woman, the absolute symbol of
glamor. Her long black hair was caught in a low bun at the nape of her
neck, her large expressive dark eyes heavily made up, an aquiline nose
and very pale makeup highlighting her strongly rouged mouth. She had
a way of holding her head tilted up and was partial to deep-cut
V-neckline dresses that accentuated her white throat and bosom. She
loved jewelry and wore ropes of pearls, long pearl earrings, two large
diamond solitaire rings and a pearl all on one finger of her very expressive hands, which were insured for 100,000 dollars. She felt her hands
were more important to her dance than her feet.

Mr. Fokine rushed to bring her a chair and with a "Verushka, please
sit down," continued to give class with his characteristic way of tilting
his head down and looking at us from under his bushy eyebrows. His
eyes had an unusual warmth as he sang away and glanced at her from
time to time. He adored her. She nodded approval, sitting very straight
in her chair, being very much Vera Fokina, the elegant beauty of the
portrait hanging above the staircase. His own added excitement made
us feel we were giving a performance, and I loved to perform!

He sincerely valued her opinion and often said she was his best critic
and collaborator as well as a source of inspiration. I have a feeling that
behind the scenes she had a strength and an influence that her outward femininity and glamor belied. There was a ring to her voice that
could also have a sharp edge.

As time went on I met their son Vitale. He wandered around the fifth
floor—where he seemed to have his quarters and where he cared for
the costumes, some of which he helped to make—and often stopped to

chat. Though he had been trained in dance, he did not seem to have much dance ambition at that time and rarely, if ever, took class. He was a kind of ugly duckling: short, stocky, not at all a dancer's body. His eyes had an expression reminiscent of his father, but instead of gray, they were intensely blue. He had a way of speaking so fast that the words seemed to tumble over one another, and a tendency to giggle, which I felt covered a deep insecurity. To balance this he had a revealing and acid sense of the ridiculous and loved to tell jokes, so that his laughter was often spontaneous and genuine.

Vitale was lonely. As the only child of world-famous professional parents he hovered in the background, brought up by nurses and governesses. He covered with wild escapades: a mixture of rebellion and a need to keep busy since he had no definite work. He tried to be on the fifth floor when class broke, I suspect so that he could talk to Esther and me. I wondered why a young man of twenty-one would seek out two dance-obsessed fifteen-year-olds and seem perfectly happy in their company. I suppose we offered the companionship of would-be sisters. With us he could be open, relaxed, sometimes even making sarcastic asides about his parents, not with malice, but with objectivity. I often invited him and Esther home with me for a good Russian dinner of pot roast and brown kasha, for laughter and warm family feeling.

One day Dad received a very agitated call from Mr. Fokine. "We have bad trouble," he said. "Big problem with Vitale. He get married couple months ago, not tell us one word. Some strange dancer, her name is Maria and now she using name 'Fokina.' Crisis!"

It seems Vitale, on one of his wild capers, had run off with this unknown dancer. Madame was in a rage: "How dare anyone use that name!" "Fokina" was hers and hers alone. She had made it world famous. She was not about to let anyone capitalize on it. "Is *scandale* —terrible woman—must stop her," begged Madame. The matter was eventually resolved by Vitale's divorce, which Dad arranged. It allowed Maria ten dollars a week alimony and included a clause forbidding her to use the name "Fokina."

One time Vitale invited Esther and me to visit what he called a "club," to which he and his cousin Leon Fokine belonged. Leon, newly arrived in America, was now Vitale's buddy. We went down the gloomy staircase to the basement floor of a ramshackle old West Side brownstone and entered a fantasy world. It was dimly lit, a red glow, with four alcoves curtained in exotic colored fabric, sheltering divans. The air was heavy, the atmosphere distinctly Arabian nights. We lounged around for a while, while I naïvely wondered what this was all about. All I could think of was *Schéhérazade*. Only years later did it dawn on me that this probably meant opium. I will never know why Vitale asked me there or what he expected. It was all very innocent. I think he wanted to show it to us because he had designed it and wanted our praise, which of course he got. We "oohed" and "aahed" and thought it all very romantic and exciting. "So original, so different from any other club-house," I said, never having seen any other clubhouse.

The many times I frantically dashed down long, windy 72nd Street to Riverside Drive always culminated in limping, painful retracing of steps to the subway home. How could I ever enjoy and really fulfill myself in dance with bleeding toes, shedding toenails, and everlasting heel blisters? I was continually nursing aches between classes. My toes never hardened, and though I loved to watch beautiful pointe work, I knew that for me it was wrong. Emotionally, it stifled me. I really did not want to do toe work any more. Apprehensively, I approached Mr. Fokine with this decision.

"Ach, Paulina," he said. "And I wanted to make you ballerina."

Ballerina, ha! I thought that what Fokine saw in me was not the cool classic ballerina. Perhaps he saw the same dramatic and emotional qualities that Madame had as well as a similar visual quality. Most probably he thought of me as a dramatic and character dancer, which of course would have been my forte had I wanted to remain in ballet. I simply could not see myself doing full justice to a role, believe what I was doing on the inside, when the externals were overwhelming. I could never be the artist I dreamed of being.

"No, Mr. Fokine, I do not want to be a ballerina. I want to be some-thing else."

Permission granted, I now began to enjoy classes fully. I swept through space with newborn freedom, worked on elevation, developed *batterie*. I even achieved *entrechat-huit*. When he gave excerpts of dances I would often do the boys' roles as well as the girls'. This certainly helped my elevation, of which I was very proud. I discovered new dimensions of movement, a new confidence born of the knowledge that I could feel the totality of every move. I was no longer hampered by aches and pains and was eager to challenge the realm of danger, rather than conform to the absolute safety of formality.

During my first year with Fokine I was given the opportunity to appear in what was called the Fokine Ballet. This company was comprised mainly of his students, some of whom were professionals, with a few guest artists. Three performances were given at the Century Theatre, an evening performance on October 23 and a matinee and evening on October 30, 1927.

For these programs Fokine revived *Les Elfes*, a company work; *Phoenix*, a solo danced by Madame; and a Suite from *Le Rêve de la Marquise*, the lead roles danced by the Fokines, who also danced *Mazurka*. Also on the program were Harlequin and Columbine from *Carnaval*, danced by Paul Haakon and Tania Koshkina, and *Voices of Spring* and *Oriental Dances*, performed by the company, which included Patricia Bowman, Betty Eisner, and Esther Rosen.

The centerpiece of the program was a revival of his 1909 ballet *Cléopâtre*. The two leads were danced by the Fokines, the slaves by Pat Bowman and Alan Wayne, and I was one of five girls in the Jewish Dance. This dance involved the use of large tambours, which at one point we had to roll to each other across the stage and catch as they rolled. Two days before the premiere I developed an infection in my left arm, with a fever of 104 degrees. The doctor said, "No performance." I said, "I must." Nothing but a straitjacket could have restrained me. With an arm that seemed to weigh a ton, dizziness, nausea, and with my first attempt at theater makeup, which produced purple and red eyelids, I went on stage. I was able to get through the dance somehow until the moment of rolling the tambour across stage. Mine went straight for the orchestra pit. I was so dizzy I never knew the difference. By the next week's performances, the doctor had lanced the arm and I made it without a catastrophe.

My second appearance with the company was a two-week engagement, February 7–21, 1927, at the Stanley Theatre in Philadelphia. This was a famous presentation house, which meant there were two performances a day of a moving picture and a stage production. The film was based on *Faust*, and as a prelude Fokine choreographed *Prologue to Faust*. Madame was an Angel and Blake Scott was Mephistopheles. We were devils and ran up and down a flight of stairs. To create an atmosphere of hell at the climax of the ballet, there were red footlights and a device for billowing smoke. One day the smoke machine broke down and we were nearly asphyxiated by ammonia fumes escaping from the pipes.

It was a great adventure: my first tour. I was not only dancing but traveling, if only to Philadelphia. Two of the older girls, Lora Da Vinci and Renee Wilde (who had an acrobatic adagio act of their own), took me under their wing. I think we were paid thirty dollars a week, not bad for that time, but we paid our own living expenses. I had earned my first truly professional salary and was bursting with pride. Every moment, whether it was eating dinner at a club, walking to the theater, or dancing on the stage, was precious. I kept wishing it would last forever.

On the train trip to Philadelphia, Madame, who suddenly became less formal, regaled us in her broken English with the wonderful story of how she had finally won Mr. Fokine. She had very beautiful handwriting, and all the senior students at the ballet school insisted she write their anonymous love letters to Fokine. "I write letters, I cry," she said. "I love him so much myself. Everything I write for girls I feel I say for me. But not tell him. I think he never look at me. I so young student. I suffer so much, but never say word." In his biography Fokine mentions he had noticed a similarity in the handwriting of these anonymous love letters, but not until years later did he learn that the letters had been written by Fokina. He did look at her, fell in love with her, and married her. All the years I knew them there was a romantic relationship filled with love, respect, and rare gallantry. Of course, Madame knew how to expect it, and he knew how to express it.

Meanwhile, my friend Esther had started taking Spanish dance classes at Carnegie Hall Studios with Angel Cansino. One of the famous dancing family of Cansino brothers and the uncle of Rita Hayworth, he was the leading teacher of the time. When Esther clicked her castanets in the dressing room at Fokine's, I was entranced. So I bought some cheap castanets and Mother made a practice dress of yellow-flowered cotton, a tight bodice and hip yoke, with wide ruffled skirts to the ankle. On went shoes with strong heels, and I started classes. The movement, the rhythm, the passion were right up my alley. Before long I was stamping away, trilling castanets, swirling skirts, shaking my shoulders, snapping my fingers, turning my wrists in true flamenco style. Should I become a Spanish dancer? Spanish dance at this time was very popular, and I loved it. I certainly had no trouble looking Spanish, and I had the fire and intensity it demanded.

At the same time, classes with Fokine continued. Looking out of the studio windows at the tall houses across the way, I had a fantasy: how wonderful it would be to live in one of those houses, get into practice clothes, and be able to run across the street for daily classes.

Because of Fokine's need for my father's legal services there was some social as well as professional contact. I was so proud when Madame invited Mother, Dad, and me to dinner. To me they were people on a pedestal, and it was hard to picture them in normal surroundings. The dining room was paneled in dark wood, the chairs were gold, upholstered in red damask brocade, the large round table was covered with a beautiful old lace cloth. The candlelight made the ornate silver shimmer and the elegant china and glassware gleam. It was a very informal dinner, just the two families, including Vitale. The food was typically Russian: borscht, roast chicken, and kasha, with baklava for dessert. Madame said she loved to cook and had cooked the dinner herself. More likely she had only supervised. It was a warm and friendly evening. We talked dance, gossiped, and Vitale kept us in hysterics with his mimed stories. These gods became human beings for the first time.

As the years went by Fokine was away more and more, traveling to the West Coast, South America, and Europe. Interest in ballet was developing. New companies were being formed and the demand for his works, old and new, began to grow. He was again in his element, delighted to be working with professional companies. He seemed happier than I had ever known him to be. His eyes sparkled; he had renewed energy. That faraway look I had so often seen had disappeared.

In 1937 he was invited by Colonel De Basil to stage his opera-ballet *Le Coq d'Or* for the Ballet Russe de Monte Carlo for their Covent Garden season. Fokine choreographed a new ballet version to a suite of music extracted from the Rimsky-Korsakov opera. This was a chance to work in the style he loved so much, Russian folklore, with its pageantry, with gorgeous costumes and a set by Nathalie Goncharova. At the Covent Garden opening the ballet was the hit of the season. Fokine was jubilant, rejuvenated. The fallow years were left behind, disappearing in the excitement of choreographic rebirth.

Fokine invited us to be his guests for the New York premiere on October 31, 1937, at the Metropolitan Opera House. We sat in his special box: Dad, Mother, and I; Vitale with his new wife Christine (whom Madame decided she had to accept), and the Fokines. It was a gala affair with all the splendor of those days — evening clothes, flashing diamonds, delicate perfumes, and the bustle and vibrations of a major premiere. *Le Coq d'Or* was a feast for the eyes. The set was in brilliant colors of orange, yellow, and red, the costumes ranging from the elaborate boyar brocades and headdresses to the oriental bare midriff of the Queen of Shemakhan. Tatiana Riabouchinska as the golden cockerel—in a gold lamé leotard with gold winged sleeves and an arched feather tail—was breathtaking. Fokine used her special qualities of sharpness, speed, and elevation to create an exciting, luminous bird flying in tremendous *jeté* leaps, sharp leg attacks, and swift movement patterns that carried her all over the stage. Riabouchinska and the beauty and sensuousness of Irina Baronova as the Queen, with long black braids and a transparent pink chiffon trouser costume, are the two strongest memories I have of the work—and Fokine standing to receive the applause and the accolades, all of us in the box laughing and crying with excitement and pleasure.

In 1934, when Fokine was in Paris, Nora's mother asked me if I would work with Nora and a friend of hers until he returned. I did not think of myself as a ballet dancer, but they felt I had the Fokine style and wanted to continue classes. By this time I had a studio of my own in the Lincoln Square Studio Building on Broadway and 66th Street and had already moved away from ballet as my personal idiom. Nevertheless it was a challenge to give those classes. They heightened my awareness of the Fokine style and helped my own search for fresh movement. Many of his basic principles were similar to what modern dance was exploring, even though the idiom was different.

Fokine never accepted modern dance. He could not see that the totality of movement he fought for, the need for involvement and continuity (he hated bows and applause during a work), his desire to be true to character, his demand for motivation, his quest to eliminate superfluous movement and displays of technique for the sake of audience appeal—all this could have been in a handbook on the early modern dance. He could not recognize the heart of modern dance because the visual aspect was so alien to his concept of what movement should look like. The clubbed-foot, cupped hand, seeking of the earth rather than air were to him ugly.

Fokine did, however, attend my early concerts. Though working in my own style, I pointed my toes, a "no-no" in modern dance. I articulated my hands, dared to use turnout when it was taboo. Moreover, I was involved with character dance. So Fokine accepted with reservation what I was doing and did not disinherit me. Occasionally in class he would make snide remarks with a pointed look from under his eyebrows as if to say, "And you are a modern dancer?" Unruffled, I tried my best to be true to his style and to absorb the artistic values that were to me his greatest contribution.

When I was in Russia only a few years later, I was saddened to see that most of his innovations in body movement had already disappeared from the formal training there. His name was still revered, but his greatest achievements and his principle that every movement in ballet should have expression were gone. Ballet had reverted to an earlier acrobatic style that now turns up everywhere.

By 1940 Fokine had stopped teaching and had moved to the suburbs. Long after I had made my career in another area of dance, my father still represented him legally. Dad never mentioned that he thought the exchange had become one-sided; I think he enjoyed working for Fokine as a courtesy.

News of Fokine's death on August 22, 1942, was a great shock. He was so much a part of my early dance life, so ingrained, that I could not believe the reality of it until I was at the funeral service at the Russian Orthodox church. The church was packed with dancers, and as the candles burned I realized that he had given me an awareness of total dance that would influence me for the rest of my life. Although I continued taking classes with various ballet teachers, among them Leon Fokine, I held on to the inspiration of Michel Fokine.

The Carnegie Hall studio building is a fascinating place. It has a long history of famous people who have lived and worked there. From the 57th Street entrance adjacent to Carnegie Hall, there is a strange arrangement: the sixth floor consists of only one studio, Studio 61, and a few steps up to the right you are suddenly on the eighth floor. On the way to my Cansino class in Studio 839, I got off the elevator on the sixth floor with Studio 61 facing me. Its fame was due to Alys Bentley, a well-known personality in the 1920s, who was its soul. Primarily a music educator, she was interested in all avant-garde movements, and sponsored music, poetry readings, and some of the earliest Isadora Duncan disciples.

With a crown of short gray hair, Bentley was a startling figure in her Grecian clothes and voluminous gray wool cape, which flapped about her wherever she went—a sort of High Priestess of the Arts. I caught occasional glimpses of her as she breezed along the hallway to her apartment next to the studio. I was especially intrigued because I often heard strains of oriental music and had heard that a Japanese dancer was teaching in "61."

The Orient had always been my first love. I was saturated in stories of the Arabian Nights (adapted for children) and swooned when I saw the beautiful Russian movie star Alla Nazimova in *Salome*. To me, she was the ultimate in exotic beauty. In my private world, I was an Egyptian princess. My bedroom was my palace—my bed draped with silks and brocades. When I went to sleep, I lay flat on my back, smoothed the coverlet, placed my arms at my sides palms down, and was lulled by the cool breeze as two imaginary Nubians waved peacock-feather fans on either side. My choice of recital piece at the Alviene dance school was an Egyptian number to ballet music from *Aïda*. Mother and I contrived what I thought was a gorgeous costume; it made me feel like Nazimova's double. And now I found myself passing a studio where I knew there was a real live Japanese—Michio Ito.

One day I mustered up all my courage and walked into Studio 61. Ito had just finished teaching a class, and there I was, staring at one of the most extraordinary faces I have ever seen. Shining black hair falling on either side of his oval face framed unusually large, luminous eyes, with a hint of sadness in them. His nose had a slight arch, almost Mayan in its contour, and a full and protruding lower lip lent a sensuous quality tinged with determination. This was not a handsome face, but a strong and beautiful face. There was an outward calm masking an inner intensity that sent an electric current through me. I just wanted to look—I could hardly speak—my first encounter with a true Oriental. Timidly I asked about classes and realized that I could not possibly fit them into my schedule.

In spring 1928 I had just finished high school and had promised my parents to go to college so that I might have a profession (they were afraid that I might not make it as a dancer). "I'll go," I said, "but only if you'll let me continue to study dance." I even suggested that I would study law, which pleased my father, but I knew that college would kill four years. Finally two very distressed parents compromised: I could take courses at Columbia University Extension and continue private dance studies as well. There was one problem—I was too young for admittance to Columbia. Here Dad came to the rescue; because of my high grades he persuaded the administration to admit me. Since I did not care about credits toward a degree, I took drawing, English literature, Dalcroze eurhythmics (with the conductor Paul Boepple, one of its leading teachers in the United States), and Russian (to understand what my parents were talking about when they wanted to hide something from my brother and me).

I could see no possibility of studying with Ito, but he suggested private lessons as a solution. Again, the question of expense. I think my parents saw the handwriting on the wall. Although they originally had been against my becoming a professional dancer, they were now my strongest supporters. Hour lessons were beyond their reach, but Dad thought he could manage six half-hour lessons. I was out of my mind with excitement.

In the fall, I started school and lessons with Ito. Instead of bothering with technique, he started out by teaching me his version of a Javanese dance. Ito made no claim to authenticity. He drew on the essential quality, not the actual steps. Whatever he did in the ethnic vein was not derivative, but it felt authentic. Until then, the word Javanese was for me associated with a vague recollection of some pictures I had seen in *National Geographic*. No matter! My instinct for anything oriental came into play. Although I had felt very Spanish in Spanish dance, in oriental dance I now felt totally oriental. I had come home to my own place and was more at ease and fulfilled than in anything I had ever danced before.

It was a time of discovery. Spanish dance had developed in me a sense of dynamics through the playing of the castanets, rhythm in the heelwork, and articulation of the fingers, wrists, and shoulders in flamenco dancing. The concentration of inner intensity generated a release of emotions which, in ballet, had to be stifled. In the oriental, there was an added dimension. I was asked to concentrate on the emotional quality with strong inner focus, while visually keeping it totally contained. I developed a new understanding of emotional quality and subtleties of movement.

I had not danced barefoot since my childhood improvisations. Now, Ito asked me to feel the floor consciously. My left foot slid around and across the standing foot, with toe pointed in, and then with weight pressing down on the heel, I slowly turned the toe out. This is the typical woman's walk in Javanese dance. Feeling the deliberate use of the foot made it come alive with a new sensation. The hand movement was just as deliberate as the walk, rotating the wrist in and then out, while curling and then fanning the fingers. The chin was the focal point of the head movement: turned to the left as the top of the head tilted to the right, then circled down, then moved to the right as the head tilted to the left, in a three-part movement. I felt the pivotal point in a new place — at the top of my spine, at the back of the head.

I was taking my last private lesson, having learned the Javanese dance to near perfection, when Ito asked, "Would you like to join my company? I am planning a New York concert and then a tour of the United States." My heart almost stopped beating. The offer had come quite suddenly; a member of his company had suddenly pulled out and here I was, with a dance meant for the program, ready and polished.

I wanted this more than anything in my life, but I would have to talk to my parents. What would they say? "New York, fine. But leave school? Go on tour for six weeks, just like that? You are too young." I could hear these words clearly, and felt that my whole world would crumble if I could not go. I had to find a way to convince them. I thought of every possible argument: Yes, I know I promised to continue school, but I can always continue when I return from tour. After all, I am not on a rigid schedule. At last I hit on it, the Achilles' heel — guilt.

It was after dinner. We were sitting in our large, cozy Brooklyn kitchen (kitchens in those days seemed the center of all family activity). Dad was relaxed after his long workday, Mother had finished the dishes. We were drinking fragrant Russian tea in glasses. I thought, This is it, and plunged in.

"Michio has asked me to join his company for a New York concert and a tour across the United States to San Francisco." I watched Mom's eyes grow round and her mouth open slightly, while Dad's eyebrows arched and then drew tightly toward his nose. Before they could answer I went on, "Here is the golden opportunity. It just happened by accident. I might never get a chance like this again. Please, you can't say no. How could you face me in later years if I said: You were the reason I never made it? You ruined my career!"

When you say this to your parents, it stops them cold. They have to think, Do we want the responsibility? It worked. Arrangements were made. Hazel Wright, Michio's beautiful blonde wife and a dancer in the company, would act as my chaperone.

During the rehearsal period I found time to take Ito's classes, and I learned his ten basic arm positions: from arm up in a "Y" position, (1) open out and bring down to sides leading with wrists; (2) raise arms to hip bones, elbows out, palms down; (3) raise arms to chest, elbows out, palms turned up; (4) lower elbows to sides of body, palms face forward; (5) extend arms forward pushing with palms; (6) fold in across chest, left over right; (7) unfold arms raising elbows, bring to eyes, palms forward; (8) open to sides, shoulder height, elbows at right angle, wrists bent, palms up; (9) keeping same arm angle, bring in over head, but not touching hands; (10) extend, stretching arms diagonally up, pushing with palms. These were first done in unison, then as a canon with one arm ahead. The changes of rhythm and body twists produced fascinating shapes.

These were the root of a movement style he was evolving that was unrelated to his neo-ethnic style. This new style relied primarily on the torso and arms. The legs were used for balance and traveling in space, rather than for isolated brilliance. His slow walking step had the dancer touch the floor first with the toe, pressing into the ball of the foot, down to the heel, with a slightly bent knee. He said, "You should feel as though walking in water." He knew how to cover space with the effortless gliding movement of the Oriental, skimming along the floor without the bouncing and shoulder wagging visible in many dancers.

From the very beginning of his career, Ito's premise was the blending of Eastern and Western cultures. This was his philosophy. He was searching for a style universal in approach, a style that could express emotions motivated by the kernel of an idea. Most of his works demanded absolute concentration and a filtering of all naturalism from an emotion, stylizing it so that it could speak universally. Symbolism and imagery were important, but expression demanded total simplicity. Although his new style was visually far removed from his oriental-style dances, it could have stemmed only from a Japanese mind. It had the purity and the clarity of a single brush stroke in a Japanese painting, and at the same time it was like a modern painting influenced by the Japanese style. These qualities have remained with me throughout my career, and I find that his was the initial influence that opened my mind to the need for exploration on my own.

Ito also had an exquisite sensitivity for delicate nuance in dynamics and phrasing. Although he usually had a basic idea and an awareness of structure, his dances were mood pieces, never literal. Choreographically he paralleled the musical line rhythmically as well as dynamically. At that time many of us did, since a conscious choreographic form was still in its infancy. The dances were very short, sometimes lasting only two or three minutes. Thematic material was minimal: one or two themes were repeated rather than developed. Some of his works showed a strong Duncan influence in their use of small skips, hops in *attitude*, and simple circular or spiral arm shapes, especially in his Chopin works and in his *Joy* to Schumann. He chose music of Scriabin, Schumann, Chopin, Debussy, Yamada, Tchaikovsky, and Albeniz for his new-style dances. However, there were certain dynamics, sharp accents, that could only have come from his Japanese background.

Company rehearsals began in earnest and lasted into the night at Studio 61. All the dances were done to live piano music. Besides *Javanese Dance*, I had to learn *Passepied* and two trios, *Arabesque #2* and *Burmese Temple Dance*, which Ito choreographed especially for this program. The trios were to be danced by Michio, Kohana, and me. Kohana was a small, dark-haired beauty with large, heavily penciled eyes, long black hair, very white skin, and a lovely body. She had been with Ito five years, one of his first students, his star dancer, and an assistant in his school. Kohana was the authority on style and repertoire.

The program consisted mainly of solo works, one duet that Michio did with his wife, and the two trios, one to close each half of the program. It seemed incredible that I, a novice, was asked to dance with Michio and Kohana, but visually it was a natural. Kohana and I were exactly the same height, both dark-haired and oriental-looking, and, with Michio between us, we created a very unusual and convincing image. I was determined to match her in dance as well. I watched her rehearse her solos and tried to absorb as much as possible.

Arabesque was a humorous dance in the Ito style, not oriental. We wore strange little caps, gloves, and velvet jackets with puffed sleeves, all in black, and short, puffed trunks. The majority of Ito's dances were conceived without specific male or female characteristics and were thus interchangeably performed by a man or a woman. Of course there were some that were definitely meant for women, that expressed a specific feminine quality.

Passepied to Delibes was a bright little dance, with a French country flavor. This dance involved more footwork than some of the others, and with my balletic training I had no trouble at all in learning it. Furthermore, it was in such contrast to the slow, evocative Javanese solo that it gave me a chance to be a little more brilliant.

Ito designed the costumes, which were stylized and constructed to allow free movement. At the first fitting for the Javanese dance, a length of batik cotton was wrapped around my hips and then drawn between my legs to trail behind me on the floor for about a yard. In order to turn, I had to kick the train gently in the direction of the turn or find myself hopelessly wrapped in a corkscrew of cloth. Another challenge was learning to balance the tall, gold Burmese headdress, which rose in tiers to a peak. It affected my entire body. If I tilted my head too much in any direction I lost my balance. I learned to counterbalance the head weight by shifting my torso in the opposite direction of the tilt. All this was exciting, more than I could ever learn from just taking classes, and taught me facility in handling strange costumes.

My excitement rose as the day for performance drew near. It was to take place at the Civic Repertory Theatre on December 2, 1928. Because the dances were so short there were many numbers on the program. Each of us alternated, thus avoiding waits between dances. The company, besides Ito himself, consisted of Kohana, Ito's wife Hazel, Dorothy Wagner (a tall, statuesque blonde), and me. The program was rather mixed; Ito chose to present more of his oriental dances, interspersed with some works in the new style as well as neo-ethnic numbers—nineteen dances in all. He used a large gold folding screen as background for the dances, and on this the stage lighting projected many colors and reflected multiple shadows, creating theatrical excitement through very simple means.

Ito possessed a magnetism that made all eyes focus on him. The moment he entered, the very air seemed to change. Space seemed infinite, and he could shape it to whatever size he wished—boundlessly open, or minutely pinpointed. In his Albeniz *Tango* Ito's body was the entire space, concentrated within the confines of his own limbs, taut, intense, lithe as a puma, ready to pounce, but always held back. In his tightly fitted black trousers, short jacket, and jaunty black-brimmed Spanish hat, he was the essence of a Spanish dancer without doing a single true Spanish step. I spent all my free time listening to every word he said, watching him at rehearsals and from the wings during performance.

When I stood alone on stage, enveloped in light, the dark expanse of the audience before me, I had a strange sensation of being larger than myself. I felt an electric current emanating from me toward the audience, even as I was withdrawing into total concentration. I also felt a return current, an energy I was receiving from the audience, and I knew that we had touched each other. I call it blue flame. I feel it each time I perform, a silent communication—to be felt, not defined.

The exhilaration of that first truly professional performance, that moment of illumination on stage convinced me that this world would be my life. Yes, I was a dancer. This is what I wanted to do, would do, as long as I could. I was committed, for better or for worse.

The reviews of the concert were encouraging, and rehearsals began for the enlarged repertoire for the tour. Michio invited Martha Graham's sister, Georgia, who was a Denishawn dancer, to do two solos from the Denishawn repertoire, a Cambodian dance and a waltz caprice. I showed him a Hungarian dance to a Liszt rhapsody that Fokine had taught us in class, and he was so impressed that he decided to include it as well (Mom whipped up a very striking costume).

The most rewarding time for me during the rehearsal period was learning *Joy*, in Ito's series to Schumann's Symphonic Etudes. The movement was buoyant and open, and the legs were used freely, including small *attitude* jumps. There was a sense of being blown through space by an unexpected breeze. The dance was light and bubbling with vitality.

Ito had designed a basic costume, which had wonderful movement, that he used for some of his modern dances and that became one of his signatures. It had a velvet bodice, bordered by a low, white silk ruffle at the neckline, laced at the center by a white silk band tied into a loose bow. The sleeves, made of the same silk, were full and gathered by an elastic at the wrist. The skirt was ankle-length, accordion-pleated white silk, slit at the sides. The bodices varied in color. Mine for *Joy* was light green.

Since *Joy* was a solo, I had a chance to work with Ito in the style that now most interested him. Watching him move, I saw that breath was an important element in the texture and the phrasing of his style. He brought to rehearsals the same intensity of concentration he showed in performance. The smallest detail did not escape him.

The range of dances I appeared in was a tremendous challenge: the quiet, lyric, gentle *Javanese*; the earthy *Passepied*; the breezy, gossamer *Joy*; the passionate *Hungarian*; the humorous, zany *Arabesque #2*; and the exotic *Burmese*. These were professional performances, so that each time I appeared on stage I had to demand the utmost of myself; each time had to be as important as the first, only better. I was sure I could handle it—and I did.

Touring in 1929 was quite different from today. Air travel was nonexistent. We went by Pullman train, with wardrobe trunks instead of valises. Eating and sleeping on a train was a new adventure. At night, when I buttoned up the curtains of my berth, I was enclosed in a private green world, with hangers and little mesh nets to put things in, lights at the head of the bed to read by, and the pulsing sound of the wheels, creating a hypnotic rhythm.

A first professional tour is a discovery, an excitement, an exploration that can never again be the same. The need to adapt to a new stage at each performance, the reviews, the changing cities, climates, and people stimulate, educate, and also fatigue. But sometimes there was frustration, disappointment, and homesickness.

I was very flattered that Kohana had chosen to share a room with me. Five or six years my senior and already a seasoned performer, she amazed me, sophisticated as she was, by finding me an interesting companion. Though I was intellectually advanced for my years, I was still a naïve teenager. She and I came from the same Russian background and, having rehearsed together, we had much in common. I was the only one so young in the company and was thrust into a group of adults. They treated me more or less as an equal and I felt comfortable with them. I skipped the adolescent years, except for the inevitable crush. I worshipped Ito, quivered each time I sat next to him, and held on to the wonder of his nearness for hours, for days. Of course I tried to disguise my feelings. I am sure he was aware that I adored him; after all, he was twenty years older.

In addition to the six dancers, the tour company included Jack Wright (Hazel Ito's brother) as business manager, and two pianists, Raymond Sachse and Manuel Bernard. The stage manager was Lewis Barrington, a friend of Michio's, who was known for his lighting. Lewis was graying and rather paunchy. Above all, he was patient and dependable. No matter what the problem with the screens and lights, they were working by performance time. He took me under his wing and often guided me to see things I would not have noticed. He was the Rock of Gibraltar for a very volatile group of people.

We started in Detroit and from there went to Chicago, in January a very windy experience of fighting to stay erect against the sudden gusts. We gave a matinee and evening performance at the modern and intimate Goodman Theatre. It had a wonderful cyclorama built as a permanent part of the stage. I had never seen a cyclorama before; its rounded form and smooth texture created a new illusion for me.

After the matinee Adolph Bolm invited us to tea, and then we dashed back for a very successful evening performance. What was then a pleasant and natural social diversion became impossible for me in later years, when staying concentrated on the mood and realm of the theater without a break was all-important. But in the beginning it seemed so easy. The physical demands were not too great, and the company in general took things rather casually. Having a good time was important.

After a well-received performance in Kansas City on January 8, where the local prop man kept running in and out of our dressing room trying to help (I now think he had other motives), we were ready at last to leave the cold north for the sunny south, with El Paso our next stop. The sunny south! When we arrived there were snowflakes falling. This was the first snowstorm in twenty years. It lasted only thirty minutes and then, behold, bright, warm sunshine! We had a lovely interval of six days before our performance on January 16—time for a little rest and fun, which we used for a trip across the border to Juárez. Since none of us had passports, Kohana and I had to go to the commissioner so that we could enter Mexico and return. We were the only two with dark hair and might have been mistaken for Mexicans trying to enter the United States illegally. Personally, I was flattered. Juárez, a picturesque Mexican town, actually felt strangely like Coney Island to me.

In 1929 very few dance companies were touring, especially a company as exotic as ours, so we were constantly invited to various social events. At one gathering, a Mexican doctor tried to teach Hazel, Kohana, and me a Mexican *jarabe*, a native dance around the brim of a hat. He said to me, "All you need is the hat in order to be a real Mexican señorita." My Spanish dance background had certainly given me an edge.

Our performance in El Paso was very successful. There had been excellent publicity and the chance to rest and rehearse beforehand. Company spirits were sparkling, revived after the initial difficulties of the first week of tour. After the El Paso concert we left at 6 A.M. for Tucson, where we danced the same night, and left again at 2 A.M. for Long Beach, California. Thank heaven for Pullman sleeping cars! Another successful performance that night, I do not know how, and we finally arrived in Los Angeles on January 19 to sleep in real beds.

Our next stop was San Francisco. After New York, it is still for me perhaps the most interesting and exciting city in the United States. We were housed in the colorful old-time theatrical hotel, the Geary, within walking distance of Chinatown. Our first evening in San Francisco, we were taken to the Chinese theater, which was a cultural shock for me, but enthralling: the strange tonality of the music in a scale I had never heard; the high-pitched, twangy voices; the men in female roles; the casual musician who sat on stage, sawing away on his stringed instrument as he smoked complacently. Most surprisingly of all, the stagehands sauntered on and off the stage, bringing what was needed. All of this was a journey into another concept. This theater had another sense of timing, and a certain stylized action making specific demands on the viewer's imagination. Years later I saw the celebrated actor Mei Lan-fang and recognized the difference between mediocrity and artistry.

I do not know how I survived all the excitement of that day. Earlier, at rehearsal, Ito had decided to teach me "his" *Habañera* to Sarasate music, and though it was not authentic Spanish dance, I loved it. There was no costume, a problem I would have to solve somehow by myself.

Our performance the following night at the Scottish Rite Auditorium was sold out and enthusiastic. Ito had to encore his *Tango*, as usual, and I was thrilled to have to encore my Javanese dance. I was the happiest person in the world, and when Ito embraced me after the performance, for a moment I reached nirvana. He had actually touched me—a holy moment.

I found material for the *Habañera* costume, designed the usual ruffled affair, and sewed it all by hand during every free moment. I was buried in strips of material, haunted by them. They had to become ruffles, they had to become a skirt that I could swish and swing and flip. Ruffle after ruffle after ruffle. Presto! Two days later, a Spanish costume.

On February 3 we left for Seattle. Our performance on February 6 was supposed to be marvelous. We thought otherwise since the audience response was rather cold. Later we were told that this was the Seattle temperament. It takes a lifetime of experience to learn to anticipate the emotional patterns of various backgrounds and cultures. A show of enthusiasm for the artist can vary from stamping feet, rhythmic handclapping, whistles, and bravos to polite applause, yet all may have enjoyed the performance equally.

Seattle was to be the end of the tour, but unexpectedly there was a request for a return engagement in San Francisco on February 28. The problem was the time lapse. Ito discovered he was flat broke. How could the company survive for two weeks with no income?

At this point Nellie Cornish, director of the Cornish School of Allied Arts in Seattle, came to the rescue. Miss Cornish was a cyclone of activity encased in a five-foot-two, roly-poly body. Everything about her was round: round face crowned by gray marcelled hair, round rimless glasses that could not hide the bright sparkle of her eyes—even her bubbling laughter sounded round. She was always looking for the new, the exciting, and the very best. When Miss Cornish, or Miss Aunt Nellie as everyone called her, discovered our problem she invited Michio to teach a guest course and to give two additional performances in the school theater.

I was happy to take some sorely needed classes. There was no company class, and I had not yet developed my regular daily discipline of working by myself. Kohana was aching to get back to her boyfriend in New York, so Ito scraped up enough money for her fare, and she left. Georgia Graham learned the Burmese trio, and I performed the *Habañera* and my Hungarian dance.

After a masquerade party one night, at which Michio had been particularly attentive to me, I sat next to him during the ride back in the taxi and could feel the closeness and warmth of his body. It was the most important part of the evening for me.

Our performance on February 22 at the Cornish Theatre was again a success. I had another solo to Scriabin's Ninth Etude. It was one of Ito's new-style works, and I was delighted to have the opportunity to do this kind of movement. I found myself pulling away from ethnic style to discover a fresh way of using my body. Almost unknowingly I was changing, with a perception of new probings that led me finally to modern dance. At that time, however, I had no thought of abandoning the dramatic and character dance for which I had a flair, and which I passionately loved to perform.

Ito had decided we would return to San Francisco by boat. We left the following evening on a small steamer of the Dollar Line. I was thrilled at this first three-day trip on a boat. Hazel and I shared a cabin. The ocean *seemed* calm, so we ordered dinner in our cabin —chicken soup, olives, toast, and tea. We ate only the soup and toast. The ocean was not that rough; we had been talking about the fear of seasickness, and it took over. The next morning we felt fine and had a healthy breakfast, then sat on deck, wishing we were seagulls, fascinated by the shape of their wings as they glided in the air. This trip may be the source of an arched armshape that simulates gulls' wings, which I occasionally use. It is the same shape as in the opening of Alvin Ailey's work, *Revelations*.

The following day, February 26, we watched our entrance through the Golden Gate, a truly majestic moment. I had the sense of entering the world cleansed and purified by the crystalline air and water. Our final performance of the tour was again successful, even profiting by being staged in the Playhouse, a smaller auditorium than the Scottish Rite. The reviewer for *The Argus* said that I, ". . . one of the most finished dancers of the company, was always lovely to look at."

Well, this was it, the end. One of the pianists departed while there was still fare money left. Jack Wright disappeared. Funds had run out, and so had he. We found ourselves back at the Geary Hotel, stranded, without enough money for fares home. The two young Ito children had been left in New York in the care of Paula, Kohana's sister, and Ito's brother Yuji. From Dad I heard that Paula had called to say they did not have money even for milk for the children. Dad, always a soft touch, gave them 100 dollars.

As for me, this was all exciting, an adventure. Michio was invited to give a guest course at a local school, which brought in enough money for the hotel and food. I took class daily, eking out my dwindling private expense money with minimal breakfasts in a cheap cafeteria. Each night we all wandered down to Chinatown, where Michio cooked a sukiyaki dinner on the little personal table stove of a Japanese restaurant. I even developed a taste for *Fun-yu*, a fermented tofu, which reeks even worse than Limburger cheese. Hazel and I would pick up a tiny bit and then suck the edge of our chopsticks with delight.

A cable came from Japan with the possibility of an engagement. In my wildest dreams I had not hoped for that, so I decided to stay on as long as I could, waiting for an answer. For diversion, Hazel and I haunted the main street of Chinatown. I knew every shop window on Grant street, every item in every shop window, every price of every item in every shop window. Still no answer from Japan.

A lecture that Michio gave on choreography was a complete revelation to me. It was the first time I discovered there was something more to choreography than having an idea, improvising, and putting steps together guided by instinct. Michio's analysis as he spoke of his works was simple. They were either a direct interpretation of music or an idea originating from the music and adapted to it. A dance could have a literary source, usually taken from poetry, and the music might be composed for it. Or a dance could be abstract. Yet during this lecture he did not seem to talk about form.

All this was very new for me, and I was bursting with a need to know more. How do you *make* a dance? Was there a theory? Or was it just trial and error? I had to get Michio to tell me more. Although we did not have money to spend, we did have time. We often gathered in Michio's room, where he sat crosslegged at the head of his bed while I, being the smallest, found room at the foot. The rest of the company draped themselves over Hazel's bed, the chair, or on the floor. He told anecdotes, Hazel amused us with her mimicry, and I tried to get Ito to discuss dance. He talked of emotion and logic controlling life, the need to discover new movement, the importance of contrast, the balance of opposition, and the nuance of shading (elements Doris Humphrey emphasized in later years). The first time I heard the term A-B-A, the simplest compositional form, I was sitting at the foot of Michio's bed, absorbing every word he said and silently worshiping him.

By now it was March 10 and we were still in San Francisco, but this day remains vivid. We were invited as guests of honor to the estate of a painter, Mrs. Seis. The house was done in Japanese style, the land-scaped grounds had stone gardens with a little red bridge arching over a bubbling brook. Many artists were present, and Mrs. Seis had engaged Lester Horton with a partner to present a short program. At that time Horton was involved with ethnic dance. His performance consisted of American Indian dances and songs, a new experience for me. The intensity of the foot planting itself into the earth, toe to heel, the bodies leaning toward the earth, the rhythmic beat made the earth come alive. As the head moved, the feather headdress took on a life of its own, quivering and swaying to the strange, hypnotic chants. A few days later I again had the opportunity to see him perform. This time he did a Cambodian dance and a Polynesian war dance, and I was fasci-nated by the unusual movement. Horton later studied with Michio.

We kept expecting word from Japan. No answer. Friction between Michio and Hazel was mounting. Hazel was very beautiful, loved par-ties, and invited the admiration of many men. Michio would sulk, which made me miserable. My adoration took on a vicarious suffering for the many problems and hardships he was enduring. By March 19 things were gloomy. The Japan prospect had finally faded, and the remainder of the company scraped together enough money to leave. The only ones left were Hazel, our pianist Raymond Sachse, and me. We seemed to do nothing but have Japanese dinners.

By this time I was flat broke and had written to Dad explaining the situation. I held out as long as possible, but even fifteen-cent movies were now in the past. Dad wired a money order for 145 dollars to cover my fare and expenses and sent an irate note for me to come home immediately. It was March 21, and still I could not tear myself away. The future looked empty and gray. Going back to school seemed dull. Ito had decided to stay on. He borrowed money for Hazel's fare and decided we must both return to New York, she to her children, I to my family. On March 27, we boarded the afternoon train. Michio bought us a large bag of junk candy. Goodbyes were hard to say. Hazel cried visibly, and I cried inwardly. As soon as the train started, the nervous tension of the last few days was left behind.

Back in New York my family was thrilled to see me and happy with my success. It was a good feeling to be home again after three months of gypsy living. Since this was the end of March, going back to Columbia was impossible. I decided it was time for me to earn some money and gain independence. The only job I could qualify for was salesgirl at Macy's department store. I took the three-day training course, put on my blue dress with a large taffeta flounce at the bottom (employees could only wear blue or black), and started to work. By the second day I knew that being a salesgirl was not for me. I had never had trouble with mathematics, but I found the mysteries of filling out a saleslip very confusing. That, plus standing all day in the hat department, was very discouraging. By the third day I had lost my desire to be independent and never returned to that job. I preferred to starve and dance. Summer-camp jobs would be coming up soon.

Ito took up residence in Los Angeles, teaching and choreographing, presenting concerts and outdoor performances at the Argus Bowl, the Rose Bowl, and the Hollywood Bowl as well as doing some sequences for films. He finally took a company to Japan in April 1931. In March–April 1937 I was booked for a West Coast tour. I knew that Michio had divorced Hazel in 1936, had been jailed once for back alimony, and later, married a Japanese woman. I found his name in the telephone book, called him, and asked him to be my guest at my solo concert on March 25 at the Biltmore Theatre. He refused at first, but I begged and insisted that he come backstage afterward. Finally, he agreed. Now that I had begun to make a name, I wanted to thank him, to tell him what a strong influence he had been in the formation of that career.

I still had the image of that striking face in Studio 61. When I saw him, I had to hide my shock. He had gone quite gray, even his skin looked gray. When I took his hand, it was limp. He looked tired and very sad. I was devastated. I embraced him and said, "Michio, I am so grateful for all you have given me. I owe much of what I have achieved in dance to you." I could feel the tears welling up in my eyes. I never saw him again.

With Yeichi Nimura / My Solo Debut

There he stood—the most beautiful man I had ever seen. His lithe, gleaming body was wet from rehearsal, a finely honed instrument; his black wavy hair was held by a hairnet and a headband. He had a chiseled face with a thin, sensitive mouth, heavy, slightly arched eyebrows, and curved sideburns tapered over cheekbones to delicate points. His almond eyes were strangely remote, shielding his thoughts. I was enthralled.

After the tour, being home had been a terrible letdown. I had been thrust into Ito's company, all of whose members were much older, but they had treated me as an equal. I had proved to myself that I was a dancer, a performer, and could hold an audience. I had met interesting people and seen interesting places. The last three months had been wondrously exciting. Now I was returning to my old routine, which seemed stale and humdrum—courses at Columbia, classes with Fokine (never humdrum), and Spanish lessons at Cansino's in Carnegie Hall.

Each time I passed Studio 61, I felt a twinge. There was a sense of emptiness, a vacuum. One day, out of sheer nostalgia, I wandered in. A young woman was seated at the reception desk. Introducing myself, I asked hopefully if there had been any word from Ito (I had heard absolutely nothing).

"You know," she said, "I studied with Ito and then became his secretary." Her words tumbled over each other, accompanied by small, fidgety movements that made me slightly uncomfortable. Her name was Virginia Ice (later, Virginia Lee). There had been no word except rumors that Ito planned to remain on the West Coast. My stomach dropped down to my heels. Was this the end? "I've heard very interesting things about you," she continued. "I'm now working for another Japanese dancer, Yeichi Nimura." My ears perked up. "He's the greatest male dancer in the world," she said with a flamboyant gesture. I thought that was a pretty arrogant statement. I had never even heard of him. "He's looking for a partner, and I think he would be interested in seeing you dance. Would you like to meet him?"

Would I! We set a time when the studio would be available for me to show some dances. I cannot remember anything I did—I must have shown him the Javanese dance (without music) and he probably tried some movement with me—but I do remember there was an instant current between us. The air about us seemed to shimmer, in the way it often does on very hot days.

This was fall 1929. Alys Bentley had taken a liking to this young Japanese, and allowed him to use the studio without charge during its vacant periods, which often meant after 8 P.M. or later. I began a twelve-hour, sometimes longer, schedule: a dance class, then on to Columbia, after which there was a period of killing time until the rehearsal. While it was warm, I sat in Riverside Park and did my school assignments. As the weather grew cooler I discovered the gallery at the Art Students' League near Carnegie Hall. There were pleasant window seats, where I could look at the paintings, get tea for nothing, do my homework, and avoid the cold. Rehearsals went on until we ran out of ideas, sometimes as late as midnight. Then I took the hour-long, weary subway ride home to Brooklyn, walked eight blocks in the dark, arriving after 1 A.M., and spent the rest of the night reliving every moment of the nearness with Nimura. My whole life was focused on those hours of rehearsal.

Meanwhile, Virginia had found a gentleman named Lee Morrison, who was willing to finance a joint recital. (Virginia was good at that. She had enormous energy and could steamroll people into doing what she wanted.) Nimura and I would perform solos and close each half with a duet based on his ideas and choreographed by both of us. The catch was that my father had to contribute 100 dollars toward expenses. Dear Dad, always understanding, did. We were thrilled and excited at the prospect of our official debut in a concert of our own. Rehearsals now had a definite goal. We worked at fever pitch on our solos and started work on the duets. The program finale, *Fantasia*, was based on Japanese scarecrows. We each wore a tightly wrapped hood with a mask attached to the back, which created a double face. I discovered that Nimura had a sense of humor—fey, offbeat, with a rarely displayed twinkle in his shadowed eyes—and the piece became light, humorous, and grotesque. I loved comedy and fell into the mood with such ease that we both thoroughly enjoyed these Japanese capers.

A three-part cycle called *Cosmic Poems* was a major work. The first part, a solo danced by Nimura to the accompaniment of a drum he carried, was originally called *Chaos*. At our second performance he retitled it *The Earth Is a Drum* (I preferred *Chaos*). The second part was my solo, *Beginning*, which I choreographed to music by the English composer Norman Peterkin. I tried to convey arousing awareness of myself and my surroundings. It had a strange sense of wonder and discovery.

The last dance was the duet *Primeval*. Nimura and I choreographed it together in a totally modern vein, the movement evolving from our very personal style. It dealt in an abstract way with the birth of consciousness arising out of chaos, and the discovery and awareness of man and woman for each other. David Freed, a cellist who had composed for Nimura before, was asked to write the music. We had choreographed *Primeval* in silence. Somehow, when we did it to the music the entire quality, the essence, was dissipated. As time was drawing short, we decided to perform it in silence—rare in 1930.

The adoration I had felt for Ito as a godlike figure, I now transferred to Nimura, but on a very human level. I was gripped by a deep-rooted identification and love that conditioned my thinking, my feeling, my very existence. I knew he was living with Virginia, who worshiped him and would do anything for him. He was shy and uncertain of his status in the United States; she was his buffer, protecting him as well as striving for his career. To her, he *was* a god and could do no wrong; he was perfect. Nimura depended on her, owed her his allegiance, and was careful to be ethical in relation to me. I am certain he knew how I felt (how could I hide it?) and responded inwardly, but there was never any open indication.

Every rehearsal was precious. It meant seeing him, hearing his voice, and touching him if the choreography required it. I would hoard each minute so that I might savor and cherish it. In *Primeval* there was an instant that for me said all. We were both on our knees, side by side, bodies facing front, arms enfolded, heads turned away. Then slowly, very slowly, we turned our heads to look into each other's eyes, and my eyes could not lie. They offered a mixture of shyness, desire, apprehension, and fear of what I might see in his eyes. His look was warm, intense, and penetrating. I always waited for that look—time and space seemed to disappear. The only reality was the touch of our entwined hands. Many years later, he admitted that he was very aware of that look, but was afraid to respond.

The date for our premiere as co-recitalists was finally set for February 23, 1930, at the New Yorker Theatre. There was still a great deal to do: costumes to be made, flyers sent out, and the program settled. Virginia busied herself with much of this while we struggled on. Winter was upon us, and it was the beginning of the Great Depression. Virginia and Nimura had practically no income, no money for food. I was one of the lucky ones; Dad still had his job as manager of the medical department for the Workmen's Circle. Mother gave me a small daily school allowance for carfare and food, and I often invited Nimura and Virginia to eat at the Automat. If I skipped lunch my remaining thirty-five cents bought a bowl of soup or a sandwich, enough to get through rehearsal that night, with a nickel for fare to get home.

Mother never could understand why I was always so hungry at night. From time to time she invited Nimura and Virginia for one of her famous Russian dinners and watched with round-eyed amazement at the quantities of food they ate. Knowing times were difficult, she supposed they were storing up until the next time.

Bad as the times were, our spirits were indomitable. We were dancing, rehearsing, preparing a program—that was what counted. I lived in a fantasy world of loving Nimura and imagining what it might be like if I knew he loved me. Outwardly he never showed any emotion; he was truly oriental in that sense. His reserve and politeness made it difficult to know what he thought or felt, and at times he was so turned in on himself that it seemed no one else existed. It was the dance and only the dance. On rare occasions I was able to pierce this protective screen and reach the man.

One day I asked if he would like to meet me at Columbia after class.

The weather was pleasant, he was free, and to my surprise he agreed. I was not sure I had heard him right, but when I got out of class, there he was. We decided to walk and ended up all the way back at Carnegie Hall. From time to time, our arms instinctively entwined as in *Primeval*, the nerve ends in our fingertips tingling. We lingered, looking in shop windows, our faces staring back at us. There were interludes of total silence when unspoken words were left quivering in the air. He was making an effort in his way to tell me something—forever left unsaid.

Our debut concert was enthusiastically received, and *Primeval* was the high point—we had to encore it. Nimura had a style of his own. His movement was large, punctuated with a sharpness of attack and an intensity that made the stage sizzle—his body was totally alive. He had a lightness and elevation that were animal-like, and a face so exotically beautiful that it immediately commanded attention. He was truly spellbinding, whether in the studio or on stage. He had the same power of concentration that Ito had, but where Ito's dances were sexually abstract, Nimura's had a powerful sense of masculinity, suggesting strength by subtle dynamics. Neither Ito nor Nimura ever claimed to perform authentic Japanese dance, but both had a quality of accent and pulse that I later realized were identical to Kabuki phrasing. *Beginning* and *Minstrelesque* were modern. *Minstrelesque*, to the Debussy Twelfth Prelude called *Minstrels*, was inspired by paintings and the quirky gaiety of the music. I followed an instinctive sense of movement, but consciously emphasized use of the hands. The footwork derived from ballet.

The gamut of my solos was large: East Indian, Spanish-Moorish. In these works I was already searching for a personal idiom, neither Ito nor Nimura.

The reviews were favorable, even though we were novices at presentation. We had not allowed enough time for costume and hair changes to fit our very short alternating solos; however, our sponsor Mr. Morrison felt that the first performance warranted a repeat, so another was planned at the same theater for March 16.

I felt my confidence growing, and the urge to explore new movement became stronger. I began to haunt the music library on East 58th Street and spent hours leafing through piano music. It had to be piano music because we were using live accompaniment. I found a work by Prokofiev called *Désespoir*, and started to choreograph a new solo, which I finished in time for the second performance. John Martin wrote of my performance in the March 17 *New York Times*: "She moves with a charming ease which hides unsuspected strength, and her style is sufficiently electric to give play to both qualities. . . . She has also a feeling for creative compositions as evidenced by her ragged *Minstrels* and *Désespoir*, which showed marked leanings towards methods of Yvonne Georgi, but was none the worse for that. . . . She has a good musical sense, is personally decorative in an exotic way, and has exceptional plastic authority for one so young in her art."

With reviews for our second concert even better than for the first, we were booked by Mr. Morrison for April 2 in Philadelphia at the renowned Academy of Music. We felt we had made it. Nimura, Virginia, and I left New York the evening before the performance in great style, a string of porters carrying costumes, drums, gongs, and a spear. We checked into the Bellevue Stratford, "the best hotel" in Philadelphia, and felt very, very posh. The entire day was spent rehearsing, and that evening we performed. We gave our best, but the theater was enormous, and, with hardly any audience, the feeling was icy. Exhausted and depressed, we returned to the hotel and called Mr. Morrison, who was to pay us. "Mr. Morrison has checked out," said the clipped voice of the hotel operator. We looked at each other in disbelief. How could he? He knew we depended on the fee to get us back to New York. Well, I thought, here I am, stranded again. We've hit bottom.

In Nimura's room, we held a war council and took stock of our finances. Neither he nor Virginia had enough money for the return fare; I did if we did not eat dinner. But what about the hotel bill? That was to have been paid by Mr. Morrison. In a panic, we decided we had better get out as quickly and as quietly as possible. We overdressed with several layers of clothing. Discreetly, with our empty valises, we wandered out of the hotel without anyone stopping us and dashed to the theater. It was still open (they were striking the stage) and we grabbed our costumes and props. Somehow, we got to the railroad station. There we sat, sustained by a chocolate bar, and waited for the milk train.

We arrived at Pennsylvania Station, a bedraggled trio, dragging drums, gongs, swords, and spear (no porters). I had only enough money to call Dad at 4 A.M. "I'm at the station. I can't get home. I have no money," I said through sobs. "Don't worry," the comforting voice said sleepily. "Take a taxi and I'll pay him when you get here." The Philadelphia reviews were excellent, but we never saw or heard of Lee Morrison again.

What would happen now, I wondered. Virginia got us an occasional benefit and started to nag me about changing my name to suit my exotic looks. My father was furious, and I, not wanting to depart too far, simply inverted "Pauline," dropping the "e" and an adding an "a." Overnight I was Nilaupa, not a very beautiful name. The only time I appeared under that name was on June 21 in a benefit performance for the New York Infirmary for Women and Children. It was held in a beautiful little Greek theater on the grounds of Greystone, the famous Samuel Untermeyer estate in New York.

From time to time we rehearsed, but there were no engagements coming up. I lingered at the studio just to be close to Nimura. He loved golf and played at the Van Cortlandt Park golf links whenever the weather was pleasant. I suddenly had a bright idea: if he would teach me to play golf, I could spend a whole day with him, away from the oppressive studio atmosphere and Virginia. Off I went to Macy's with a list from Nimura of the basic clubs (a birthday present from my family). There was the long subway ride to Van Cortlandt and then the whole day for us just to be two simple people enjoying the fresh air and making casual conversation, as he tried very patiently to show me how to hold the driver, how to swing, and what the other clubs were used for. We walked together from spot to spot as he drove his ball—he was an excellent player—and I diddled while he waited patiently. We went only about three times, but for me they were days to savor over and over. After that I never used the clubs again.

I spent summer 1930 giving concerts and staging numbers for reviews at Green Mansions, a summer camp in the Adirondacks that was famous for its cultural programs. One of the staff members was Lou Bunin who, besides being an excellent painter, was involved with a marionette theater. I was so intrigued that I learned to handle marionettes and often took part in his shows. He also was kind enough to paint some muslin to look like stylized Javanese batik for *Altar Piece*, a dance of dignified ritualistic quality I had based on Ito's style, as well as some borders on a Russian costume for *At the Fair*. Both of these works from the February concert remained in my repertoire for many performances.

At the end of the summer I dashed back to Studio 61. Virginia said, "I have some good news." I waited. "Nimura has the possibility of being in a Broadway show. I also mentioned you, but of course if you are in it you will have to be billed as his assistant."

Until then we had been co-recitalists, partners with equal billing.

This would be a step down. My mind was in turmoil, and I could feel the blood ebbing from my face. Anguish metamorphosed into anger. I drew myself up to my fullest five-foot-one-inch height and said with a slight tremolo as I forced back the tears, "Virginia, I'll never be anyone's assistant." I turned my back so she would not see the tears brimming. Holding my head high, I strode out of the studio, got on a subway, and sobbed all the way home.

I had in two minutes cut off my professional association with Nimura, and with it any chance of seeing or being near him. Though I was shattered and numb, my gut reaction was that, at any cost, my artistic integrity must come first. The pain and the frustration lasted a long time. What hurt most was that Nimura had allowed this to happen and never said a word. An interesting partnership had broken up, and for what?—a show that never materialized. As time passed, hurt turned to bitterness. I would show him that I could stand on my own. I was nobody's assistant. I would give a solo concert.

My family recognized that I was going through a crisis and was at a breaking point. They knew I would have to find an answer, some way of continuing in dance. I needed their help morally and financially. We held a war council. They, too, were furious with Virginia after all the friendship and support we had given, and agreed that I must give a concert of my own. Dad offered to help with the business end and Mom with the costumes. But first I would have to build a complete solo program, no mean task for a teenager.

I rehearsed at the Whitehead Studio in Steinway Hall or at the Cansino Studio, when it was free. We rented the Guild Theatre, the most popular for dance recitals, for a Sunday evening in December, and I began to work feverishly. It was now late September, and since I was keeping only *Nilamani* and *Minstrelesque* from the old repertoire, I had to create an entirely new program in less than three months.

I had recently seen Harald Kreutzberg, Yvonne Georgi, and Mary Wigman during their first appearances in New York, and was very taken with their dance qualities. Their versatility—dramatic, lyric, semiethnic—in a very personal dance style was fascinating. Kreutzberg's quality of movement, his elevation, and his subtleties made him a new kind of male dancer. Georgi was heavier, earthier. But it was Mary Wigman who made a stunning impression. Hers was an approach to dance I had never experienced. Apart from her movement idiom and costuming, the strongest impact for me was her use of percussion.

I decided to do a work in that vein. In a little basement music shop on West 48th Street I found secondhand instruments and bought several Chinese items—three beautiful gongs, a tom-tom, a set of wooden temple blocks, very old temple bells that looked like bowls cascading down on a red cord—as well as a drum and a Turkish cymbal. I had a portable rack made for these instruments and started to work on my first truly modern dance piece. My accompanist, Irwin Jaeckel, and I composed as I choreographed. The percussion created an entirely new movement reflex for me. My motif was turmoil bursting forth in violent movement, sharp attacks, darting arms, sudden body shifts, and diagonal stage designs. I was newly aware of space up, down, and around me. I called it *Upheaval*.

From the time I begin a dance, I simultaneously begin to see the lines of a costume and the colors. Mother and I went shopping for fabric and constructed a costume on my body. Practice skirts were made to be sure the costume lines would not hide the movement. Dad and I designed the brochures. Birdee Rose, the sister of a school girl friend, did some color sketches for display, and I used one of them on the brochures. Friends and family were drafted to help in the mailing. Dad sent them to all his doctor friends and included tickets, which they felt obligated to buy. Even though the concert was ostensibly under the sponsorship of the Arthur Judson management bureau, we did almost everything ourselves.

Finally the great day arrived: Sunday, December 7, 1930. The theater was available for just that one day to do lighting, spacing, and then the performance. David Rossi, whom I had met at summer camp and who had studied at the Yale Drama School, offered to be technical director. We had to use whatever light was available: footlights and borders in red, blue, and white, and four floodlights on stands, two on each side of the stage. These and a set of black velvet curtains to dress the stage were our total equipment. The entire light plot consisted of a change of colors in the floods, always remembering not to use the same colors from both sides, in order to give modeling to the body (one of the lighting principles of the time).

I was functioning on nervous energy, and there was no time to indulge in fears. During the opening piano interlude, as I waited in the wings, I was not sure where my legs were. Once on stage, I was home. The performance went perfectly, even the costume changes. Except for one intermission and one piano interlude, there were no long pauses between the dances. I saw to it that the costumes were designed with change-speed in mind. Mother, who helped me make the changes, knew every hook and eye (no zippers). We choreographed the changes so she would hook my dress while I did my hair. Everything was rehearsed carefully at home, time and time again, but we did not allow for the shaking hands that dropped hairpins and skipped hooks. Nevertheless, I sailed through the evening with the assurance and arrogance of youth. The house was well filled and enthusiastic, and I was swamped with the bouquets of flowers traditional at a premiere. I was excited and happy. In the back of my mind was the triumphant thought: I did it. I've shown him!

The following day the reviews were raves, particularly John Martin's in the *New York Times* and Mary F. Watkins's in the *New York Herald Tribune*. I was happy, tired, and felt the usual letdown after a major creative and performing effort. I allowed myself a week of lolling around the house, reading, enjoying boredom, and wondering what next.

It was Sunday morning, December 14. Through a sound sleep I heard shouting. I woke up to hear Dad calling from the foot of the stairs, "Pauline, Pauline, wake up. Something marvelous is here! An article by John Martin in the *Times* drama section—two columns!" Dad bounded up the stairs two at a time and plopped down on my couch. There it was, a headline: "The Dance: A New Talent." It said in part: "When a young dancer with the manifest gifts of Pauline Koner rises above the horizon with a sweep . . . one realizes with misgivings how inadequate the resources of the dance world are to enlarge itself by fostering of rich young talent when it appears. . . . She has already exhibited her unquestionable right to stand alone. She can build a dance far better than the average, she can perform it with complete authority. Her only need is maturity."

Dad read it aloud in his best histrionic manner. Although I had hoped for good reviews, in my wildest dreams I had never expected this. I read it over and over, each time in disbelief that John Martin was talking about me; no, there it was, the same each time I read it.

I was only eighteen years old. I had hung on tenaciously to my pride, which forced me to pursue a lone way. Although I had overcome the thought of Nimura the dancer, I still was facing the fact of Nimura the man. During this period, there was a kind of mutual blackout. Virginia had effectively cut all communication, and I was too hurt and too proud to make any overtures. So I concentrated on plans for a concert the following year and numbed the hollowness of my heart.

I needed to create an almost entirely new program, this time not in desperation, but fired with a zest to explore the new avenue of modern movement that had created my success. I began to experiment and discovered the conscious use of breath. My movement wanted to start from deep within and find its own way through the body, out of the body and into space. The more I let this happen, the stronger and more vital it became, whether lyric or dramatic. At that time I was working by instinct, having no other source. It was no longer making movement; it was movement-making.

Because blue laws forbade performances on Sundays, the only night that theaters were available, dancers were forced to break the law. When the Sabbath League threatened arrest, we organized the Concert Dancers League to fight. Dad offered his services gratis to any dancer arrested under the Sabbath Laws. Helen Tamiris and Agnes de Mille headed the organization, and with the help of lawyers the law was changed. At several meetings I saw Nimura at a distance. We studiously avoided contact. My pain was still there.

Meanwhile, the prestigious Arthur Judson Concert Bureau had decided to manage me. In those years each dance performance was an event. There was a seething undercurrent of excitement. We were involved in searching, experimenting, exploring, and danced against all odds. The public did not take to the modern dance idiom easily; they wanted to be entertained rather than stimulated or challenged. Financially, there was absolutely no help. It all came out of our own pockets, and we were always paying off the debts of our last performance even as we planned the next. If an offer came along to dance for nothing, not even personal expenses, it was grasped simply for the chance to appear.

Such an opportunity came when Gluck-Sandor and Felicia Sorel organized a concert series for the benefit of the Dancers Club. Theirs was one of the first loft theaters I can remember, a lovely large studio-theater on 56th Street just west of Sixth Avenue. This series, considered important, included the well-known Swedish dancer Ronny Johansson, the Elsa Findlay Group, Sophia Delza, Esther Junger, and me. I had just given my concert on March 3, 1931, when I got a call from Edwin Strawbridge. He was commissioned to stage Prokofiev's *Le Pas d'Acier* for the League of Composers' annual major presentation and wanted me to participate.

I knew Strawbridge by name—he had a school on East 59th Street and a small touring company that primarily gave performances for children—and the League of Composers was a prestigious organization that sponsored contemporary music and unusual productions. I accepted happily, without even asking about financial terms. Strawbridge had me in mind for "Steel." I thought, In *The Age of Steel* it must be an important role. It turned out to be nothing special.

When I walked into the studio for the first rehearsal, I stopped short, stunned. There was Nimura, working with Strawbridge. He too had been engaged. I nodded and disappeared into the dressing room to pull myself together. Here was the opportunity to reestablish contact.

In the beginning, rehearsals were separated. He was cast as one of two "Efficiency Experts," Eddie Strawbridge as the other. I never knew if Nimura would be there or not. Each day was a fearful question mark; each night I rehearsed imaginary scenes of confrontation. Then the day came when a full company rehearsal was posted on the bulletin board. I came early to warm up. The colossal company of fifty-eight dancers arrived in dribbles. The first day passed in utter confusion. There was no chance for personal contact until final run-throughs, when I was late leaving one day and suddenly there was Nimura in the studio. He too had waited until the crowd cleared.

"Hello, Nimura. How are you? I'm delighted to see you in this ballet." Nothing could have been more stilted.

"I'm fine, Miss Pauline. How are you?" The answer was just as conventional as my question. But the barrier had been broken. We were two people again, instead of two zombies trying to avoid each other. Now everything changed for me. I tried to schedule my time so that there might be a moment of meeting, a word, eye contact, a nod. My anger had long ago disappeared, when I recognized that our break was for me a beginning. Now I wanted desperately to resume our friendship, if one could call it that. Since our roles had little contact, the encounters were few, but our conversation became a little less formal.

Le Pas d'Acier was under the general direction of Lee Simonson. The scenario was so complicated that I was never quite able to understand it. It involved a group of laborers (with universal implication from Egyptian times to the present), three peasant figures, a belt of Coal, Iron, Steel, a cross section of the bourgeoisie, Blue Cross, dowagers, flappers, a labor leader, a financier, boy scouts, and soldiers. The two efficiency experts, whose headdresses consisted of dial telephones, were the catalysts. The premise seemed to be the takeover of mechanization.

There was a series of ramps on which most of the movement took place. I had to jump from a five-foot-high ramp to the stage, and each time I panicked about jamming my ankles.

The production, co-sponsored by the Philadelphia Orchestra Association, was conducted by Leopold Stokowski. We were to open at Philadelphia's Metropolitan Opera House on April 10, 11, and 12, and then move to New York's Metropolitan Opera House for April 21, 22, and 23. During the technical and dress rehearsal, we found that working on the ramps and on various levels was more hazardous than expected. The stage was a mass of confusion: lights being hung, Lee Simonson in a tizzy about the construction, and poor Eddie trying to pull his ballet together. Finally we started the run-through with orchestra. Stokowski wore a white silk rehearsal shirt with Byronic collar and full sleeves cuffed at the wrist, which accentuated his hands as he conducted without baton. His halo of white hair and sharply chiseled features created a theatrical effect of which he was keenly aware. He stopped and started, repeated sections, waved his arms, shouted at the musicians, at us, and generally threw temperament around. Time did not seem to matter. (The musicians' and stagehands' unions were not what they are now.) We rehearsed until 4 A.M., by which time we were numb with fatigue and sore with muscle cramps. Everything seemed worse than when we had begun.

Somehow the premiere came off with kudos. My costume was a gray unitard, the first I had ever worn. A cubistic helmet covered the face to the mouth, with an eye opening that blocked peripheral vision and made working on the ramp twice as difficult. I felt like a medieval knight in armor rather than Steel.

After the third performance, the call for departure to New York was 8:30 A.M. The company was to meet at the main railway station in Philadelphia. This was it! I would have a chance to tell Nimura that I was no longer hurt and that we could be friends again. I found a seat in the train and made sure the one beside me was empty. I scanned the car. The train moved—no Nimura. Bitter and disappointed, I felt the tears brimming. The train stopped at the suburban station just outside Philadelphia. I did not bother to look up. A figure brushed past me, a familiar scent, and I quickly called, "Nimura, here is an empty seat."

He sat down, out of breath. He had overslept, missed the train, but caught a cab and was able to make it to this station in time. A small silence, and then words. We wiped away the unpleasantness between us. We could meet and talk. I could telephone, and so could he. Soon after the performance he did just that.

"Miss Pauline, I am giving a concert at the Roerich Museum on May 19. I would like to invite you to be my guest artist to do the *Cosmic Poems* and a Spanish duet."

"Of course, Nimura. I would love to."

How ironic. Our collaboration had been shattered because I was to "assist" him. Now I was to be his guest artist. Much had happened to me and I was totally independent as a dancer. Nimura had tried to find new partners, evidently not too successfully, and was still doing essentially the same repertoire. He discovered that he needed me artistically. Needed me!

The summer heat of 1931 was so oppressive that I gratefully accepted an offer to dance at Camp Scopus in July and August. It meant income and a chance to be in the Adirondack Mountains, away from New York. The entertainment staff consisted of Clifford Odets as social director, in charge of presentations; Mordecai Bauman, a young baritone from Juilliard, and me. I was to give one concert a week and participate in the musicals (I even sang in *H.M.S. Pinafore*). During July I got the bright idea to have Nimura invited for a weekend to share a concert with me. He agreed. I was bursting with excitement and anticipation. He came alone, and was his usual reticent self. We spent a lazy afternoon stretched out on a blanket on a hillside, drinking in the sun and watching the cumulus clouds shape our dreams.

In October, Nimura decided to expand and rented a studio with living space in what was called the Lincoln Square Studio Building between 66th and 67th Streets. In mid-afternoon the studio was idle. I was working on my new program and needed a place to rehearse. Now I called Virginia, whom I had avoided, and offered to rent the studio for two hours a day. I would have ample time for work, and of course I had an ulterior motive. Nimura was only one closed door away.

I created every possible opportunity to attract his attention. The record player would not work, or I needed to ask a question about studio schedule. Sometimes it was just a greeting on arrival or a goodbye on leaving. At times the frustration was so overwhelming that I burst into hysterical crying, curled up on the studio floor, hoping in the back of my mind that he would hear me through the thin partition and look in to see what was wrong. Sometimes this did happen. There were even a few ardent moments, an embrace, a kiss. He had the most wonderful body scent—strange, spicy, nutlike, lingering in memory. Dressed in practice clothes, Turkish-style trousers and low-cut sleeveless cotton top, his tan-gold skin was satin smooth. I tarried as long as possible in the dressing room and office after rehearsal. Sometimes I was invited into the apartment to chat or watch him play cards with his Japanese friends; sometimes we even had dinner together, the three of us.

A young girl named Elizabeth Hathaway had begun to study with Nimura. Her background with Pavley-Oukrainsky in Chicago was ballet, yet Nimura began slowly to groom her as a possible partner. She was absorbed in Nimura's style and determined to learn it. I was asked to teach her *Primeval*. She herself has said that she found my version of the work impossible to perform. I was secretly pleased when Nimura dropped it from his programs and substituted *Life Perpetual*; it was ours, only mine and his, born of veiled feeling, momentarily revealed, privately meaningful. Elizabeth assumed the name Lisan Kay and became his partner while they were abroad, a partnership that lasted for the rest of his life.

Now my major interest was preparing for my second solo performance, scheduled for the Guild Theatre on December 6, 1931, one year after the first. I worked very hard on the new program, choreographing eleven new works, all but one in the new area of movement I was exploring. Strangely, although I had pulled away from my earlier styles, I still felt that beautiful hand movement was essential. At a time when a turned-out position was taboo in modern dance, I refused to set myself any limitations; I pointed my toes whenever the movement demanded it. I was not "in," but then, I never wanted to be. I was criticized for this approach, which was considered too balletically influenced.

Eleven new works were a little too ambitious. Some were good and others fair. Nevertheless, by now I had definitely established myself in the field. The Judson Management had booked me for concerts in Appleton, Wisconsin (because of a raging blizzard I arrived there just in time to get on stage), and Altoona, Pennsylvania. I still needed the studio and continued to rent it.

One day in the dressing room a tiny, red-haired girl asked if she could talk to me. She was very intense, spoke hesitantly with a European accent, her blue eyes tear-filled. "I came to take classes with Nimura, but his style is not for me," she confessed. "I have seen you. I would like to study with you. Please, can you help me?" I explained that

I worked alone and was not teaching in the studio. "Yes," she said. "But maybe you could work alone with me. I must study," she said desperately. "I have been teaching Hebrew at the Montessori schools in Newark, and teach songs to the kindergarten children, but I feel dancing for children is very, very important. I've studied a little and I know that dance is the most important thing for me."

Her desire to dance was so great; I could remember and identify with her. This was the beginning of a deep and binding friendship. I had never had a really close girl friend. Her name was Corinne Chochem. We had many interests in common, and lessons stretched into conversations, dinner, and concerts. She later studied with Graham and Louis Horst, became an authority on Hebrew folk dancing, had a group of her own for years, and published two books on Palestinian dance. She married a well-known Israeli painter, Yehoshua Kovarsky, and became interested in painting. After her husband died, her own career as a professional painter blossomed under the name of Corinne Kovarska. She is brilliant, warm, intelligent, dedicated, and is as close to me as a sister.

The emotional strain of working in Nimura's studio, constantly aware of his nearness yet farness, became too much to bear. I had to put distance between us or face emotional disaster. In spring 1932, with the money I had earned on tour, I decided to go to the Near East. I discussed my problem for hours with Corinne in a little Chinese restaurant. She had recently returned from Palestine, where she had worked in a colony, and she urged me to go there. Deep in my heart I found it terribly hard to leave. I knew there was one thing I had to do to survive. I was a virgin and obsessed by the notion that I belonged to Nimura. If I did not give myself to him totally I was afraid I would never be able to relate physically to another man. It had nothing to do with how Nimura felt about me; it was my personal madness.

About a week before departure, there came a time. It was my last day at the studio. I knew he was alone in the apartment. I knocked at the door with some vague excuse about farewells, and the fact that I was really leaving dawned on him. He suddenly took me in his arms, but it was hardly a glamorous moment. The fear that Virginia might return hung heavy in the air. It spoiled any possible sense of intimacy or emotional closeness. In a way I felt, Thank Heaven, that's over, now I can go on. But I did not go on. I remained all evening, unable to tear myself away. Some people arrived. I was sitting on a window ledge, a little forlorn, looking out. Then I heard a voice, Nimura's voice, saying aloud, "Too bad I have spoiled beautiful flower." He was playing cards. No one took any notice. I glanced at him, our eyes met. No, Nimura, I thought, not spoiled, *liberated*.

The following week I left for Egypt. I did not see him again until 1936. Now I could face him without the inner tremor and I said, very quietly, "You know, Nimura, I'm cured. I asked you to come to tell you I do not love you any more. You do not have the hold on me that you had."

I do not know if he believed me. The spell was broken, but I was tied by the memory. Through the years, at times when I was very depressed, I would drop in at Studio 61, which had now become Ballet Arts, run by Virginia and Nimura, and then I would leave, feeling lighthearted and free.

One day in the mid-1970s, I had tea with Nimura. I think we talked more openly than we ever had in our lives. He finally admitted that he had a strong feeling for me. "Nimura, I don't think you really know how to love, to give of yourself from within." He acceded, "I think perhaps you are right."

In 1979 I was at a reception after a performance of my company, when a member of my board said, "I saw your name in the *Times* yesterday, the obituary column, in reference to a Japanese dancer." I stood very still. My heart contracted. I had spoken to Nimura only the week before. He was very ill, sounded desperate, and had asked me for the name of a doctor. When I got home the following day there was a message on my machine. It was Lisan. "Nimura passed away at 2 A.M., April third. I thought you would want to know."

Lisan invited me to speak at the memorial service at a Buddhist temple. I talked about the electric presence of the man as performer, the magic of the man as person. I wanted to celebrate the artist, the dancer, the man. When I heard someone say "Mrs. Nimura" to Lisan, an unforgotten ache cried, "No! Mine! Mine!!" I had never known that they had been legally married. The memory of a long-ago love was very much alive.

This page, clockwise from top: Samuel and Ida Ginsberg Koner at the time they met. Pauline, age 4. Michel Fokine and Vera Fokina in the twenties. Opposite: Michio Ito in his *Dance Caresse* (1926).

Opposite: With Yeichi Nimura
at the Untermeyer Estate,
1930. Below: *Upheaval* (1930).
Photo, Maurice Goldberg.
Right: *Chassidic Song and
Dance* (1932). Photo, Alban.

Opposite: *Spanish Impressions* (1933). Photo, Thomas Bouchard, © Diane Bouchard, courtesy Diane Bouchard. Left: *Bird of Prey* (1933), Russia, 1936. Below: With Russian students from the Lesgaft Physical Culture Institute of Leningrad in improvisation on the beach, 1936.

Improvisation on the beach near Leningrad, 1936.

The Solo Years

Egypt and Palestine

From the very first time I went to the Metropolitan Museum of Art as a child, I was magnetically drawn to the Egyptian rooms. The mummies, painted mummy cases, hieroglyphic figures, costumes, headdresses, and jewelry of turquoise, coral, and gold were spellbinding. I haunted those tombs. They were places of mystery, enchantment, and ancient rituals. Without definite plan, I booked passage for Egypt.

Since I had no dance commitments until February and March, I set no rigid time schedule—I would play it by ear until my funds ran out. I wanted to make contacts, dance in faraway places, do research, see ethnic dances, and absorb other cultures. These would be more important than any formal college education. It frightens me now to think how, not yet twenty and without any experience, I had the temerity to take on such a venture. It did not frighten me then. Even my parents' apprehension did not stop me.

I packed my costumes and music, all my percussion instruments, my summer and winter clothes, and on June 8, 1932, boarded the ocean liner *Champlain* for a midnight departure. There was the typical send-off with family and friends, the warning whistle for visitors to leave, the vibration of the ship's motors telegraphing departure. I was on my way. As I watched the dark swirling waters I came face to face with the rashness of my venture. Very much alone and surrounded by silence, I stood on the deck and defied fear.

Slowly the ship came alive. No one could sleep; soon we were talking and getting acquainted. This trip was for me a time of transition. Until now, I had been so involved in school, in dance, in performance, and in my feelings for Nimura that a social life had been nonexistent. I had not experienced the normal growing-up activities of girls my age. On board this ship I was thrust into a whirlwind of activity: walks on deck, mild flirtations, full-dress parties and dances every evening until the early hours of the morning. I loved social dancing and was constantly in demand. I discovered how it felt to be attractive to men. Word got around that I was a dancer, and I found myself in the midst of a coterie of admiring, gallant young men. I was honestly surprised and thoroughly enjoyed it with the naïveté of an innocent. It was all fun, and I had not known fun since early childhood.

The final night, June 15, was the gala: balloons, paper hats, tooting horns like New Year's Eve, and, when the bar closed, a glass of champagne in someone's cabin. Then up to the top deck. Since arrival was scheduled for 6 A.M., I simply decided to stay up the rest of the night and watch the sunrise with a friend.

By the time I boarded the boat train with all my baggage, I was a wreck. Fortunately, Per Bromberg, a Swedish engineer I had met on the boat, was also going to Paris. I gratefully accepted the offered shoulder and dozed on and off the entire five-hour trip from Cherbourg. I had planned to spend a few days in Paris, but knew absolutely nothing of how to go about it. We were both so green that we did not even know one could buy a guidebook. We simply knew the names of places we wanted to see. We tried all afternoon to find the Latin Quarter, never knowing that we were there all the time. The same happened in Montmartre. We did find Notre Dame, the Louvre, the Tuileries Gardens, and the Eiffel Tower. I sat in open cafés for the first time, sipped liqueurs, and watched the people stroll by.

Little by little I learned to cope. I tried to use a public telephone, but did not know the mechanics. I asked for help and suddenly there were seven Frenchmen, all talking at once, trying to be helpful. Finally one who spoke English came along, but by that time I had deciphered the French. Then the handle of my costume valise broke, and I needed a piece of steel wire to fix it. After trying several stores, we ended in the bathroom fixtures section of Samaritaine, a well-known department store. I spied just what was wanted, but could not make myself understood. An interpreter was called, a distinguished-looking gentleman who could not speak English. I was desperate. Then he said, "Ponimaete po-Russki?" I burst out, "Da, da," in my best Columbia University accent and explained what I wanted in pidgin Russian. He understood! —a meter of steel wire. We waited. Then one of the managers of the store, dressed in a frock coat, arrived with a pair of pincers and cut off a piece of wire attached to a pillar holding a display item. They did not have wire to sell; he simply took it from their fittings. When I wanted to pay, he said, "Mais, c'est un cadeau, Mademoiselle."

One of the purposes of my stay in Paris was to meet the concert manager, Ysaye (brother of the famous violinist Eugène Ysaye), and to interest him in booking me. I did see him, a charming gentleman, but at first he was not very encouraging. Modern dance concerts in France at that time were practically unheard of. However, after I explained that I also did Spanish and oriental dances, he warmed up and asked for circulars and pictures. He would try to get in touch with some organizations to see if there was interest and arrange an audition for managers on my return through Paris. I was pleased. In the end, it never happened.

On the evening of June 20, I took the night train to Marseilles to catch the boat for Alexandria. After some confusion at the Cunard office, I boarded the *Champollion* and, wonder of wonders, got a lovely cabin to myself. It was a small boat with friendly passengers—wealthy Egyptian cotton plantation owners, Indians, and people of various other nationalities. My nationality seemed to puzzle everyone; I suppose I was not what one considers a typical American.

The passage past Stromboli and through the Strait of Messina was awe-inspiring. A little past midnight we sighted the volcano, which sporadically spewed a small shower of flame and glowing matter. Then we picked out tiny sparkling lights that signaled our arrival at Messina —the famous Scylla and Charybdis, made by civilization into a simple and easy passageway. The lights along both shores, Sicily on one side, Italy on the other, scintillated. In spite of the beauty, the new impressions, the many people, the distance, my feelings for Nimura were always there, always beside me. I placed my hope in time.

The final evening aboard was, as usual, party time, and a rather wild one at that. It became a key to my stay in Egypt. I was invited to a champagne party by Roger, a tall, elegant young Egyptian with chiseled features and long, velvety lashes that shaded brilliantly dark eyes. He was truly handsome. The party was on deck, the host a wealthy plantation owner. Champagne was brought up in cases and we drank it out of water glasses. The sea was tranquil, the moon full, and the champagne very bubbly.

I felt wonderful, completely forgetting my misgivings at the prospect of landing alone in a strange country and a very different culture, not knowing what might happen. The champagne made me heady. Without much thought, I kicked off my slippers and began to dance. I was wearing a red plaid taffeta evening dress with a very full skirt and a tight-fitting bodice—wonderful to move in. I danced in silence, using various mood colors for dynamics and just letting it happen. There was a hush. I could feel the excitement of those around me, but I was dancing for myself because I *had* to.

When I improvise, I enter a dimension of "within-ness." It is a state of self-hypnosis; all the external falls away. What is left is a burning awareness of an inner absolute. I do not know what I am doing, how I am doing. I allow heartbeat, pulse, breath to take over. These feed rhythm and motion and mind. Time, space, and energy synthesize and I dance. Afterward, it takes time to re-enter the world.

When I stopped there was dead silence, then wild applause and voices: "You must dance in Alexandria. We cannot allow you just to pass through and disappear." Someone else said, "I know a newspaperman. Call me up and I will give you his name and telephone number. I'm sure he can do something." Roger thought his father, one of the wealthiest men in Alexandria, might be able to help. I was thrilled and happy. Things happen in strange ways.

I found a temporary hotel and finally managed to reach the newspaperman, M. Matelon. He was a writer for the daily, *La Bourse*, seemed to have many connections, and promised to do all he could. He first found me a place with a charming private family, where I had a lovely bright room and meals as well. A young Arab boy brought me sweet Turkish coffee with a roll for breakfast. I asked to have fruit for lunch; I was served fresh figs, dates, and mangoes, and developed a passion for them.

To those accustomed to Egyptian traditions regarding the protection of women, it must have seemed strange to meet a young girl traveling alone, feeling quite free to go about where and when she pleased. Most Egyptian women were veiled or traveled in carriages or cars; I liked to walk and to see the city. However, I found that wherever I went, men stared at me openly and at times lecherously. I bought a wide-brimmed white straw hat and filmy blue silk sun veil, transparent enough for me to see through, yet opaque enough to shield my face from stares. I never went out again without it. When I had to travel by carriage it required a certain technique. The drivers were native-born Arabs, but one always had to direct them where to go. I learned the Arabic words for right, left, and straight ahead, and managed as well as I could.

Alexandria was a city of extremes. There was the posh—the beautiful beaches on the Mediterranean, the luxurious gardens teeming with patterns of lush color and heavy with the perfume of tropical flowers, sumptuous homes with their cool marble floors and shaded windows, droning ceiling fans creating a lazy breeze. Then there was the poverty —the haggard faces of the hungry; children with trachoma-infested eyes; people sleeping at noon in whatever shady spot the street could offer, their faces and eyes blackened by huge flies, which they never even bothered to brush away; and beggars in tatters everywhere, asking for *bakshish*. The general filth and lack of sanitation appalled me. No one seemed to care. No one did anything. This was Egypt. You just did not look or see.

Matelon was not one of the wealthy clique. A journalist and gifted poet, he was also singularly interested in helping others. It was almost a mania with him. He always cautioned secrecy, and his manner was at times stealthy. I was waiting to hear from him about developments. He said he knew a commander of police who might sponsor a recital, but there always seemed to be confusion about appointments.

Most of the time I spent touring Alexandria, visiting friends, and sitting in cafés eating a strange, very sweet ice cream that hung from the spoon in dribbling shapes. There was also a water ice in ultravivid shades of pink, orange, and green that was very refreshing on a hot, muggy day. I continued social life with Roger and his friend Raymond. We went sailing in the Bay of Alexandria, where people owned their own floating cabins, and I went swimming for the first time from Raymond's cabin. The lavish life of cars, sailboats, and floating cabins was one I had never before encountered.

This was not an easy time for me personally. There were days of exhilaration and days of depression, of fear. What was I doing in this strange country trying to get engagements? I thought at times that I must be mad. There were so many obstacles, so many hazards. I had no pianist, stage manager, or lighting technician. How could I handle this alone? I had arrived on June 25. It was now July 5. At last, a definite concert date was set. My dream to dance in the East was coming true. The performance was to take place at an elegant club called Le Pré-Fleuri, just outside the city. They agreed to build an outdoor stage in the garden. It was to be a special event for the elite of Alexandria.

My first need was a pianist. Someone recommended Mario Antolini, who was playing nightly in a casino to earn money, but who was really concert caliber. We met and established immediate rapport. He was an excellent musician, sensitive to phrasing and quick to learn. He could also improvise with imagination. Next I needed a place to rehearse. I had met by chance a Mme Barda and was surprised to find that she spoke American English and that she was, in fact, Pauline Vincent, an American dancer who had performed American Indian dances in vaudeville. She had married an Egyptian gentleman and was happily settled in Alexandria with two lovely children. She found a local studio for rehearsals. Pauline, her friend Lilian de Menasce, and I became a threesome, happy to share our mutual interest in dance. It was rewarding to find women friends with whom I could be relaxed, and with their influence in Alexandrian society, many problems were easily (and some not so easily) resolved.

The performance was set for August 6, so I had about a month to pull things together. The program included a Palestinian dance, *Ya-Lel*, and *Chassidic Song and Dance* for which I had to find a singer, five more ethnic-based dances, and four modern dance pieces, one of which was very modern. Now I settled down to a daily rhythm of rehearsals, designing a flyer, and many social activities. I was taken to a Syrian café where I saw *ouled nail* (belly dancing) for the first time. I felt it was important to see it, even though it was a little odd for a woman to go to such a café. The place was so heavy with smoke you could cut the air. I drank thick, syrupy Turkish coffee and watched the most amazing display of isolated muscle control: stomach and hips moved independently, while, with elbows bent and hands joined above the head, the two index fingers made a snapping sound. The music was also new and entrancing to me.

I was not much interested in the young men I met, except as company for dinner, the cinema, or swimming. I was still bound by time past, and when I realized that M. Matelon had formed an emotional attachment to me I was disturbed. I wanted him as a friend and adviser, not as a lover. I decided to speak honestly and openly, allowing him to make his own choice. It was painful. I did not want to hurt him, but I had to make it clear that I could only meet him on a friendly or business basis. A day later I received a letter, scribbled in pencil: he understood my point and though it would be difficult, he felt that he wanted to continue to help me. He did nothing to hide his anguish, but he recognized the logic, and from then on our association was strictly business. I could not bear to look into his eyes.

As rehearsals progressed with Antolini, I found him more and more interesting. Slight of frame, sandy-haired, delicate-voiced, but with the emotion of his Italian ancestors, he was artistically stimulating and personally refreshing. We began taking long walks after he finished work at midnight. The city was still, the air cooled by sea breezes and perfumed by the intoxicating scent of the night blooms. The mystery of this land, its thousands of years of history, seemed to come alive. We held hands, no more. I liked him very much, but only that. He never allowed his deep personal feelings to intrude. He introduced me to interesting music by contemporary French composers and tolerated my stumbling French with humor and patience. As signal for our late-night walks he passed under my window and whistled the opening two bars of one of my waltzes. It became his personal signature.

Preparation for the concert did not all come easily. The effort to find adequate lights and curtains was a major project, and supervising the construction of the stage and the hanging of equipment was nerve-wracking. At times I was so disgusted with the inefficiency, I was almost ready to call it quits. There were days of utter exhaustion, when I questioned why I was doing all this. The answer was always the same: the need to dance, to perform, was a driving force. I knew that if I could not face the difficulties involved I had better give up. But I was not going to give up. I had committed myself to this performance and I would do it, no matter how difficult the mechanics of pulling it together.

The heat, the rehearsals, the anxiety about performance, and sudden waves of helplessness frightened me. The more surrounded I was by casual acquaintance, the more isolated I felt. There was so little in common, artistically or emotionally. I was prey to spells of homesickness. In the dance world too I was alone—a soloist. To pull myself out of these depressions, I plunged with forced energy into the daily discipline of work, rehearsals to polish every detail, aiming for the perfection one can never reach. Antolini was always there to help, his suggestions both artistically and theatrically valuable.

The sixth of August! At last it was here. The newspapers had been full of advance notices about this unusual event. The curtains were hung, the lights in place, the piano in place, and at 10:30 P.M. the performance began. The night was cool and very breezy, something we had not counted on during the warmth of afternoon rehearsals. Antolini was a hero, coping with music that kept flying wildly about in the breeze. Fortunately, he could play most of it from memory and sailed through without catastrophe. The elegant audience was responsive and so were the stray donkeys, braying in the distance. I had to do two encores; strangely, the most successful numbers were the two on Jewish themes. The newspaper reviews were raves in French, English, Italian, and Greek—I never did see the Arabic ones. All of them said this was a first; Alexandria had never experienced or seen a performance like it.

Because I had not yet performed, as promised, for my original Egyptian sponsors from the boat, I was invited by Roger to a soirée on August 11 for the cream of Alexandrian society as well as artists, intellectuals, and the press, at the home of his father, Morice Aghion. I chose to wear a green chiffon costume and give an "Evening of Improvisation."

This venue was much nearer to my idea of what a performance in open air can be. The garden was designed in ascending terraces and surrounded by a huge wall, over the top of which one could see the rounded domes of mosques nearby, one lonely streetlamp, and several tops of buildings in oriental style. It made a perfect setting. To one side a small terrace formed the stage, with the old wall fringed by shrubs and greens for a background. In the foreground were two tiny cypress trees, which made the space quite private and gave one the impression of looking into a woodland plot.

I danced, but not my usual repertoire. Antolini played beautifully and I danced to his improvisations. It was experimental, but the audience appreciated it. They said the effect was entirely different, as of course it should have been. I do not know how I dared to think of doing this in 1932; I was risking my reputation before a very select audience that had never witnessed anything similar, but it was a chance to experiment and to discover. The Italian paper wrote a long column, a paean to the evening, which was the highlight of my Alexandrian adventure.

However, I was strangely depressed when it was over. Perhaps my mood reflected my reaction to all this luxury in contrast to the struggle of artists to survive. I had received only thirty pounds for the Pré-Fleuri concert, which was barely enough to pay the expenses of my eight-week stay, yet I was surrounded by people who had so much with practically no effort.

After two months in Alexandria, I felt it was time to move on, to say goodbye to my friends, and to reach my original destination—Cairo. Off I went, determined to see the Pyramids, the Sphinx, and the famous museum. Tutankhamun's tomb had recently been opened and there were many wonderful treasures to explore.

I stayed at a small pension and at dinner met two very nice engineers who spoke English. My first visit was to the museum. I was a late riser, so that by the time I got there it was closing for the mid-afternoon heat. I was the only person walking in the white-hot sun; the entire city was closed and sleeping. That first day was a complete washout, but I learned that whatever you wanted to do had to be done before noon or after 4 P.M. So I went to the museum each morning with my drawing pad, attempting to absorb as much as I could. One day I was sketching one of four alabaster jar covers carved in the shape of a female head. I noticed people staring at me and wondered why. The heads were painted with the traditional Egyptian eyelines and tinted lips. Not until I got back to the pension and looked in the mirror did it dawn on me—I looked like those jar heads!

If you want to see the Pyramids, I had heard, you must go *au clair de la lune*, by the light of the full moon. Off I went alone on a long trolley-car trip, full of anticipation. I arrived at twilight. This must be a mistake, I thought. I must have come to the wrong place. The entire area was overrun by people picnicking and playing popular tunes on portable gramophones, the babble of voices filling the air. The place looked like an amusement park. Was this what I had dreamed of, the mystery, the sacred Pyramids? I fled back to town, almost in tears at all my shattered childhood visions.

The next evening I mentioned it to my engineer friends. They insisted that I go back with them late one afternoon. This time we went by car and arrived before sunset. No one was there except a forlorn cameraman with a camel for the tourist trade. Naturally I had my picture taken on the camel. We went into the Pyramids, where anachronistic bare electric light bulbs lit the passageways. There I was, looking at the Sphinx in all its silent majesty, the nearby Pyramids arousing memories of the suffering of those who had built the magnificent tombs.

At this moment the sun, a huge globe of red fire, was about to set. I felt a need to embrace what I saw. I ran up a small embankment, raised my arms, and gave myself over to the total experience: the silence, the timelessness, the immense open space, and the thought that my ancestors built all this, that it was part of me.

Now it was time to go to Palestine. Why Palestine? My lack of a Jewish upbringing made me rather curious about roots. Corinne had urged Palestine to me all winter. I also had friends there, Eda Pollack and her husband. It was comforting that for part of my first trip abroad, so far from home and family, I would not be totally alone. When I arrived in Tel Aviv, Eda invited me to stay with them until I was settled.

Tel Aviv was a tiny city hugging the Mediterranean and nestled alongside the old Arab city of Jaffa, with its minaret-crowned mosques visible in the distance. There were people of every description: dark-skinned Yemenite Jews with velvet eyes, long expressive fingers, and exquisitely embroidered dresses; Arabs in flowing caftans and keffiyehs; Europeans of every nationality. Old customs mingled with new. Donkey carts and buses constituted most of the traffic; private cars were few. Orthodox Jews prayed on Sabbath eve. Young settlers from the kibbutzim—energetic, sunburned, work-steeled bodies, and minds honed by the difficulties of survival—had a look of life in their eyes and a warmth in their heart. The spirit of youth was everywhere, singing and dancing in the streets. It was a city of pioneers. The atmosphere breathed enthusiasm, hope, and progress. I felt vibrantly free, as if I had shed an invisible layer of skin, and proud of my Jewishness.

I was in Palestine at a fortunate time, during a breathing spell between the 1929 and 1936 disturbances. At least it seemed so on the surface, but there was always an undercurrent of fear. The kibbutzim kept *shomers* (watchmen) to prevent pilfering of grain by the Bedouins or to warn of the occasional Arab ambushes. But generally, things seemed relatively peaceful.

My friends' apartment was a small one on Hayarkon, the street that runs along the Mediterranean. Sleeping on the balcony under the stars, I heard the camel caravans coming in from the north on their way to Jaffa, with their jostling camel bells and the chanting calls of the drivers. The first few nights I jumped up to watch the shadowy forms as they passed beneath my balcony, the camels gently nodding their heads. I was not dreaming. This was real.

Since the city was an intimate community, it was easy to meet actors from the famous Habimah Company and from the Ohel Company. I picked up some Hebrew phrases from them, although many spoke English because Palestine at that time was under British mandate. Concert dance in Tel Aviv was practically nonexistent, and performances almost unheard of, although Rina Nikova had a dance school and a year or two later Gertrude Kraus from Vienna established the first modern dance school. Yet I managed to convince a local manager to sponsor a concert—a rare occasion indeed—to be given at Mograbi, the home of the Habimah, and the only decent theater in Tel Aviv.

I started rehearsals with the pianist Nachum Nardi. It took about a month to pull the program together. It was very eclectic, and included my two dances based on Jewish themes, *Ya-Lel* and *Chassidic Song and Dance*. It was daring to present these works, which had been created in the United States, where people knew the real thing. I could only rely on instinct. I believe in Jung's theory of the collective unconscious, and somehow my guts told me I was right. As for the concert, I remember making up, I remember devouring a bar of chocolate halvah (a rich sweet made of ground sesame seed), but I remember little about the performance itself, which must have been a success since I was engaged for others in Rechovot and elsewhere. My name became familiar in the community.

One of the main reasons for this trip was to explore the native dance and music. I decided to settle in for a while and found a room with a private entrance in a little cottage right at the edge of the Mediterranean. From my windows I could see the sunset sky streaked with color turning the waters a shimmering crimson and purple, then sudden darkness—night falls rapidly in the Near East. The rhythm of the waves was the first sound I heard in the morning and the last at night. This is where I lived for six months. When I left I could not sleep at night—the quiet was too loud.

The only cooking device was something called a "primus," a small metal stand about sixteen inches high, with a single burner on top and a container for kerosene on the bottom. Lighting it was taking your life in your hands; it terrified me. Besides, my mother, saving me for art, had neglected to teach me how to cook. My room was quite a distance from the center of town, and restaurants were few and not very good. How could I manage? My dresser Pnina, who had become a good friend, offered to come daily and cook dinner, which consisted of the same menu: fried liver and potatoes, prepared on the devilish primus. In addition, a doctor had recommended that I eat two *lebens* (yogurts) a day. It was my introduction to what is now a staple for most dancers.

Word of my performances got around, and I was invited to visit one of the colonies situated out in the countryside near a small Arab village. Without a definite plan, I took castanets and a Russian peasant costume and off I went. I arrived in the late afternoon to much excitement; my hosts told me they had invited the neighboring Arabs to come to dinner. As evening approached I saw a band of Bedouin men and boys coming across the fields. We all had dinner in the main dining room, which also served as the recreation room of the kibbutz. After dinner the tables were pushed aside and a clearing was made at one end. I had been introduced to the Arabs, and now we invited them to dance. What a wonderful evening! They did a dance called the *debka*, singing and accompanying themselves on a hand drum. The men formed two facing lines, their arms on each other's shoulders. The dancer on the right end of each line, acting as leader, held a handkerchief high in his right hand. The movement, in a four-bar phrase, consisted of left heel forward, back to place, right heel forward off the floor, bend knee and hop on left foot, take two steps to the right, followed by tight jumps on two feet facing left then right. The pattern was constantly repeated traveling to the right, but since they moved in a circle, the two lines continued to face each other. They became a wheeling diameter. The idea was to increase the tempo, indicated by the waving handkerchiefs, until the movement's sharpness and bite created a heady excitement and exhilaration.

Now it was time for me to return the courtesy and dance for them. On went my Russian costume, and I did a Russian peasant dance in silence because I had no accompanist, but that did not bother me. To hold the intensity of a dance in silence, I simply created my own inner rhythms. Then I did a Spanish dance, with castanets and heelwork as accompaniment. They had never seen dancing like this before, and I doubt that they knew what to make of it. We had a wonderful party afterward.

The Arabs promised that the women would come the next morning to show me their dances. They arrived well scrubbed and wearing their dark Bedouin dresses brightened by embroidery, with blue tatooing on their faces (a sign of beauty), and children trailing after them. One of the women was a beautiful sixteen-year-old with large burning eyes and heavy braids; as the tribal chief's favorite, she was weighed down with heavy silver jewelry. The women's dances were not nearly so interesting; again the circle, but very simple movement, quite gentle and languid. In turn, I showed them my dancing which, because of its freedom, astonished and may have embarrassed them. After lunch, we said our goodbyes. What surprised me most was the warm relationship between these villagers and the colonists. At that time the Arabs seemed grateful for the help, the medicines, the food, and the new ways to make the land come alive. Everyone was friendly and comfortable, at least on the surface.

To see these dances done nontheatrically in a truly native milieu gave me a feeling for their temperament: the character, the dynamics, the basic elements, the true heart of the movement. I think one can best approach an ethnic style for artistic purposes by trying to absorb the characteristics of the people themselves, their tempo, rhythms in speech, and music. Even if the real movement and steps are not used, it begins to look real, it takes on the flavor rather than the fact.

I absorbed style from watching Yemenites talk. They had an unusually sharp attack in hand movement and an intense use of the entire body. Bracha Tzvira, Nardi's wife, was a famous Yemenite singer, one of the first to give concerts in this style. She taught me a Yemenite song, which I later used for a dance called *Yemenite Prayer*, singing the song myself. I laughed when I heard a story circulating in Palestine that I was not American at all, but a Yemenite who had studied in America and had now returned.

(I did return, but not until December 1979, when I staged my work *Cantigas* for the Bat-Sheva Company. Palestine was now Israel, and Tel Aviv a bustling European city. Most of my familiar landmarks were gone, but I did find my friends' house with the balcony I had slept on. Mograbi Theatre was a tired-looking movie house, and luxury hotels occupied the site of the little beach cottage where I had lived for many months. I found out that the artist Chaim Gliksberg's portrait of me in the white straw hat I bought in Alexandria hangs in the Tel Aviv museum.)

And then, that first trip to Jerusalem, as though I had been thrust back by a time machine. Something inexplicable happens when one first sees men praying before the Wailing Wall. There is a root-pain in the heart. Thousands of years of suffering are condensed in these lamenting old Jews. As they prayed, their rocking bodies seemed transformed into an ancient dance ritual. I left my own little prayer on a piece of paper, tucked into a crevice — an old belief that it might be answered.

I had chosen this trip abroad because of an intense desire to see and experience new places and new people, but deep within I knew there was the greater need to put time and distance between Nimura and me. My feelings for him were self-destructive. I had to break the hold, and this made me very vulnerable.

I met Alexander Pen at dinner. My friend Eda had invited him. That night, the room seemed charged by lightning. Pen was a fascinating young Russian, a gifted poet, with a velvet-rich voice. Tall and spare, his training in boxing had developed a sinewy muscular aliveness that was visible through his open shirt. A jaunty cap pulled down toward his right eye shadowed a high, open forehead. Sharp cheekbones pushed against burning dark eyes and the twisting of his thick brown eyebrows framed eyes with an ever-changing expression. A lean, fine-boned nose and a strong jaw highlighted a voluptuous mouth. Yes, this was a strikingly handsome man, whose vitality was provocative. At age twenty-six, he seemed driven by a restless energy and need, which I shared. There was instant attraction. Long after dinner Pen sat on, talking and enchanting us. I knew then that I would stay longer than I had intended.

He began to drop in daily, usually in time for dinner, and since there was no privacy until I moved, we took long moonlit walks along the Mediterranean. He recited his poetry, lyric poetry inspired by the Palestinian landscape. One of his poems, "Kineret," had become a popular song, which, with the help of some cognac, he sang in a lusty rich baritone that hung in the night air. We meandered along the ocean road, caressed by the cool air. The world seemed far off.

Our problem was communication. He spoke Russian, German, and Hebrew, but not a word of English. I spoke English, Yiddish, and a smattering of Russian and French. What finally evolved was a mélange of Russian, German, and Yiddish, with occasional Hebrew thrown in for good measure.

Pen was not specific about his past. He was a *bezprizornik*, one of the children orphaned in Russia between World War I and the Russian Revolution. They roamed the country in wild bands, stealing, looting, terrorizing the countryside. They lived with, and by, brutality. He often talked about this period of his life, but was very vague about his general background. How he got to Palestine in 1927 or for what reason he came I never found out. I could only speculate about what he did, where he went, or what his life was like aside from my own contact with him. This much I did know: he drank heavily, had a wife and child, was given to wild swings of mood, and was the acknowledged lover of Hanna Rovina, the leading actress of the Habimah Company, who was fourteen years older than Pen. What he truly felt for me I could not know.

I was captivated by him, all my emotions engaged. I could relate to him without having to mask my feelings. I longed for his company, but without a telephone there was no way to keep up communication. Quivering with anticipation of his unannounced visits, afraid that I might miss him, I ventured from home only when necessary. At the same time, I was trying to grow artistically, to understand my inner needs — and to stretch my meager finances. His constant mood changes swept me along, but the toll was heavy. All I could do was try to hold my balance. In my cottage by the sea we were very much alone in the same room at times, but there were also times when, curled in the protective warmth of his arms, I would lie awake consciously to feel every moment of nearness. For this short interval, I was not alone.

Letters from home began to arrive, demanding that I return. Under a Columbia Concerts contract I had two commitments to fulfill, and one I had already refused. Another, and I would lose the contract. I began to talk to Pen about going home. He reacted with unexpected enthusiasm: "How would it be if I come to America with you?" I would have him all to myself! Did I have enough money left to pay his passage? I thought I could swing it. Jubilantly, he applied for a visa. A few days later he appeared in my doorway, his cap pulled low to hide the desperation in his eyes. "They won't give me a visa," he said.

It was a bitter evening. A brooding silence hovered in the corners of my room. I shivered with cold. He sat there numb with shock and disappointment. Finally, I said, "I have to leave in one week. I have a deadline. Suppose I rent a car and we take a trip for a few days? We'll go to Kineret and you can show me Palestine."

Wherever we drove there were new orange groves. History breathed from the earth, the rocks, and the mountains. I stood on the shores of the Sea of Galilee and was proud of my heritage. Everywhere there was a sense of timelessness and immediacy juxtaposed. There was joy in the moment, but I learned that spending twenty-four hours a day with someone you think you love reveals unknown traits. We had no true communication. The constantly changing moods were difficult, and the ever-present sense of parting filtered through. At night I awoke, my face wet with tears. When I asked if he loved me, he answered in Russian, "I have an 'abstract' love for you." To this day I wonder what that means.

As the days passed Pen brooded more and more, and finally a complete pall settled over us. I was leaving, but that was not what really mattered. His plans were shattered. No America. No escape into a new life. Now I knew that for Pen I had simply been a fresh experience, a moment of hope during a dark time.

This was March 1933. I had been away nine months. I had escaped one continent in order to search and discover on another. Now I was leaving again—again an escape. As the shore of Haifa receded I discovered the truth: Pen was fading fast. As America approached, I trembled at the thought that I might again see Nimura.

When I arrived, he was gone. He had given up the studio to embark on a European tour. I rented that studio and held on to the memories.

Interim

This was the first studio of my own, the start of breaking away and testing my independence. I knew it was rash; I had no income, just the first month's rent paid. One wall had many windows, plenty of light, so I painted the others a deep blue. Mom and I found some fabric of the same color and hung curtains to create a space for a dressing room and a room of my own, where I had a desk, a chair, and a couch. Nimura had left excellent brass barres along one of the walls and a single standing floor mirror in a gold frame. I set to work organizing classes, which I hoped would pay at least the rent, telephone, and electric bills. Whatever little remained would be subsistence money.

The greatest luxury after years of renting studios by the hour was time—I was now rich in time. No more anxiety about wasted minutes on an uninspired day or meeting deadlines, which has always created a block for me. I was a night person and found my most creative hours after dark. Now I could work until midnight and not have to travel afterward. In the beginning I stayed in the studio two nights, then three, and slowly it grew until I was home just on weekends. Mom loaded me with food and slipped a few extra dollars in my hand when I went back.

Often with no idea in mind I would play a record, some favorite piece like Beethoven's Seventh Symphony, and simply improvised for hours. I was dancing for myself, with myself, out of myself—purified, fulfilled, transcended—and late at night I would fall asleep, very tired and very happy. Exploring without a guide, I needed to find an amalgam of the various styles I had learned that would breathe "me." I did not know then how many years it would take. This I did know: I did not want to be derivative. I never took a modern dance class—not with Martha Graham or Doris Humphrey or Louis Horst. From the very beginning I was a loner.

Corinne came very often and stayed for days. We ate in our favorite Chinese restaurant, commiserated with each other and laughed with each other. There were also days of despair, when my heart and mind played games. The immediacy of this studio kept memory alive. In the heartbeating stillness of a sleepless night, at unexpected moments in the day, Nimura's captured image in the mirror became a luminous presence.

The world was looking grim in 1933, but then an unexpected call would change the picture for me. One was from Edwin Strawbridge, who asked me to dance as his partner for two performances at huge Lewisohn Stadium in July. Strawbridge said that he had chosen symphonic dance music—dances from Beethoven's *Prometheus*, Borodin's *Prince Igor*, and the like—which meant he had to create works specifically for this occasion. I danced the female lead in four pieces and contributed much of the choreography for Saint-Saëns's *Danse Macabre*, which was a duet. Eddie had assembled a group of forty dancers, including Ruthanna Boris, whom I remember as an intense, dark-haired young girl with burning eyes. I do not know how it was pulled together so fast, but Eddie had tremendous energy, strong nerves, and infinite patience, so I found him very congenial to work with.

To my great surprise, the billing was to read "Edwin Strawbridge, Pauline Koner and Company." Rehearsals progressed at fever pitch, with all the usual last-minute hysteria of costume fittings and consultations with musical director Hans Lange. The final orchestra rehearsals, midday in the hot sun of July, were exhausting. A special stage was built for us in front of the orchestra shell, with a green gauze curtain hiding the orchestra and providing a backdrop for the dance. Of course we were worried about the weather and listened to the hourly reports (postponements are shattering). July 18 arrived, a sunny day, and the afternoon dress rehearsal went well. As I was making up for the performance, someone shouted, "It's begun to rain!" The rule was, if it rained until 8 P.M. there was a cancellation.

I went on making up, praying for the drizzle to stop, concentrating on my performance, trying very hard not to be distracted. At 7:30 the sky cleared. The stage was dried as the stars asserted themselves. By performance time the evening was perfect, pleasantly cool and clear, and, most wonderful of all, the stadium was packed. Thunderous applause came from 12,000 people. The sound washed over us in waves, enveloped us, stimulated us.

In order to reach an audience in an arena that size a performer has to enlarge his movement and intensify his emotions. Physically it was tremendously demanding, but the fatigue at the end was also exhilarating. The following night the audience was 15,000, the largest of the season. We gave not the usual second-night letdown performance, but one freer, fuller, and richer. It did not add up to any personal creative growth, but it was important performing experience.

In August Doris Humphrey and Charles Weidman gave performances at the Stadium for the first time. Doris had given birth the month before to her son Charles Humphrey Woodford, so she appeared in only one number. I had never seen any of her works, and the dance that overwhelmed me was *Water Study*. Performed in silence, the dancers' bodies were metamorphosed into rhythmic, undulating waves, receding tides, swirling, swooshing eddies. The dynamic buildup *was* water. I have never since seen the work performed like that. The whole program stirred a cognizance of something new, something unknown, something I did not explore until many years later.

The result of the Stadium concerts was an offer for Strawbridge and me to share a concert with the Don Cossack Choir, with which I had appeared the previous December at the Waldorf Astoria. We would use part of our Stadium repertoire: *Danse Macabre*, the *Polovetsian Dances*, and the polka from *The Bartered Bride*. I shuddered when I heard we were going to the cold north of Bangor, Maine, in October. Cold is my worst enemy. Still, sharing programs with Eddie was a happy experience. I enjoyed him as a person—generous, warm, honest, and not interested in playing dance politics. He was a respite from the constant struggle alone.

That struggle continued with two solo recitals, one at the Schubert Theatre on November 5, 1933, and one at the Little Theatre on April 29, 1934. These fulfilled the requirement for an annual recital, but their impact was not too great. I was moving in two directions simultaneously, the modern and the neo-ethnic. It was difficult to leave behind what came to me so naturally and try consciously to integrate my multistyle dance background. Nevertheless I was working toward a stylistic synthesis, so that even dances with an ethnic root would be far removed from authenticity by distortion, invention, and stylization.

The years 1933 and 1934 were full of experiment and creation. I did *Rondo* to Mozart and *Waltz Momentum* and *Bird of Prey*, both composed by my accompanist Harvey Brown. This last dance was a step in the new direction and remained in my repertoire for quite a few years, as did *Dance of Longing* set to percussion; Lord Berner's *Three Small Funeral Marches*—*For a Statesman*, *For a Canary*, and *For a Rich Aunt*; and *Cycle of the Masses*; adding to the original *Upheaval*, an introduction to percussion called *Awakening*, plus a finale composed by Brown called *Liberation*. So much for my modern trend. In the ethnic style, I did *Yemenite Prayer*, a *Debka* by Zeira, based on the Arab dance; and Gaillard's *La Maja Maldita*, a new Spanish dance.

One day in 1934 I got a call from the office of Leon Leonidoff, producer of shows at the year-old Radio City Music Hall: "You have been highly recommended as a possibility for one of our shows, one of your Spanish numbers." I was to make an appointment for an audition. Having rarely auditioned, I was terrified. An engagement as a soloist at the Music Hall meant a great deal, professionally and financially. I wanted it desperately. So I packed the red velvet costume I had designed, which was totally different from most Spanish costumes. It was a one-piece dress fitted along the body and flaring into ankle-length fullness, one long sleeve, the other arm bare. From one shoulder a two-inch band of gold metallic ribbon was appliquéd, winding around the body in corkscrew fashion to the edge of the skirt. This created a very unusual look, especially during turns. Taking my gold shoes and castanets, off I went. I was ushered into a huge studio, where Leonidoff was waiting with his assistant, Russell Markert, founder of the Rockettes. Harvey Brown played for me. They seemed impressed and said they would let me know shortly.

I waited and hoped. Then the call came: I was hired for their next show, and invited to come look at the set design. One look was enough to make me wince: an eight-foot-high platform, eleven feet deep, twenty feet wide. "Suicide! It's impossible to dance on such a shallow space. I can't do it," I said, choking on the words. I knew I was risking the engagement, but I had no choice. "We'll think about it and let you know," they replied. I waited and worried, consoling myself that at least they had invited me.

The call from the Markert office said, "We've come up with something else—plenty of space for you!" The "something else" was really something else! This time it was the entire open stage, 100 feet wide. I was sure it was done with malicious intent. Somewhere on stage right, at an upper level, there were some figures in Spanish costume on a balcony, lit behind a scrim. There I was, five-foot plus, making my entrance through the center of the front curtain, a huge gold affair rising from floor to ceiling of the Music Hall stage. Thank goodness for the red costume. I danced a few bars on the apron, then the curtain drew apart and I had the entire stage alone. Feeling like Alice in Wonderland in her miniature state, I had to reach an audience of more than 5,000. The heelwork and small castanets had to be heard above the orchestra.

I never worked so hard in my life. With four shows a day, and five on Saturday, I felt more like a track runner than a dancer, but at least I did not have to worry about falling off a platform. Instead, I had to worry about enough breath to last through the dance.

Dancing in a presentation house was a new experience. One actually lived there. I had a private dressing room with couch and shower. Between shows I could read and relax, or see new movies in the "preview room." There was a cafeteria and if I wanted to go out for dinner I did not remove my theater makeup; I simply put on dark glasses. Makeup stayed on all day. I put my base on at home at 10 A.M., went to the theater with dark glasses, and finished the makeup there. At 11 P.M., after the last show, I was too tired to take the makeup off. On went the dark glasses, home I went, and peeled the makeup off like a mask.

There was no other life but the theater. Once home, I fell into bed, dead tired, hoping to recover enough energy for the next day. I was at Radio City only one week—the hoped-for holdover of the film never materialized—but I did get the magnificent fee of 250 dollars, many months of studio rent.

I spent summer 1934 again at Green Mansions. This time I was asked to bring a small company of three or four dancers. I had had little experience choreographing for others, but accepted apprehensively. Working with a group proved challenging and instructive. Not knowing how to begin, I used motifs from my solos and expanded them. The variety of work was interesting: one dance concert and participation in a weekly musical.

The end of the season was nearing when I was told there was a cable waiting for me in the office. When I opened it I thought, Someone is playing a joke; I'm sure this isn't real. It read: "Have possibility concert tour for two months in Russia. Dad."

But it was real. Mom and Dad had celebrated their twenty-fifth anniversary with a trip to Russia to find old relatives and visit their birthplaces. Dad had taken my press book, just in case, and had approached the Soviet concert bureau, Gometz. They were interested, particularly because I had been a pupil of Fokine. With that as a background I suppose they felt they were not gambling.

I cabled acceptance immediately. Letters followed and terms were fixed: I would receive a round-trip ticket, a two-month guarantee for concerts at 1,000 rubles per concert, with a six-month option to be negotiated. The concert bureau would supply a pianist, an interpreter, and possibly a cellist to play short intervals, and would provide all transportation. It sounded too good, and I waited for the bubble to burst. There was nothing in the offing at home, and I was extremely curious to see Russia.

I was thankful for the Russian I had taken at Columbia; at least I could read and write it. It was daring to think of performing in Russia, a country attuned exclusively to ballet, except for the impact of Isadora Duncan and one or two minor efforts to modernize dance which had never taken root, yet it was the most exciting moment of my life.

Russia

I did not believe it would happen. Communication was very haphazard, but I busied myself with preparations. Costumes, music, instruments all in order. I tried to put together a wardrobe that would be practical and serve all occasions, both cold and warm weather. Fortunately I had a raccoon coat, the kind fashionable on college campuses. I filled a valise with all the woolens possible, and then stuffed every available space with cleansing tissues. I had heard paper was scarce. So was makeup; I made sure to take a well-stocked case.

Then one day there it was, an authorization to Intourist for a round-trip ticket to Moscow with a request that I come as soon as possible. On November 10, 1934, I was aboard the *Ile de France*, bidding tearful goodbyes to my family and friends. As I waved to my family and the dark span of water began to separate us, a sense of loneliness and desolation overcame me. I stood there watching the white flutter of my mother's handkerchief until it disappeared, and felt a tear trickling down my face. But I loved ships and being on the water. Soon I was enjoying the pleasures of an ocean voyage, living in the moment, dismissing all apprehension.

In Paris I was met by an old friend, Sidney Bernstein, who was studying at the Sorbonne. For my three-day layover he had found a hotel on a narrow little street near Notre Dame. A poste restante letter at American Express told me that Nimura was in London, so I would not be able to see him. Paris would be very dull, but not all that dull. Sidney introduced me to the student life—eating in small bistros, sipping a glass of wine in cafés, and listening to violent arguments.

The evening of the third day I boarded the train, with all my luggage on the racks above, and prepared for the journey that would take me across all of Europe and on to Moscow. I was worried. Hitler was more and more powerful in Germany, and anti-Semitism was rampant. I knew the train had to pass through Germany. I had an American passport with a Russian visa, and I was Jewish. Visions of being dragged off the train on some trumped-up pretext haunted me. When we stopped at the German border, I heard percussive steps and the crisp voices of customs officials demanding documents and shrank into the corner of the compartment, quivering inside. I handed them my passport, holding on to its tip as long as possible for fear they might take it and not return it. They leafed through it slowly—I never looked up—and then it was shoved back at me. I did not stop shaking until we left Germany and entered Poland.

When we came to the Russian frontier, I boarded the Russian train that would take me to Moscow. Again passports, customs, and surprise when they learned that I, a dancer, had been invited. They treated me with great respect. In fact, I was the first American dancer to be officially invited after President Roosevelt's recognition of the Soviet Union. A representative of Gometz met me on arrival in Moscow on November 24. Confident that I would understand Russian, all I could get was the greeting; the rest was too fast. The representative escorted me to the bureau to meet the officials and then took me to the Metropole, a prerevolutionary hotel. The trip had taken three nights and two-and-a-half days, and I was thoroughly exhausted.

The Metropole, the finest hotel in Moscow, was situated on a square diagonally opposite the Bolshoi Theatre. Elegant as the hotel was, with its broad hallways, impressive lobby, red carpeting, and crystal chandeliers, very few rooms had a private bath. My otherwise large and cheerful room did not, but it did have a telephone. There was a control desk on each floor, where keys were left with a very efficient lady who monitored the floor. There was no such thing as room service, but one could always have a pot of tea or hot water brought in. The first days I had my dinner in the Metropole dining room. An elaborate remainder from an earlier era, it had a live orchestra that played many current American tunes, sometimes with a singer. There was not much on the menu in the way of meat or chicken, and fruits and vegetables were scarce now that it was winter. I settled on a dish called *russky salat*, which consisted of a mixture of cold, canned vegetables with potatoes and whatever else was available, bathed in a sort of mayonnaise. With this and all the coarse black bread I wanted (I loved it; the Russians hated it) I was able to survive.

My first impression of Moscow was mixed. The city exuded a tremendous energy—people everywhere on the go to work, to market, to the theater—but they were drab. Their clothing was a no-color faded gray-black, bundled-up on shapeless figures, the women's heads bound in kerchiefs, the men in fur hats with flaps turned down over their ears. The mist of people's breath in the dry cold air clouded their faces. On the other hand, there was the Metrostroy, the newly opened subway. One traveled down steep escalators deep into the earth to discover these palatial stations. I never had to ask which station I wanted; each was individualized by its design. Equally impressive were the immaculate streets. Small containers were mounted on posts, and all litter, cigarette butts, and scraps of paper were conscientiously dropped into these receptacles. When I remarked about this I was told, "But these are our streets, we must keep them clean."

My arrival coincided with a terrible moment historically. On December 1, 1934, Sergei Kirov, president of the Leningrad Soviet, was assassinated. Kirov's liberalizing policy had made him very popular, so all Russia was shocked. The tremendous public funeral was a very elaborate, moving production, with Stalin one of the chief mourners (perhaps hypocritically; they had been rivals). I watched the funeral procession in Moscow from my hotel window. It lasted five hours. Many thousands of people demonstrated their sorrow by parading to Red Square, and the State Academic Theatre of Opera and Ballet, the old Maryinsky in Leningrad, was given the added name Kirov.

Gometz assigned a young woman, Valentina Mikhailovna Genne, to be my interpreter, companion, and tour expediter. Valya had been married to an American, and soon became my close friend, helping me through many difficult times. A pianist, Arkady Pokras, was recommended, and we started to rehearse. Rehearsals went well. Arkady took to my music with zeal, and by December 11, I had a final run-through in preparation for a very special event. Before my official premieres, Leningrad on January 1 and Moscow on January 17, I had been invited to give a private performance at the Klub Mastera Iskusstva (Masters of Art Club). This was a club solely for members of the arts: dancers, actors, stage directors, musicians, film makers. Each major profession had its own club. Many of them were housed in old palaces and had restaurants (with better food than publicly available), game rooms, and a small theater. I was told that all foreign artists were requested, as a courtesy, to appear at Mastera Iskusstva. Although it would be a trial by fire, I had to accept.

The stage was miniature and had no special lighting. Dancing almost in the faces of the leading artists of the country, I tried to forget my fears and plunged in. Well, there were bravos! applause! speeches, curtain calls, and encores! The next day, all Moscow was talking. I was dazed—when you live through a very trying performance, it becomes a blur. All you can recall is the result: success, elation, failure. It is a built-in protection for artistic survival. Overnight I had become a celebrity, passed upon by the leaders of Moscow's artistic world, and was looking forward to my Leningrad debut. Now the cold, long waits in line for a taxi, a bus, or a train, or even to buy some salami and bread in a food shop seemed of little importance.

Lines—there were lines for everything, very disciplined ones. You took your place and waited interminably. Transportation was most difficult and often walking on the ice, which covered the streets permanently throughout the winter, was faster. Perhaps this was one of the reasons why people were always late for appointments. I was grateful for my raccoon coat, and bought *valenki*, crude boots made of felt, clumsy but warm. I learned to walk in them by shuffling along flat-footed on the ice.

In Moscow I met Vsevolod Meyerhold and was invited to his theater. Meyerhold, who had parted with the traditional and become truly avant-garde, was one of the leading stage directors of his time. I saw four of his plays and found them almost choreographed. What struck me most was his stylization of gesture. He was an anti-realist, strongly influenced by dance and music, and believed that all elements of a production should be integrated. There was a kinship in what he and 1930s modern dance were doing.

When I arrived in Russia, modern dance as we know it was unfamiliar.

Isadora Duncan had come and gone, and had instigated some attempts to introduce new forms—mechanistic dance by Nikolai Foregger and erotic displays by Lev Lukin and Kasyan Goleizovsky—but they were not having much success. By 1931 most of these trends had died out. Ruth Page had appeared briefly as a guest of the Sophil Society in Moscow in 1930. Anna Sokolow came on her own and left disillusioned. Dhimah was there, also on her own, trying to form a group. Locally, some hardy souls were trying to have a say. The Russians, steeped in their age-old love and admiration for ballet, were hesitant to accept a rival, except for their native folk dance.

I came to Russia to introduce American dance, but I would first have to establish myself as a dancer and an artist to gain universal confidence and acceptance. Russians are famous for their love of character and folk dance as well as dramatic quality. If I could get my peers and the public to accept me on that basis, my modern works would be viewed with more sympathy.

Program building was a delicate and subtle affair. The pattern was to open with the buoyant Mozart *Rondo* and Harvey Brown's *Waltz Momentum*, both of which used much torso movement, then oriental and Spanish dances. Sandwiched in were two altogether modern works, *Bird of Prey* and *Three Funeral Marches*. As time went on, I added more modern works; acceptance gave me confidence. I always had to end with a Spanish dance, which seemed to be expected. It assured an ovation and many encores. The Russians, who appeared to know only balletic *demi-caractère* Spanish dancing, were overwhelmed with the castanets, the heelwork, and also the passion of flamenco dancing. Emotionally this was close to them.

A sleepless night on a stiflingly overheated train brought me to Leningrad, a striking city of many islands linked by bridges. Because it was a planned city it had a symmetry and an architectural unity rarely seen in other Russian cities—broad boulevards and open squares, impressive old houses, and eighteenth-century palaces. The principal color of the city was faded yellow with white neo-Greek columns (columns everywhere).

The first performance turned out to be a nightmare. The Philharmonia was a beautiful concert hall, home of the Leningrad Philharmonic Orchestra and certainly not meant for a theatrical presentation. White marble columns along the sides defined the boxes and red plush seats filled the center of the auditorium. Overhead, two rows of elaborate crystal chandeliers hung from the ceiling. The stage was an open platform framed by the pipes of the organ. On either side of these pipes was an arched-columned doorway, curtained in red velvet, the only entrance to the stage. This was where I was to make my debut.

On the day of the concert I quickly assessed the place and decided I could manage with no front curtain by using blackouts. They promised they would bring in some lights. As for the background, that was it: the organ and two red-curtained doorways. I waited, no lights. I rehearsed with the pianist, who was at one corner of the stage in open view. Still no lights. "Don't worry," they kept assuring me, "the lights are coming." It was past 6 P.M. I was hysterical, refused to dance. My first public appearance in the USSR. Much depended on it, and there were only obstacles. We delayed a half hour with the house packed. By then I knew there would be no lights.

I went on, giving the entire performance with nothing but the light from the crystal chandeliers. They could be switched on and off for my entrances and exits—that was it. I forced myself through it by telling myself that this was a new experience. If it succeeded it would be the true test: my dancing was strong enough to stand on its own without theatrical trimming. I hardly had that much faith in myself.

It was a great success. People yelled bravo until I was deaf. Encore after encore. Finally, I ended by improvising, and that too went marvelously. I was too tired and aggravated to be happy about it. The next night I had some light—one projector, plain white light, placed in the center aisle at the back of the hall. It was much better. All the dancers and artists came to this second performance. They too were enthusiastic. Tatiana Vecheslova, Vakhtang Chabukiani, Andrei Lopukhov, Sergei Koren, and others from the Maryinsky came backstage to congratulate me and invite me to come watch their professional class. When I arrived the next day, they applauded me. Some of the Maryinsky dancers adopted me, especially Lopukhov and Koren. We became a close-knit little group, and I always had entrée to the performances.

I gave one more concert, at the House of Culture, on January 6. A strained muscle forced me to postpone my concert at Tea-Dom, the theater club. I was supposed to return to Moscow, but tired and depressed, I decided to stay a bit longer. The next day I learned that the train Valya and I would have taken had a fatal accident. Fate works in its own way.

When I got back to Moscow on January 10, I found myself without a place to stay. Sylvia (Si-lan) Chen, a Chinese dancer I had met, was kind enough to offer a haven. I spent the night there, while a room as big as a peanut in the New Moscow Hotel, quite a distance from the city center, was found. This was just when I was preparing for my official Moscow debut, and a comfortable room was essential. The constant difficulty in finding comfortable hotel accommodations was nerve-wracking, but I discovered that with persistence you could get what you wanted.

Coming from the United States, where a few sparse concerts a year were the norm, I was overwhelmed by the sudden switch to continuous performing. Only the instant success compensated for the terrible toll on my strength. I was working on nervous energy and facing the hardships of living in a country that offered few amenities. To be dancing, performing, was enough to keep me happy for the moment. I had little chance until much later to discover what normal Russian life was like because all my friends were artists, who were revered and had special privileges. They received top salaries and better living quarters; some even had dachas. All dance education was paid for, and in addition students received a stipend for living expenses. I knew that this had existed since the earliest days, but now I was surprised to discover that all education, especially higher education in the universities was also covered in the same way.

On free evenings I went to the theater or the ballet. Tickets were very cheap and were always sold out, but I was lucky to be invited as a guest most of the time. Intermission was a ritual. People were dressed in their best, which meant that there was a little more color added to the badly made clothing. Faces were bright and gay. In the spacious lobbies there was always a buffet serving sandwiches, tea, and stronger drinks. People availed themselves of the buffet or promenaded in a large circle, all in the same direction, as though taking part in some ancient rite. They were a wonderful audience. If they liked the performance they applauded, stamped, clapped rhythmically, and shouted bravo; if not, there was a silent, icy chill. They were never an unknown quantity.

I was amazed at the number of theaters in Moscow: the Meyerhold, the Kamerny, the Maly, the Moscow Art Theatre, the Vakhtangov, the Nemirovich-Danchenko, the Gypsy Theatre (which specialized in Russian Romany plays, performed by gypsies), the Moscow Government Jewish Theatre (where classics were performed in Yiddish), and many, many others. The Jewish Theatre was state-sponsored, as were all the theaters. Anti-Semitism did not exist, as far as I could see. The great actor Mikhoels played King Lear in Yiddish. My pianist and my cellist, whom Gometz had recommended, were Jewish.

I had my official Moscow premiere on January 17, 1935, in a real, fully equipped theater, the Kamerny. It was sensational. People yelled and roared. I had to give three encores, during the last of which I got a paralyzing cramp in my leg and had to improvise with the castanets until I could get off the stage. This concert had all of Moscow talking.

On the nineteenth, after traveling all night to Leningrad, I gave another concert at the Philharmonia. It was not a personally satisfying performance, although the huge sold-out house seemed pleased.

Leningrad kept me very busy, yet I did not seem to run out of energy. Two days after the Philharmonia concert I saw Chabukiani and Vecheslova in *The Flames of Paris*, and the next night gave a small party for my Leningrad friends. Everybody was merry. We drank plenty of wine and had a wonderfully relaxed evening. On the twenty-third I gave a concert at Dom Pechaty, the Press Club, with such success that I was asked to do a repeat the following night.

Meyerhold invited me to the premiere of his staging of *The Queen of Spades* on the twenty-fifth, and on the twenty-sixth I gave a concert by special invitation in the Theater Club. The place was packed; half could not even get in. The applause was thunderous and prolonged. Afterward, we had a delightful banquet and I was asked to dance again.

As a result of my guest appearances at the artists' clubs in Moscow and Leningrad, I was given honorary membership, which allowed me the use of the club's restaurant, recreation facilities, and the privileges of regular members.

As time went on two problems became very apparent: eating and staying in shape. The food situation was pretty grim. The basic Russian diet consisted of cabbage soup, potatoes, salami, black bread, *prostokvasha* (yogurt), tea, and naturally vodka. Occasionally some chicken or morsel of meat was available. I got tired of eating in restaurants and sometimes preferred to eat in my room, so I waited in line in front of a *gastronom* (grocery) to buy a hunk of salami, black bread, and yogurt. With the money I was earning, 1,000 rubles per theater concert, I could also buy all the caviar I wanted, wonderful blue cans of Beluga caviar. The only difficulty was that these cans were one kilo each and no matter how much you like caviar that is just a little too much; I bought it if I was entertaining friends. I also frequented the dining rooms of the theater clubs. There, one could always meet interesting, like-minded people to talk to, and this saved me from the waves of homesickness that were becoming more frequent.

Staying in condition was a little simpler. Since I had to have the discipline to work alone daily, I developed my own system, based on what my own body needed. My movement intrigued the dancers at the Leningrad Choreographic School, where I was again invited to dance; they all tried to imitate what I did. It was fascinating that the studio in which I demonstrated was raked to the same angle as the Kirov stage. This meant that the body alignment was adjusted for that slant. In the beginning, dancing on raked stages was quite a challenge. I had to adjust my center of balance and tilt back to stand erect. Turns were really difficult. Since my engagements were in various halls and theaters, some with flat stages, some with raked, I was constantly having to adjust.

January 29 was a day I would look back on as a key to my constant delay in returning home. I was invited to a party at the Astoria Hotel, and found myself at a table with Vsevolod Pudovkin and Natan Zarkhi, two outstanding artists in the Soviet Union. Pudovkin, one of the leading film directors, had just received the Order of Lenin; Zarkhi was a poet, playwright, and scenarist for Pudovkin. We felt an immediate rapport. I danced with Pudovkin all evening. He was an excellent dancer, and moreover he spoke English, giving me a respite from the strain of steady Russian. Due to my success, everyone in the place knew me, and people constantly stopped by the table with congratulations. For the first time in those early, difficult Russian days I had fun.

I had seen Pudovkin's film *Storm Over Asia* in New York and been most impressed. In person, it was his vitality and energy that struck me. The inflection of his speech, his flamboyant gestures, his changes of mood were surprising and stimulating. He was filled with an element of the unexpected. Everything he said or did was underscored with an intensity that was electric. He was lean, above average height. A shock of dark air, well groomed to begin with, usually ended up tousled, with a single lock claiming his high forehead. Heavy eyebrows arched midway and then wandered away, and his eyes, so warm, could be sparkling or deeply searching. His lips, normally tightly pressed, could broaden into an irresistible smile. His ears were large, giving the impression of always listening. Pudovkin's face was full of mobility and continually changing expression.

Zarkhi on the other hand was totally different and probably the perfect complement for Pudovkin. Zarkhi was short and had a high, broad forehead that blended into his round-topped, balding head. There was always a twinkle in his eyes, as if he were enjoying some hidden joke. He was gentle, with a warm, enveloping smile. I found him relaxing and entertaining, with his wry, sparkling humor.

In the next couple of days I started a thrilling series of lectures and classes for teachers of the House for Artistic Training of Children, and performed—rather badly because I was deathly tired—at the Theater Club. On February 1, I danced at the Philharmonia. Everything went wrong the one evening I wanted to dance well because Pudovkin was there. He was tremendously impressed in spite of all the problems. Afterward, we talked all night about sound as a counterpoint rather than a parallel to visual experience, about the distinction between rhythm and meter, about thematic material and how to attack it. He used imagery to emphasize his ideas and talked of "rhythmic montage" as essential. Pudovkin and his famous colleague Sergei Eisenstein were diametrically opposed in their method of editing. The French critic Moussinac wrote that a film by Eisenstein resembled a cry, while a film by Pudovkin evoked a song. He was strange and impassioned, brilliant and inspiring. I found new impetus for work.

On February 9 I gave my farewell performance at the Philharmonia. In a span of twenty-one days I had given eight concerts, two lecture-demonstrations at the Maryinsky School, and five classes at the institute for teachers, in addition to rehearsing and social activities. When I was leaving to return to Moscow, Lopukhov, Herman Pavlovitch, the director of class at the Maryinsky, and others brought candy and gave me quite a send-off at the station. With the warmth and friendship of these people, I felt less lost, less homesick.

My next performance, a repeat at the Kamerny Theatre in Moscow, would not be until February 17, so I decided to use this time as a breather. Moscow in midwinter was a shimmering, crystalline cloak of ice. It was bitter cold, but dry cold unlike the dampness of Leningrad. I did not feel it too much until I tried to touch my nose and could not find it.

Settled again at the Metropole Hotel, I decided to contact Pudovkin, who was also back in Moscow. He visited and we spent the most delightful evening I had yet had in Russia. I was quite taken with him. The next day, I waited all evening for a telephone call from him. There I was, falling into my old pattern of waiting. I knew I would not be able to call him too often for fear of being recognized. There was his wife and a maid who might answer. I knew I was still looking for an escape from Nimura. I knew I was still vulnerable, and besides my ego was flattered. What was I letting myself in for?

Pudovkin was headed for a rest home in Uskoye, not far from Moscow, where he and Zarkhi often worked. Valya mentioned that her father was at this place; she thought it would be nice to visit him. So did I. When we arrived, Zarkhi was there, but not Kin (my secret name for Pudovkin). We learned that he was expected any minute, and at long last he came. All afternoon we stayed outdoors sleigh-riding and having pure fun in the snow. After dinner I spent some time alone with Kin and thought he showed real interest in me. I was slipping under his spell, and though I felt worldly, I was no wiser than I had been.

On February 17 I gave the concert at the Kamerny. I did not dance exceptionally well, but was very encouraged at the manner in which *Dance of Longing* was received. It was a modern dance work to percussion accompaniment using my Chinese gongs and bells. It was influenced by Wigman, especially the costume of green-gold metallic cloth, with a fitted, long-sleeved bodice, open midriff, and long, full skirt. Another performance, on February 19, was part of a review of theatrical dancers, headed by the Commissariat of Public Education, to evaluate trends for the training of mass dance in the USSR. One response, printed in *New Theater Magazine*:

> Koner's performance added weight to the arguments for the new forms of plastic dance training that the development of the mass dance in the USSR has so urgently made necessary. . . . [It] showed how necessary it is for the new Soviet dancers to study dance attainments in other countries, of which, up to now, little is known here. The conference stressed the fact that the center of development of the new dance has shifted definitely from the classical ballet and schools—which served a valuable purpose in introducing the masses to the art of the dance and handing down the art heritage—to the plastic realist schools and the mass forms of dance and dance training which now demand maximum attention.

Though I was aware of each individual success my concerts had won, I did not perceive the overall effect. All I knew was that very little dance from the outside world had been seen, so there was keen interest and lively discussion about everything I did. This forced me to analyze for myself what I thought modern dance was, but I still had much to discover before I could formalize a theory.

My original contract was for two months, with a six-month option. Since the first two months had been so successful, discussion was underway to take up the option. I wanted to continue the same financial terms, but now they balked. Decisions came slowly. I had the feeling that no single person wanted to make the decision; it was passed around. I had quite a few unpleasant discussions with the concert bureau; disturbed and tired as I was, I wanted to know my future plans. I knew that continuing the contract would mean touring the country, a daunting prospect in 1935, when there were more people than facilities, last-minute emergencies, a lack of efficient organization, and often things left simply to chance.

Through it all I saw Kin from time to time. The old excitement before such meetings was not there and I thought my feelings for him could not be real emotion. Perhaps I could no longer feel the kind of love I had once experienced. It was a quandary, and I hoped it would not turn out to be another foolish experiment.

Without any resolution of my contract, I was booked for three concerts in Kharkov, once the capital of the Ukraine and the home of many intellectual institutions, on February 25, 27, and 28. On the train, to my utter dismay, I found that my makeup case was missing. I could not remember if I had taken it along or forgotten it in the excitement of departure. (Checking in and out of hotels every few days, with all the luggage, costumes, instruments, and personal belongings, was a major undertaking.) I spent a sleepless night and then put through a wild call to Valya, who was still in Moscow. She arrived in Kharkov on the day of the first concert with the irreplaceable case. The concerts went very well.

Back in Moscow on March 3 I learned that Gometz still had not made a decision. I whiled away the time in Kin's company and at the theater. An impossible performance I gave at the totally unequipped Press Club was balanced by making some interesting new acquaintances there.

At long last, Gometz settled the contract. I would receive 1,000 rubles for Moscow and Leningrad, 800 for Kiev, and 700 elsewhere. This was considered top salary. Some workers probably got less per month than I did for one performance, but my cost of living was on an entirely different scale. The first glow of excitement, success, and newness was beginning to wear off. Fatigue, frayed nerves, and constant anxiety about performing conditions were taking their toll. In spite of that, I was eager to see more of this vast land, meet the people, and study the different cultures. There was talk of my going as far as central Asia. The word "Orient" rang in my ears. So I gambled.

In the meantime Pudovkin was occupying my mind more and more, although I was trying to convince myself that this was just an adventure, nothing serious. He was still working at Uskoye and, as I had a few free days, I offered to present a concert at the rest home. This time I went alone and thus had a chance to discover a new Kin—sensitive, soft, and responsive. He was a person I could admire, respect, and learn from. In turn he respected me as a person and an artist.

How wonderful it was to talk, to exchange thoughts and inspiration, to lose oneself in wild enthusiasm and the surging flame of creation. The few days I spent in Uskoye were a revelation. I was falling in love with Kin and at the same time wondering if the agonizing moods of doubt, waiting, hoping, desiring, which strip the ego and leave it bare, were desirable.

When I returned to Moscow to prepare for the tour, Gometz announced a postponement. I did not have to leave until March 27, so a whole week of vacation was ruined. To fill the time I participated in a *sborny konzert*, a mélange of singers, actors, and dancers, each performing one or two popular numbers. These were arranged for special workers' celebrations and events. The general attitude of all the performers was, We do this as *khaltura*, potboilers. No one worried too much about the staging—sometimes just a house light or minimal stage light, the same for everyone. On a big holiday there might be more than one on the same day. I danced so badly that it shocked me out of my dreams of love into the blank realization that I must work, and work hard.

The day before I was scheduled to leave, Kin finally called. He had a way of calling quite suddenly and coming on the spur of the moment. Without realizing it, I found I was always waiting for his call, often afraid to make other appointments for fear of missing him. He never became monotonous; he always had new energies, new interests, and new enthusiasms. He was passionate, yet understanding. It was reluctantly that I left for the tour of the Ural area, the outskirts of Siberia, with Sverdlovsk as my base.

Sverdlovsk was a funny little town, two or three main streets with very modern architecture, old broken-down houses on the remaining muddy streets. The concert in the Delovoya, or Business, Club was a huge success. I was surprised that in such a provincial place the *Dance of Longing* should be so well received. But even here, in a small, not-too-developed city, there were opera, ballet, and theater companies. The arts had a high priority everywhere in the Soviet Union. Since there was little else to do between my performance dates, I got a liberal education in theater and opera and a challenge to my Russian. A production of *Boris Godunov* was particularly fascinating because of the authentic sixteenth-century costumes and set, Tatar in origin.

There were also the usual secondhand stores, where one could see old furs and semiprecious stones like amethyst and malachite. I was earning money steadily and sometimes had to carry it in a small valise, so I could indulge my passion for old costumes, jewelry, and especially little embroidered caps from Tadzhikistan, Uzbekistan, and Georgia. A palatine that consisted of twenty-four Siberian sable backs, edged with sable tails, was expensive by Russian standards, but I was working hard to earn my rubles and would not be able to take them with me, so I bought it.

The tour continued in places where Russian dancers rarely went. On April 17 and 18 I found myself in Chelyabinsk, south of Sverdlovsk. It was a tiny factory city, where the only place for a performance was the circus arena. I looked and shuddered. At one end there was only a square raised platform, but at least there were some spotlights. Backstage, among the animal cages, I found a space to use as a dressing room, and worried that the lion might roar during quiet moments in the music. Somehow I gave two performances there, practically in the round—a novelty.

Communications between Gometz and the local concert bureaus were not always the best. Sometimes I wondered if the locals knew anything more than, She's coming. It was stupidity, inefficiency, and inadequacy at every step. My endurance was fraying. I argued with my accompanist and felt stagnant doing the same dances over and over. Even a long-awaited letter from Kin was more an appeasement to my ego than a welcome relief.

Besides the professional wear and tear, the unbalanced diet was making me physically tired and weak. I developed carbuncles under my arm, which made it difficult to move. I was homesick, very much alone, very lost. Upon return to Moscow, I had the boils pierced, and felt better. There was also a surprise: after five years, I received from

Nimura what, for him, might be called an ardent love letter.

I had suggested Nimura to Gometz, thinking his style would be appealing to the Russian audience, and they were interested. I wrote to him, saying I might be able to arrange it, but made it clear that he would have to come alone. His response was that Virginia and Lisan would have to come too, so we did not meet after all. I felt relieved. The strength of Nimura's presence had faded for me, outstripped by Kin's keen mind, crazy spirit, and sparkling brilliance. Still, the effect of Nimura's letter after all those years, tragically funny in a way, made my nerves tingle and blood surge.

Spring came to Moscow with May 1; the air smelled of it and the city seemed bursting with life. The great parade celebrating May Day began with a clangor of sounds: the striking of the Spassky Tower clock in the Kremlin, the music of the Internationale, a roar of cheering and cannon salvos. At Stalin's arrival, the massed army, horses, tanks, and caissons changed from static tension to rhythmic movement. It seemed as if all of Red Square had begun to move—power, strength, victory, and joy.

May was a month of ups and downs. Illness caused depression, but the contentions with Gometz were finally straightened out. Work with a new pianist, always a difficult process, almost drove me mad. Nevertheless, it was spring, with days in the country—and love.

Pudovkin and Zarkhi were working at Abramtzova rest home, so I tried whenever possible to get there. We had days of incredible happiness, days of beauty and languor. We shared ideas and plans. I watched him and Zarkhi in the midst of work, creating, their eyes shining and bodies filled with vibrant energy. From shapeless ideas they formed sharply outlined characters with problems, happinesses, and sorrows. One beautiful morning Kin related to me the entire plot of a scenario. He could have paid me no greater compliment.

When not in the country I was preparing my summer concert tour that was scheduled to start in June. Since I had a surplus of rubles, and was desperately homesick, I hit on an idea I hoped would solve both problems. I wrote to Mother and suggested, if she could pay the fare, that she should come to spend the summer with me and bring my brother. It would be a good chance for Marvin and me, so far apart in age, to get to know one another. Mother answered that it was a wonderful idea; they would come as soon as school closed. I could hardly wait.

At the end of May I was invited by the Committee of the Government Academy of the Bolshoi Theatre to give a private showing for the company and school at the Mali Theatre in Moscow. It turned out to be a day of hard luck and bitter anguish: the drumsticks broke, the castanets broke, the accompanist was unprepared, and I was dead tired. Here I was, dancing for my peers, and gave probably the worst performance of my Russian stay. I could only hope that, as theater people, they understood that accidents happen. A concert at the Theater Club the next day was smoother.

I met Kin at Abramtzova again, a meeting of pure happiness. Then, a week later, I visited with Andrei Gontcharov. Kin had introduced me to Gontcharov, an impressive portraitist who was enthusiastic about painting me. He did a wonderful full-length portrait and gave it to me as a gift when I left Russia. This particular evening was something of a situation because Kin was there with his wife. I had never met Anna Nikolaevna; she had written cinema articles during Kin's early career, acted in some of his films, and exerted a strong influence on many of his decisions. She was attractive, probably in her late thirties, which to me seemed old, although at forty-two Kin never seemed old.

I was not annoyed by the situation—rather, happy and confident —but Kin hardly spoke. All evening his mood was strange, sullen, and morose. Just as they were leaving, he made a beautiful gesture: he solemnly recited a poem I had taught him, Poe's "The Raven." Only Valya and I understood. Did he really mean "Nevermore"? My doubts came and went.

The summer tour that began in Archangel and the months following it were a kaleidoscope of scenes, impressions, elations, depressions, and all too often frustrations. Through it all I kept up detailed journals, the only way to sort out the myriad events.

June 8–9, 1935. Arrival at last in Archangel. A private motor boat across the glorious Dvina. Eleven at night and the sun just setting —white nights. People singing, laughing in the streets all night. Sleep impossible.

June 11–13. Concerts here very successful, even though at the first one the projectors didn't work, and when they did, the curtain broke down. Archangel is a lovely little port town on the White Sea, clean, airy, and cheerful. The streets are always filled with people—young, laughing, and gay. I thought we might be able to fly back from Archangel to Moscow—I so want to see Kin—but impossible to make connections. After three consecutive concerts, and I rather exhausted, we depart for Ivanova. Concerts, concerts, concerts; I'm filled to the throat with them. The train is stifling, with pounds of dust. There are three classes: first, very deluxe, is *mezhdu-narodny*; second, *myagky*, means "soft"; third is *zhutky*, or "hard" because rows of wooden seats are jammed in to capacity. We are in *zhutky* for five hours.

June 16–18. The Ivanova audience is crazy. They really don't know what my concerts are about. We can't wait to finish this last one, and then I'll be back to Moscow and Kin. Great excitement; Mother is already on her way with Sonny.

June 18–20. After eleven long, painful days I am with Kin in the cool, fresh countryside. Each meeting grows more tender. He has said so openly, which is remarkable. At last I can really believe in his sincerity.

June 24. Suddenly I must leave, a change of dates. No time for the train; I must fly. Kin is busy all day with his work, with only an occasional minute to talk or to caress. He is sullen, gloomy, fretful because I must go. I promise to write and am solemnly promised to be answered. A passionate parting, a snapshot put in my bag, and I'm off in a rickety old buggy, wanting to jump off and run back swiftly.

June 25. Four o'clock out to the airport. Seven o'clock onto the already quivering plane—only eight seats, no pressurizing, no heat. Up into the sky, with a marvelous sensation of defying gravity, and then calmly watching the earth through morning mists. My first air trip.

June 26. My twenty-third birthday. For twenty-three I've seen and done a good deal. This birthday is in Sverdlovsk. Where might the next one be? It's lonely, away from family, friends, and Kin.

June 27–30. Left for Berezniki, north of Sverdlovsk, and had an awful accident on the train. Slammed my finger in the heavy door and fainted for the first time in my life. The train is called *kulturny poezd*, the culture train. My compartment was spotless, with flowerpots, table, lamps, and curtains. Berezniki is as dull as can be. I'm living in the theater because there is no easy way to get back and forth from the hotel. It's so lonely. I miss Valya and can't wait until Mother and Sonny come. The concert went well, and tonight is sold out to the engineers of the Kombinat. I had no idea that such out-of-the-way places were part of my contract, but it's too late to do anything but suffer through.

June 30–July 2. Second concert went even better, but I'm dying of loneliness. Life here is dirty and dull. I have to remember that I am doing something to forward the understanding of dance art. On the bus going out to dine alone, I asked directions from a sparkling, green-eyed girl. She offered to lead me, and out of longing for human companionship, I invited her to join me. Afterward we crossed the river Kama to visit the city of Usolye, in existence since the time of Ivan the Terrible. It is old and quaint. On the way back, we met an old railway worker, who pointed out a charming little house: "It's so beautiful, it resembles an Italian villa. I suppose it is the home of some specialist from the Kombinat. Our children will study, become specialists, and they too will have such homes." Such hope in the face of such hardship!

July 3–8. Thank God I'm back in Sverdlovsk. After Berezniki it is heaven. I've met Professor Lelio Zeno. He's from Argentina and has discovered a new treatment for burns. He is intelligent, urbane, and fortunately speaks English. I expect to get in touch with him in Moscow.

July 8. Excitement. Anxiety. At last the moment has arrived when I can see Mother! I waited all day, then missed the train. They arrived and found no one to greet them. Our meeting at last was so emotional: tears of joy, kissing, laughing, shrieking, talking all at the same time. It feels like home again to have Mother always near to talk to; to have Sonny annoying, yelling; to have breakfast served and clothes washed and mended. I have become more attached to Mother than ever, and shall miss her tenfold when she leaves.

July 9–14. Showed Mother and Sonny around Sverdlovsk, introduced them to my friends, and generally led a family life. Mother brought news from Kin by way of Valya; he sent three letters I never received. Since Berezniki I haven't given one concert. The bureau promises only one, on the fifteenth. On the thirteenth I gave an impromptu talk to a group of Komsomols from Ural-Mash, the big factory. I tried to describe America, while remaining sensitive to their point of view. There was an article about it in the next day's newspaper.

July 16–17. In the evening, we left for Krasno-Uralsk. At five in the morning we changed trains and began to feel an intuitive withdrawal from our destination. Arrived and beheld a village—dirty, muddy, solitary, and eerily desolate. We were installed as usual in the Dvoretz Kultura, the Palace of Culture, and were apprised of the news that we weren't expected and weren't wanted. When they had learned we were to arrive, they had telegraphed and phoned to ask for a delay. They were told we had already left, which was not true. I was furious. We decided to give the first concert anyway, and think about the second. To my surprise, the people seemed thirsty for artistic diversion and loved the performance. I spent a frantic, sleepless night chasing bedbugs. Finally, toward morning, I got a couple of hours of exhausted sleep by putting two hardbacked chairs together.

July 18. A strange uneasiness. The air vibrating with hidden menace. I, trembling with irritation, an unaccountable heaviness oppressing me, asked Valya to cancel the concert. She promised to do something, but left me waiting without an answer. I thought I would go mad. The strange mood kept mounting. Not knowing what to do, I sat reminiscing about Kin and our relationship, looking at the picture of him and Zarkhi he had given me. Why do I need them both together? I was not able to disassociate them, so taking scissors I meticulously cut them in two. Valya insisted I give the concert. In a fit of hysterics, which I also could not explain, I packed and left. At the station she overtook me, and I returned, but somehow, something in me was shattered. I was determined to leave immediately after the performance. A special little railroad jitney was obligingly lent to us by the wife of the factory director; it was the only way we could make a connection to Sverdlovsk without waiting another day. After a thrilling ride, despite the fact that I was deathly tired, we caught a train to Sverdlovsk and traveled third class. Arrived the nineteenth, a physical and mental wreck.

July 20. Decided to leave for Moscow: Mother and Sonny by train; we by plane. Took them to the train, which was three hours late, only to discover that there was no possibility of seats. Our plane tickets were already bought, but I could not leave Mom and Sonny alone. After a week of crises I was pretty near the end of my string, so I started a scandal. The station master and all the clerks ran about wildly —nothing! Then the ticket agent walked in unconcernedly and asked, "What shall I do with three extra tickets?" How we pounced on her! After much aggravation, we saw Mother and Sonny off, and made our way to the airport. Weather conditions did not permit a takeoff and we were told to wait—indefinitely. Could not sleep from nervous excitement. Finally, twelve hours later, we at last took off for Moscow.

July 21. Impossible to complete the trip to Moscow because of darkness. We stopped in Kazan for the night. I begged that we continue, but was voted down. We went into the city, and there discovered a friend, who casually said, "Did you hear about the awful catastrophe in Moscow three days ago? There was an auto crash. Zarkhi was killed and Pudovkin. . . ." Three days ago—the day I cut apart their photo. I clapped my hands over my ears. This was the final touch to make my world crumble. Sobs wracked my body. No one knew what had happened to Kin. Rumors flew. He was killed. Badly hurt. No definite news. The next day, word was that he was not killed, but severely injured.

July 22. Arrived in Moscow—no room! No place to sleep. We ran around trying to find a room. Desperate to know what happened to Kin. Tension gnawing. Went to his house. They would not let me in. How can I manage to see him, to reassure myself that all is well? I cried uncontrollably. On the telephone a voice, a strange voice. It is Kin, but I do not recognize him. He asks me to come. I almost fly. White flowers. Valya and I arrive. He is relatively unhurt, physically. Only his eyes, frightened eyes, like those of a child to whom something terrible has happened that he cannot explain, dimmed with a veil of pain and sadness.

July 22–26. Spent these days with Mother and Sonny in Moscow. As usual the train on which they arrived was late—but earlier than we were told, so we weren't there to meet them. I rushed like crazy to the station. Up and down, in and out. Didn't find them. Called the Metropole; they were there. I got there; they were gone. Rushed to the Vostok Hotel and found them at last. Saw Kin almost every day. Went to his house, too. And he came to me.

I left for Tiflis and he came to say goodbye. Tiflis is a four-day, four-night trip. No places but third class, with a promise for first class as soon as we are underway. My temper already boiling. We're off. No other places! It's impossible to ride four days in the "hard" car. Frantic arrangements to get off at the next station and return. Rushing up and down the train, witnessing unbelievable sights: hundreds of people with children, baggage, and food galore. Finally, for a special premium, the conductor has given up his compartment in first class and we can travel comfortably. Heat unbearable. No dining car, but at every station the local people stand by with roast chickens, bread, and whatever is available in the area. It's a sort of game: dash out, buy food, dash back, and survive until the next stop.

July 31. Arrival in Tiflis. Again I am obsessed with a passion for the Orient. I seem to be thrown back three years to the time I was in Alexandria. The cities resemble each other. Tan-skinned people with burning dark eyes fill the streets. The heat is oppressive. The hotel is ugly and depressing. I wonder how it will be possible to dance; clothing sticks like glue. I am sending Mother and Sonny to Borzhomi, a resort.

August 2–9. The concert on the fourth a tremendous success. The weather luckily is delightfully cool. The following day Mother left for Borzhomi. I followed. Valya had an accident on the plane to Tiflis and punctured her eardrum. She is miserable and nervous. Also in a nervous state, I am unable to cope with her. Borzhomi is a relief—cool, almost cold, with the mountains of the Caucasus so near they seem to press on one's head, but the atmosphere seems close and uncomfortable and my sense of movement is impaired.

August 9. Back to Tiflis to find Valya ill in bed, the concert canceled, and Baku impossible. A reversal of plans and a decision to go to Kislovodsk, a famous resort.

August 12. Off on a bus like an oversized, old-time car, with about eight seats, open sides, and a black hood. Through one of the world's most beautiful mountain passes on the road leading from Tiflis to Vladikavkaz across the Caucasus. Towering, eerie, majestic mountains, wandering mists, deep valleys, river beds, rushing rivers. The air biting, with a strange effervescent sparkle. Two legs wiggling in mid-air, then more and more legs. A hole in the seat of some of the pants. Ragamuffins doing handstands and begging for *karandashi*, pencils. They're all along the ridge of the mountain.

August 13. Kislovodsk. No room in the hotel. A strange, ugly room without water or light is substituted. This is a place, though, of open space and bright light that does not scorch, only caresses. Met an official, Vladimir Michaelovitch, who shortly declared ardent love for me. I truthfully said I could not accept. However, he suffices as an escort and helps me through difficulties. Mother is leaving soon. I dread the moment as if it were the plague. Haven't heard a word from Kin and am worried at this silence.

August 21. Mother leaves today. My feeling of isolation is again obsessing me, especially after having had them with me. Sonny is already a man. Who knows when I shall see them again? I have no home here, no family, and few real friends. The last few minutes are sad. Trying to stay in control and acting the worse for it. Mother is really suffering, and I would give anything for her to stay on. Poor thing. She has had many discomforts here and would have many more if she stayed.

August 23–25. Concerts in Essentuki and Pyatigorsk went well. Awfully tired.

August 31. In Kislovodsk, arrived at noon for rehearsal. Stage set with a tremendous mechanism and the operetta company rehearsing full blast. I request the stage, and am brusquely refused. I go to the administrator and request the stage be clear by two o'clock, which is promptly promised. Arrive at two to find the same condition as before. In a tone higher, I demand the use of the stage. Is it really possible that people can deny that evening's performer a rehearsal on a strange stage that has a terrific rake? It is possible. Back from the administrator with a promise to have it at 2:30. An exact repetition of earlier, except that this time I lose my temper altogether and yell full voice. The administrator also gets his share. By this time I am shaking with rage. Rush home choking, sobbing. I cannot stop. My hands are paralyzed—I cannot open them. My legs too! Three hours. So weak. I can hardly talk. My eyes and lips are swollen, my body leaden. I do not want to see or hear anyone. I cannot dance, and cancel—a first. There is a scandal.

September 2. After two days of nightmare spent mostly in bed, at last I am able to leave. At 2:30 P.M. I am told there are no tickets, but it is impossible to stay any longer. I must get out of this awful hell of my emotions. I go to the train agent. He tells me to return later. I return later and beg him to take me. He does not know. There is no place. I offer to stand. He will take me. Once on the train I find a seat with no trouble.

September 3–13. Arrive in Sochi and no one meets me. How can it be? I go to the hotel. No room for me at all. Gometz can do nothing. I am desperate. At last a room is arranged in the hotel, beautiful, with a balcony opening on the Black Sea. The sound lulls me to sleep, creates an undertone to my dreams, and wakes me in the morning with its rhythmic swishing, gushing sound. Luscious sunlight to dry out my aching body and bedraggled mind. Sochi is one of the most beautiful Black Sea resorts, with wonderful beaches: one for those who prefer to wear a bathing suit, one for nude men, and one for nude women. You have to pass through them, no matter what your choice of beach. Unpleasantness with Valya, but kept at arm's length.

September 7–8. Excellent concerts, shared with the actress Natalia Alexandrovna Rosenel, the former wife of Anatoly Lunacharsky, the first Commissar of Education.

September 13–15. A last-minute surprise: must go to Moscow alone. No one to meet me there, no room reserved, no visa! Met friends on the train who took me to the Metropole. No luck. Hectic two hours of racing around in pouring rain trying to find a place to sleep, and finally plumping down in the Metropole and refusing to budge until they arrange a room. They have.

September 15–October 4. Got in touch with Kin and he came to see me straight from Uskoye. The ache of all these months disappeared. Although I fight desperately against the hold he has over me, it seems useless. When I love, I love with all my heart and being.

Hectic days and sleepless nights trying to get a visa. Finally, settled for one month. Gometz is making dirt for Valya, and of course I am vitally concerned. Our mood is one of depression and desperation combined. Everything is going wrong. Financially I am very low, and for the first time here, must count my "pennies" and live on a strict budget. I shall very soon be worrying about my next meal. Hotel living is prohibitive. Some friends have found me a room in a private apartment, but there's no phone, and that complicates matters.

There is a possibility of going to Leningrad to teach. I am invited by the Lesgaft Physical Culture Institute. This means cutting off all my connections and creating a plan of life all over again. There are so many pros and cons for leaving and staying. I am bewildered. If I go, I will probably have an interesting experience and financial security, but must leave all my private life behind. If I stay, perhaps I am missing an important step in my artistic life.

October 5. Danced at Dzerzhinsky Club, named for the Bolshevik revolutionist, and all the men came in flocks. We had a banquet and danced afterward. But it was all hollow. I saw Kin this afternoon and had a strange feeling of impending loss. His wife arrives tomorrow from vacation. Now I shall see him less than ever.

October 16. Today a wild rush from morning to night, occurrences tumbling over one another. This evening, further word from Leningrad, urging me to come immediately. Bang, clash, run, push; tickets, tickets, tickets. Within a half hour, a mad trip to Leningrad. A feeling that my luck has turned and perhaps all will be well. The Institute offers me terms that will solve my financial difficulties perfectly, and a visa extension as well.

December 24. During this interval, so many things have occurred. After all the excitement, I received permission from Moscow to have my own group. Meanwhile I have been working for the Lesgaft Institute. Their dance department is the nearest thing to modern dance, in that they dance barefoot. Graduates are qualified to teach dance in the educational system. My hotel bills are covered and a car is sent each day to pick me up and take me home. The regularity of the schedule is a needed change. My work, though inhumanly tiring (I have to teach in Russian with no translator, but body language is universal), is stimulating and creative. I want to use new possibilities and incorporate all my theories. For this reason I will inaugurate the use of films in teaching, also excursions to museums and concerts. The pupils are young and fresh, a new type of youth, full of desire to work and strength to accomplish. I will be able to create an interesting company with them. I have tried to choreograph a new solo—joyous, hopeful—but it is awful. It is impossible to think creatively; I am too involved with the mechanics of living and confused by the various theories of aesthetics surrounding me, especially classical ballet. I am stimulating others, but find no real stimulation for myself.

Undated, 1936. In the lapse of time I have continued my work in Leningrad. The film experiments are undertaken, a paper will be started. The formation of a Moscow group is hopeless, so I will concentrate on Leningrad. I want to study sculpting and music and film directing.

Emotionally I have lived through a crisis. My love for Kin has constantly grown. What can I do against it? He can be satisfied with the few times he sees me since he has a home life besides his work. My nerves are drawn to the breaking point by his unpredictability. January in Leningrad gave me a warning that all was not well. He was nervous, I was tired, and our contact seemed to be broken, more ordinary. Although Lelio Zeno has made no advances, and I have only a surface attachment for him, in my desperation I use the idea of him as a safety line. I convince myself that I can forget Kin and hang on spiritually and emotionally to Lelio. It helps me at this low point. I have even thought of marrying him—wild!

Moscow—supper—champagne: "A toast to my new husband!" An exclamation from Kin's wife: "Really I must tell Vsevolod you have been unfaithful to him." She knew. I, trying to be witty and sound casual: "Oh, that happened long ago."

February 1. I am supposed to be back at Lesgaft today, but they have postponed until the thirteenth. Anxious day, waiting for telephone call. Nerves tense. I want to keep Lelio close and for that reason goad him on. He evidently has some private problems I know nothing about. I do not know what to do, and give him the choice of continuing our friendship or not. He has refused to choose.

February 3. Still the suspense of waiting. Then, snap—collapse. The only outlet to cry day after day. Doctor's diagnosis: overwork and nervous exhaustion. An immediate rest necessary.

March 3. In Suchanova, an architects' rest home, I have had a beautiful and complete rest. Learned to ski, play billiards, and sleep in fresh air on a balcony. My desire to dance is returning slowly for the first time in two months, and with it my faith. If something unpleasant does not happen, I will be completely well.

March 10–31. Back in Moscow, red tape and finally a room, a pigeonhole in the Savoy, but any place with a bed and a lock on the door is heaven. Kin came the evening of my arrival. I feel wonderful, full of the old spirit, though as yet no strong desire to dance. People are always dropping in to see me. I have my share of *pokloniki*, people who enjoy being around an artist to help and admire without demands. Their visits overlap and they try to outstay one another. I don't worry or wait for phone calls. My new philosophy is foolproof.

News from the Institute—another postponement. Kin is ill. The last days of my stay are spoiled after all. Beginning to feel low again and fighting it with all my strength. Went to see Kin. We had a long talk about our relationship. Our great tie is our extreme hypersensitivity to each other. Kin said he had a strange feeling that somehow I would change. He didn't know how or why, but regretted it. I too feel it. Anna Nikolaevna adores my black hat. She asked if she might copy it. What else could I say but yes.

Undated. A Moscow conference of Workers in the Arts was convened to promulgate Socialist Realism in all the arts. Valya said we must try to attend the session on theater. When we arrived it was impossible to get through the crowds outside. Police were trying to maintain order. Valya said, "Take out your passport." I waved my green passport wildly in the face of the policeman near us while Valya shouted, "This is an American dancer. You must let us through." The policeman opened a path for us. Valya impulsively grabbed the hand of a tall, distinguished man who had been standing beside us: "Sergei Sergeyevitch, come with us." She dragged him along. When we got into the theater she said, "Pauline, meet Sergei Sergeyevitch Prokofiev." What an honor! The hall was packed and the only empty chair was on the crowded stage. Valya told me to take it, and I asked Prokofiev to share the chair with me. Afterward I asked him if he would like to come to a rehearsal, and he accepted.

Undated. Anna Nikolaevna arrived at the rehearsal during which Prokofiev was present. He is a strange man, striking, very self-centered, secure in his poise. Distinctly sensitive to art and very cultured. I was ill, a sore throat and cough. Anna brought me to her home and I spent the rest of the day there. I felt comfortable and cozy and delighted that Kin was near. I saw him in his own surroundings and understood why he could never leave them. Something in me numbed—not my love, but a hidden hope to have him for myself. I did not envy, I even began to like Anna, to be attached to her. She is a lovely, warm, handsome woman. I understand how Kin can still be so much in love with her.

April 7. A party for me at Kin's. How I danced. He will never forget me or that evening. I danced with him. I danced alone with music and then without music. I danced as I rarely dance—capricious, scintillating, sparkling, and at moments tragic. Every accent, every line was a silent message. He knew and answered.

April 8. Kin came. I am happy and I want to go back to Leningrad. I *must* go. It is a superstition. I must go tonight. There is a ticket. I leave triumphant. Lelio and Valya take me. A spoken goodbye by phone to Kin. He hopes to come to Leningrad, but I don't believe it. I have decided to concentrate on work. I want to work again. Only work counts because that is always sure and faithful. Everything else must take second place. It must and it will. This is my truce with myself and my emotions. Once more, I have taken the initiative to go away. Am I growing stronger or weaker?

I arrived in Leningrad on April 9 and was installed in a little suite with a private bath at the lovely old Astoria Hotel. I asked if I could have a piano, and in a few days had an upright in my room. I renewed old acquaintances, enjoyed talking with Lopukhov, Koren, and the other dancers. Walking with them one morning in Theatre Square, I was introduced to a young girl with sandy hair, sensitive face, small features, no makeup, and carrying a bag of practice clothes. Lopukhov said, "Pauline, this is Galina Ulanova, one of our leading young ballerinas." She was twenty-six at the time, but looked like a teenager.

Life took on a more continuous rhythm than I had had in more than a year. My students were wonderful, close and dear friends. In their enthusiasm they even managed to understand my primitive Russian. They loved to talk, and one day I told them in a stern voice to stop their chattering and get down to work. They did, but with a startled expression that seemed to hide something. After class I asked, "What was that about?" They answered: "In Russian you said, 'Grab your knees with your elbows and hold on to the chandeliers'!"

There was to be a Physical Culture Parade on July 12, for which I was asked to prepare a project. After two days of plans and sketches, I came up with the idea for a star-shaped platform, with movement on the center plane, the five sloping points, and the ground level. It would start with a waltz, moderate to a march, and end strongly and joyously. My plans were accepted with enthusiasm. Here was a challenge; my first opportunity to work on group choreography. There was so much yet to learn and always so little time, but the desire for the new, to experiment, gripped me.

We decided to have music commissioned, and I suggested Shosta-kovich. He lived in Leningrad. I thought he might be interested in a project of such popular appeal. Despite the recent storm of criticism against it, his opera *Lady Macbeth of Mtsensk* was still being performed in Leningrad, if not in Moscow, and his teaching position was still secure. I called him and he agreed to discuss it with me. He was a thin young man of thirty, rather shy, a lock of blond hair falling over his forehead, and blue eyes shielded by heavy horn-rimmed glasses. I described the project in my poor Russian and he listened carefully, then most politely said, "I would like very much to do this, but you see I am very busy with several commissions and a symphony (it was his Fourth) and could not possibly do this at the moment." Very disappointed, I nevertheless saw that it was asking a lot for only a single performance.

At the end of April I was suddenly confronted with the question of whether or not it was ideologically correct to dance on the emblem of a star. I felt it symbolized the force for the new generation. Besides, the work would have to be a very theatrical spectacle to have impact in the large square in front of the impressive Winter Palace. But everyone was extremely wary of chancing criticism. My plans went crashing, and with it, my mood. I had no middle range, emotionally.

After three days of depression I slowly developed an alternative. I was not happy with it. Just some brilliant movement that would catch the eye. I used a mass of dancers and rehearsed them in the large open stadium of the institute, while I stood on a balcony with a microphone and broadcast instructions.

The time was passing swiftly, and I was anxious to finish the project and go home. I wanted desperately to get back to America and to my family. One day, Serafima Alexandrovna Bortfelt, who was in charge of the dance division, said, "Tovarich Koner, the administration has authorized me to ask you whether you would be interested in returning next fall to continue your classes at the Lesgaft Physical Culture Institute. Your course has been most successful." My first reflex was, I will be able to see Kin again. Then I began to reason: would I have any obligations for the future season in the United States? I would not have to return until October. The dance in the United States was mainly activity under the WPA program, and those plans were already set. I would have to start all over again establishing myself after this absence, and that would take most of the coming season. Here, a job would be waiting. Leningrad was an interesting city. I wrote to Kin, who seemed pleased with the idea, and decided to accept.

Final rehearsals were hectic with costumes, sound, and coordination, and at last the day arrived. The performance on the great Palace Square was quite a spectacle, and the newspaper reviews were excellent.

I gave most of my things to my friends and left a trunk packed with my purchases of lovely old china and books at the Astoria until my return. I had heard rumors that there were political trials going on, but knew very little about them. I was excited about going. Leavetaking was not sad; I had a return ticket in my purse. The Russian ship sailed from Leningrad across the Baltic and the violent North Sea. To walk the decks, one had to hang on to the ropes, but I loved it. I spent several days in London, then took a ship home to my beloved New York.

This letter came from Pudovkin not long before I left Russia:

How terrible that I cannot see you before you leave. There is nothing that I can do. I must be in Moscow all this time. I hope that you can come here at least for one day, it is easier for you. . . . Write about your voyage. Write about everything. It will be interesting how all will look to you now. Only don't write what isn't true. I hope the time before your return trip will pass quickly for you. It is terribly sad that I will not see you for so long a time. . . . Well, . . . we will see each other in four months. Don't forget me.

I received one more letter in September, before foreign correspondence from Russia was curtailed. Then all communication stopped.

Transition

I arrived in New York the end of July 1936. How luscious the fragrance of that first orange as I peeled it and the little drops of juice burst forth to greet me on my return home. The flowers on the dark blue wallpaper of my bedroom seemed to reach out in a welcoming embrace. The comforting pleasure of my own bed, my plain white dresser with its flattering beveled mirror, my window facing the little back garden with the pink rambler roses along the fence of our funny little row house in Brooklyn, the delicious smells coming up from the downstairs kitchen, the sounds of mother preparing dinner—all this seemed a luxury I had never before appreciated. The 8 P.M. doorbell. Dad was home from work. So many things I had taken for granted suddenly thrust their identities upon my consciousness. It was good to be home!

It took time to adjust. I wandered around the house the first few days saturating myself with the feel of home. I had been away a long time —too long. For the moment I put away all thoughts of leaving these comforts and immersed myself in the conscious sense of family, home, the security of knowing I could always ask Dad or Mom for advice, and the joy of seeing their happiness at having me with them. They were proud of my success and of my return contract, but for the moment we decided to put it out of our minds. That was one of the few happy summers of my life. There was something to look forward to, so I could indulge in relaxing and replenishing within.

But summer passed all too quickly and I had to think about preparations for returning to the Physical Cultural Institute in November. I sent the usual application for a visa, and with the engagement definite I was certain it was only a formality. The return letter from the Soviet Embassy said, Visa denied. No reason. Immediately I wired the institute and asked them to apply. The answer was the same, and again, no reason.

This was when the Stalin purge was gathering impetus. There were trials and denunciations filling the headlines, and foreigners were no longer acceptable. Although my immediate reaction was shock, deep down I felt relieved. Returning to the USSR meant work in the field of dance, but infinite difficulties in living, and certainly emotional crises. I had not had the willpower to say no because of the emotional tie, and had rationalized it as a need to function in dance. But I knew in my guts why I had wanted to return. Fate had taken it in hand and I was grateful.

Once over the initial shock, I needed to think about reactivating my career in the United States after the year-and-a-half hiatus. I was too young and naïve to see that I could have capitalized by writing a book about my Russian experiences. Besides, it was dancing that was important, not spending time with words.

I had been abroad at the time that the Dance Project, a branch of the Federal Theatre Project, organized and subsidized by the WPA, was in full swing. Dancers had become socially conscious: there was the New Dance Group (one of the long-lasting ones) and many workers dance groups; the First National Dance Congress and Festival, which included a cross section of many kinds of dance and dancers, critics and managers, opened on May 18, 1936, and continued a week.

Unaware of the tremendous strides dance in America had taken during my absence, I was unprepared to return to this new dance world. However, there had been some publicity about the Russian tour. I had also given a few lectures and written some articles. With these as a springboard, I was able to get sponsorship from the California Dance Guild for a few concerts in Los Angeles at the Biltmore

Theatre, on March 24 and 25, 1937, and in San Francisco at the Curran Theatre on April 4. I also was invited to give guest lessons at the San Francisco Opera Ballet School, directed by Willam Christensen, on April 1 and 2.

This gave me a little time to think of some new pieces. I was terribly tired of the old works, felt a brewing dissatisfaction with the ethnic styles, and decided to synthesize some of my Soviet impressions into dance movement. The Soviet week was five days of work, the sixth was Free Day, and the seventh day started a new six-day cycle. A weekend as we know it did not exist, which I found very confusing. But Free Day was always a day of relaxation and celebration. So I decided to do a work called *Free Day*, a bright dance, to the music of Lev Knipper. In contrast to that I did *Lullaby to a Future Hero*, music by Nikolai Myaskovsky, in which I tried to capture the earthiness, the strength, and the sense of hope that I had seen in some of the Russian women.

The advance press in California was disconcerting. I was called "Soviet Concert Dancer" and "Russe Dancer." In fact, my program was eclectic: Soviet, Palestinian, and oriental themes and modern dances. Dance concerts on the West Coast were quite rare, and modern dance in 1937 was having an even greater struggle there than in New York. Most of the newspaper reviewers were surprised that my program was so successful and the audience response so lively. Vivian Fine, a composer-pianist who played for the Humphrey-Weidman company, had agreed to be my accompanist and her musical support was a great help.

In San Francisco I met John Bovingdon, an active dance *amateur* who had visited the Soviet Union at the same time I was there. He was planning to drive to New York and suggested that I drive back with him, see the United States, and share expenses. Although I had toured to some extent, typically I had not really seen the country. Now, in mid-April, as we drove across the desert the expanse of endless space as far as one could see stimulated a new sense of dimension, a vision of openness, of height—the sky with no obstructions. I had a feeling of America I had never before experienced. The Grand Canyon was sculptured shapes, depth, rhythmic curving lines, varied colors, tones of reds and browns—infinite variation and dynamics. An opposite experience was a trip down into a coal mine in Pennsylvania—darkness, narrow tunnels, space utterly compressed, strange fumes, and shadows of men, dark forms with lights on their caps, hammering away in this no-world. I came away frightened and depressed.

Home again, it was time to make long-term plans. Artistically I was dissatisfied with myself. By now, Martha Graham had a strong group, Doris Humphrey and Charles Weidman had an excellent company, Anna Sokolow had already begun to appear on her own. Since I did not stem from any of the modern schools, I had to evaluate what I had done alone and how I wanted to change. It was time to establish my own identity by creating a style different from existing styles. I drew on the speed, precision, elevation, and turns from ballet; the smoothness in covering space and importance of the hands from oriental dance; and the rhythm, dynamics, and elegant body line of the Spanish. I began to evolve a style that used spiral movement, sharp attacks countered by lyric phrases, and suspension. I isolated parts of the body, especially the hands, seeking shapes I had not seen before. I sought movement that would adapt to any theme. If I chose to use an ethnic motivation, I used the flavor, not the fact of that movement. Improvising for hours, I could see the slow change. A totally new program would have to be prepared for a New York recital. I did not set a deadline. As soon as I had something worthwhile, a date could be set.

The most important immediate problem was space. I needed a studio where I could plunge in and work as long as I pleased. I finally found an old loft at 94 Fifth Avenue between 14th and 15th Streets. It was a fourth-floor walkup over a cafeteria, whose stale, oil-fried fumes reached even that height. With the help of an acquaintance in the lumber business, I acquired a hardwood maple floor, built two small partitioned rooms, installed a shower, and bought some secondhand furniture, including an old icebox that needed block ice delivery, and a two-burner gas stove that sat on a table top. I hung the blue curtains from my old studio across an alcove, creating a small dressing room, and placed the mirror against a wall and the metal barre on the opposite wall. Presto! I had a small studio. The place was bright and cheerful, and I looked forward to working and living there. In spring 1937, loft living was more or less a novelty.

One day in August the telephone rang: "My name is Trude Rittman. I have just arrived in New York, and the National Council of Jewish Women suggested that I call you. I have played for the Jooss Ballet in Dartington Hall, and taught music theory. They thought you might need a composer/pianist."

Trude came to my studio. She was a thin girl with short, brownish hair, and wore heavy glasses. She spoke with a rich, lovely voice and had an excellent command of English. We immediately took to each other. She needed work. I had no funds to engage her on a regular basis, but wanted her to compose music for some works I had in mind. I also gave her a list of people to contact, one of whom was Agnes de Mille. Trude did write music for some of my pieces, but she made her career working for de Mille, arranging the dance music for all her Broadway shows. After that she collaborated with Jerome Robbins and Lerner and Loewe, so she did not need my meager assistance, but remained a good friend and valued mentor.

The rent and other bills were quite a problem. I was trying to organize classes, which would take time, so I decided to let one of the loft rooms to help tide me over. A charming girl had come to take class —she could afford only one a month—and was looking for a place to live. I let her have the room for whatever she could afford. Her name was Gertrude Weissman, and since I had been struck with the name Trude, I immediately dubbed her Trude Weston. I enjoyed her companionship, but even with her small contribution toward the forty-five dollar rent, the economics of life were still grim. A class cost only fifty cents, and there was never a fixed income.

We made the acquaintance of three young artists living in the next building, also on the fourth floor. They were having as hard a time as we, but their apartment had a real kitchen. One day, they invited Trude and me to share a meager dinner. During our conversation, we hit upon a great idea. What if we pooled our resources and had dinners together? They were great cooks, I would do the marketing, and Trude and I would do the dishes. It worked perfectly. In order to save walking up and down four flights we devised a special route. A glass doorway from my room led onto the fire escape, its handrail exactly level with the boys' window ledge to the left. We found an old door, laid it across the fire escape rail at an angle, and secured it to their window ledge. It made a bridge with a four-story drop underneath and no rail for support, but we hugged the wall and there was always a hand reaching out to help.

Our everyday life regularized, but the world was in turmoil. The rumblings of World War II had begun. Nazism and Fascism were making headway at an accelerated pace. The Civil War in Spain was raging. The American Dance Association, a consolidation of the New Dance League, the Dance Guild, and the Dancers' Association, was organized and sponsored many fundraising concerts between 1937 and 1939.

Individual dancers, including me, gave studio concerts—every contribution helped. I presented *Tragic Fiesta*. Martha Graham did her famous *Deep Song* on the subject of the Spanish Civil War. Artists felt they had something socially important to say—important to all, not just to themselves. What was essential was that these works be works of art, not just propaganda (some were, some were not). It was a time of vitality, involvement, and caring, a sense of human responsibility for others.

With all this activity I was not taking class, but still meticulously did a barre, practiced daily, and worked constantly on new dances with the ultimate goal of a big New York performance. The American Dance Association sponsored two concerts at the Humphrey-Weidman Studio Theatre on West 16th Street. The first, on June 8, 1938, was shared by Jane Dudley, Sophie Maslow, and me. This concert gave me a chance to try out some of my new works. *Summertime*, from Gershwin's opera *Porgy and Bess*, was an open, sunny dance of lyric Americana, using jazz dance patterns. *Song of the Slums* was one of my socially conscious works. There also was the *Suite of Soviet Impressions: Sailor's Holiday, Lullaby to a Future Hero,* and *Harvest Festival*.

One of the pieces I was planning, *Dances of Yesterday*, was Spanish in texture, but modern in its stylized movement and presentation. It was in three parts, to music composed by John Coleman. I had three platforms constructed: a flat square, a taller cube, and a two-foot-high circular platform five feet in diameter. Each part of the dance was done on a different level and portrayed a different mood of Spanish flamenco dance. The basic costume, of gold satin with purple and magenta, had a bare midriff and one purple sleeve—very modern. The whole concept was visually theatrical, and unusual for a Spanish dance.

Combined with *Tragic Fiesta*, it became a suite I called *Lejenda* (the program misprinted it as *Legenda*). *Tragic Fiesta* used an authentic flamenco song with castanets. I sang part of the song while I moved, as a lament for Spain. The addition of my own vocal sound increased the texture of the movement. The costume was long and black, with a magenta midriff and the circular skirt lined in magenta.

China as well as Spain was very much in my consciousness. *Among the Ruins* mirrored the horror and devastation of a Chinese civilian caught in the bombardment by Japanese war planes.

Surrealism also intrigued me. I had seen Jean Cocteau's film *The Blood of a Poet*, and the images he created were provocative, especially when a figure walked on the edge of a molding or pulsating mouths suddenly appeared on a body. A satire on surrealism would be a challenge and make a good program balance, so I created a work called *Surrealist Sketches: Study of a Nude and Pas de Deux*. Henry Brant, a young modern composer, devised a piece in which he used some of the sound and percussion instruments I had acquired, especially an old-time auto horn, a bird whistle, and a slide whistle.

The costume for *Study of a Nude* was a hot-pink semicircular skirtlike device, with a huge eye appliqued in front, that hung from my neck to my knees. My legs were in black tights, and the costume exposed just one arm, so that the only naked limb was my right arm. I had found some pinkish metal out of which I cut narrow eyeglass frames. I stared at my nude arm throughout the dance and used extreme non sequitur movement.

The *Pas de Deux* was a technical dance, drawing on my ballet background. I wore black leotard and tights, with a short white tutu around my neck, and my hands were encased in white satin toe shoes. The arms and the upper body were the girl, the legs and torso, the boy. There were moments when the arms, extended up, paralleled the boy's movement, but inverted so that "she" looked upside-down, while with the legs the "boy" did the same movement right side up. This created the illusion of two people. In *arabesque*, with one arm and its pointe shoe touching the floor, the other arm stretched forward, it looked as if both characters were doing *arabesques*. Of course, at one point, I had to show off my ballet technique by having the "boy" perform a series of eight *entrechat-six*.

By fall I had enough material for a major New York concert. It had taken almost two years to create a program that I felt was entirely new and different. I had not been seen in New York in a solo concert since the season of 1934–35. It was frightening to plunge in again after such a long absence. Again a family conference. Dad thought I needed a press agent. Alix Williamson was recommended. I engaged the Guild Theatre for Sunday night, January 8, 1939. There we were again —shopping for cloth, Mother helping me design the costumes and sewing like mad, and I working until I was ready to drop to pull together a very demanding program.

About one week before the concert, Alix called to say a reporter from the *New York Post* was coming to interview me. At the appointed time I opened the door to a young man with a photographer at his side. We talked about many things, serious things, things important to me—

about my views of modern dance, its need to be meaningful as well as good art and good entertainment. I made the point that I was not particularly interested in abstractionism—how could I be, having so recently listened to lectures on socialist realism in Russia? The interviewer asked questions, which I answered in my most "intellectual" vein and added a summary of the upcoming program.

In the midst of all this, one of my artist neighbors appeared on the ledge of my back window, yelling, "Hey Pauline, can I use your telephone?" "Not now," I told him. "Come back later."

And we went on with the interview. I obligingly got into costume for some photos. I took it all in good faith that I would be "quoted," and that my serious approach to modern dance, on which I definitely had focused the interview, would then appear in the *New York Post*.

I was flabbergasted when, on January 6, I opened the paper to find a feature story with a picture from the *Surrealist Sketches*. The byline was Earl Wilson, who for many years afterward wrote a famous gossip column in the *New York Post*. After our hours of serious discussion, Wilson had written a snide "kitsch" story that was evidently funny and silly enough to hit one of the wire services, and it appeared in newspapers throughout the nation. I was appalled at the misquotes and the use of verbatim language that was definitely not mine. There it was, with a double-column photograph at the top of the page captioned "She Hates Abstract Dancing."

Miss Pauline Koner's dance studio is upstairs over a Fifth Avenue pool hall and there, while barefoot, she declared bitter war today upon *la danse moderne*. A neighboring young man was standing on a fire escape just outside her window squalling, "Hey, Pauline, howza 'bout using your telephone," at the historic moment. "Scram for a while," Miss Koner bid the young man, who did. Miss Koner then explained that she had been running around barefoot like this for weeks because she is going to open her big war on modern dance with a recital at the Guild Theatre, Sunday night. She went on to imply that if anybody wants a smack in the smoocher, they can get it by connecting her with the modern dance. . . . "I have a strange idea about dancing . . . I think the audience should be allowed to understand what you're dancing about."

I was devastated, furious, aghast at such misrepresentation of my ideas. Artists are often at the mercy of those in the press who can, by distortion, create what may be a great story for their byline, and to hell with what happens to the artist as a result! With the performance only two days away, I tried not to let it get to me, and felt that those who knew me would surely understand that this was simply somebody's gimmick. How wrong I was!

One of the boys next door had a battered secondhand car, and I lashed my platforms to the side to take them to the Guild. Physically, I was in fine shape, give or take the nervous tension. The evening went better than I had expected. The props and the platforms worked, costume changes were smooth, and above all, I danced well. I know when I dance well or badly—that night I danced very well, and the audience was enthusiastic. We piled the platforms back on the old car, packed the costumes, and I came back to the studio exhausted but exhilarated. I definitely felt I had made a huge step forward. Toward morning, I finally fell asleep.

Always apprehensive about reviews I hesitated to run out and buy papers, hoping somebody would call with the news. The morning was strangely quiet. And then a paper was brought. There it was in the *New York Times*, a review by John Martin. He had taken at face value that I was anti–modern dance because of the Earl Wilson article, and the review was a critical response to it rather than an evaluation of my program. Martin knew my work. He had always been encouraging and constructive. This time, he launched an attack that destroyed me. Dancers who had been at the performance called to tell me they thought it was the best thing I had done. They found it one of the most interesting concerts of the season. Other reviews were critical, positive, and some enthusiastic. But what did that matter? It was John Martin of the *New York Times* who counted.

Paul Stoes, a prominent concert manager who had offered the possibility of a tour, called and apologetically said that without a positive *New York Times* review it would be impossible to book the tour, even though he personally felt the performance was excellent, the program very exciting. I was bitterly disappointed and frustrated. I felt helpless. My anger grew. I wrote Martin, explaining how I was misquoted. I said that as a newspaperman, he, of all people, must know the distortions possible in the press. I received a polite letter in return:

> Thank you very much for your letter. I am sorry if you have been misrepresented, but it would have been difficult to draw any other

conclusion from your advance publicity, which repeatedly referred to your determination to depart from "the more arty and abstract dancing generally connoted by the term modern."

Unfortunately, I have not the space to print your letter, but I shall try to run a paragraph on the subject.

He never did.

Stop! I said to myself. Give up and try to find an easier, more satisfying way of living your life. For nine long years thereafter, except for an occasional performance, the solo concert dance was a bleak, almost frightening area for me.

In 1964, when *Dance Magazine* chose me as one of the recipients of its annual award, I was asked whom I might suggest to present this award. I thought for a while. On November 30, 1963, I had presented a new solo at my concert at the 92nd Street YMHA. It was called *Solitary Song*, and was one of the last dances I choreographed for myself. Martin had already retired from the *Times*, but I had invited him to the performance, and soon after received this note:

Just a line to tell you how much I enjoyed your concert last night. You can't imagine how nice it is, after thirty-five years of sitting in sphinx-like immobility to be able to applaud when the spirit moves me.

The new solo is a beauty. There are some phrases there (motor phrases, I mean, not just musical ones) that had me jumping out of my seat. This seems to me to be a work right out of the top drawer. . . . But there. I am writing a review. Habit is so strong.

Of course *The Farewell* left me moved and shaken once again. A truly lovely work.

Thank you for inviting me.

Why not ask John Martin to present the *Dance Magazine* Award? This was of course after seventeen years of excellent notices from him. He did it, and after the presentation party I said to him, "You know, John, I once wanted to shoot you!"

"Why" he said. "What did I do?"

When I told him, he could not even remember the incident that had almost destroyed my life.

New Paths

Fritz Mahler

It was Fritz who had the courage to bring me the disastrous Martin notice of January 9, 1939. We had been friends for two years. He tried hard to comfort me and to rationalize. Being a performer himself, he well knew what my reaction would be.

I met Fritz Mahler in an odd way. Trude Rittman was giving a small Christmas party. "Pauline, I would like you to meet a friend of mine who has recently arrived in the United States," she said. "He is Fritz Mahler, the symphony conductor." The evening of the party I arrived late and he had already gone. Just one of those things not meant to happen, I thought. The next morning a telephone call came. "I'm sorry I missed you last night," said a man with a heavy Viennese accent. "Trude has spoken so much about you. I would very much like to meet you." I was curious, so we made an appointment. I wondered what the meeting would be like. I had never had a blind date before, but as we had heard about each other, it was not totally blind. That Saturday night I entered the main lobby of the Radio City Music Hall, expecting to see a glamorous Viennese conductor. Instead there was a short man in a typical European black homburg, a too-long, navy-blue overcoat, and thick-lensed, horn-rimmed glasses shielding almost invisible blue-gray eyes.

He introduced himself. I responded in a rather small voice, with even smaller enthusiasm. "We must go outside to the personnel elevator," he said. "I have tickets for the mezzanine from one of the directors here who is a friend of mine."

We were escorted to posh reserved seats. With an elaborate stage show and a film, there was no need for conversation and when he tried to hold my hand, I found reason to occupy it with a small lorgnette I used for viewing. After the film we stopped to have a drink at Child's Restaurant. Not knowing much about cocktails, I remembered hearing about a "pink lady," a sweet drink with grenadine. I ordered one. He did, too.

We had a little time during our drink to talk about music, and this I found fascinating. His English was good, and I had coped with enough foreign accents to have no trouble understanding him. He took me to my studio, and I politely said goodnight. I thought, Well, that's that! I really was not interested. The following morning he telephoned.

"I enjoyed so much our evening. I hope I may see you again." His voice was soft and gentle. He had telephoned. Little did he know that he had found my Achilles' heel.

"Perhaps," I said, not too enthusiastically. "I'll see what my schedule is."

He called again. He called every day. And soon we were having dinner together or going to concerts. The very first concert he took me to included Schoenberg's Quartets, something my musical background had not prepared me for. On the other hand, he had little exposure to dance, especially modern dance. Fritz became part of my social life, and we established a friendship based on a mutual interest in music, the arts, and the world situation. Whenever he came to the studio, my dog Shutka (Russian for "joke") would not let him sit close, but always wedged between us.

After my emotional turmoil in Russia, I had made a decision to avoid hurtful situations. What I was looking for was the comfort and the assurance of being loved as well as companionship based on mutual interests and respect. I wanted desperately to be cared for—which certainly would be a change. Fritz's daily telephone call proved that he was aware of me. Whether we were together or not, he was concerned. Our friendship grew, even though temperamentally we were at opposite poles. I began to depend on his companionship, his calls, our concert-going, and discussions of our work.

Fritz, a second cousin of Gustav Mahler, was born in Vienna where his father Ludwig was professor of oriental languages at the university. Coming from a family with a great musical tradition, Fritz majored at the University of Vienna in musicology and history of music under Guido Adler, and then studied composition and instrumentation with Alban Berg, Arnold Schoenberg, and Anton Webern at the Academy of Music.

Although he played the piano, he did not start as an instrumentalist. From the beginning, his main interest was conducting. At twenty-one, he was engaged as assistant conductor at the Wiener Volksoper, and then conductor at the National Theatre in Mannheim (where he lived in the home of Trude Rittman's parents). For two years he led the Berlin Radio Symphony. In 1930 he became conductor of the Danish State Symphony by winning a competition, and also directed the famous Danish Radio Chorus. Invited to the United States in 1936 to conduct a series of concerts for CBS, he decided to make his home in New York, the political climate in Europe being what it was.

During our friendship I saw a great need to improve Fritz's rather old-fashioned European wardrobe. We bought a tweed suit to replace his somber dark ones, shortened his coat, replaced the homburg with a felt snap-brim hat, and I bought ties that brightened his appearance. More than that, whenever he had to write or needed a press release, I became the co-author. What I gained from him was a wonderfully enriched knowledge of music.

I still could not shake off the pall that enveloped me. It seemed that only a drastic change of some sort, a change that would occupy my mind in a totally different environment, would be the only solution. I thought that marriage might be the answer. Fritz had been a confirmed bachelor. He was living with his mother, who ran the household, and quite recently his sister and niece had come from Vienna to live in the apartment. It was not easy for a conductor to start a career all over again in a new country during a depression. He was coaching opera singers and guest conducting from time to time.

One day, during a discussion about our careers, I casually said, "Fritz, have you ever thought of marriage?" He looked a little startled. With his financial situation precarious, I was sure he had pushed it far back in his mind. He looked at me through his thick-lensed glasses and said, "Maybe one fine morning I'll ask you." My nice Jewish parents seemed eager for this, long before I even mentioned the possibility.

One fine morning in early spring 1939, Fritz asked, "Pauline, will you marry me?"

"Yes," I said, "but perhaps we should agree on some things first."

We were honest with each other and mature. At thirty-eight, he was eleven years older than I—for me that was a positive value. We each had an established career and knew its demands: dedication, isolation, tensions, disappointments, and, we hoped, successes. Knowing myself, I made it plain: "No children." I love children, but to have a child means giving time, energy, and all of oneself. If I divided myself between dance, Fritz's career, and a child, I knew the child would suffer. We made a pact that our careers must come first.

Before we married we lived through a crisis. Fritz developed a staphylococcus infection in his throat. He was terrified because Alban Berg had died of such an infection. Fritz's temperature rose to 104 degrees and I called Dad. He got his best nose-and-throat specialist to come. Penicillin was prescribed, and I was told to watch carefully; if his fingertips turned blue, I was to call immediately. I sat vigil through the night, and the next day the worst was over.

On May 23, 1939, we were married at the summer City Hall at the New York World's Fair. Of course we got lost driving there and barely made it. Fritz knew Mayor LaGuardia, who prided himself on his musical interest, and the mayor performed the simple ceremony. When he stuck his glasses on his forehead and asked me the question, "Do you promise to love, honor, and obey?" I was so nervous I could hardly say, "Yes." We were a small group—Mom, Dad, Fritz's mother, his sister Hedi, Alix Williamson, and my friend Corinne. The wedding dinner was at Enrico's in Greenwich Village.

I moved into Fritz's apartment at 260 West 72nd Street, which now housed his mother, sister, niece, and the two of us. We had two rooms: his studio where he taught and a studio bedroom where I did my living. His mother, whom we called in Viennese fashion "Mutti," ran the household, which included cooking her Viennese specialties. The house was always fragrant with the aroma of freshly brewed coffee, which no matter how she explained it I was never able to master.

Mutti spoke only a few words of English. I understood her because of the Yiddish I had heard as a child, and got by speaking a kind of pidgin German. My job was to wash the dinner dishes. Mutti was horrified when she heard me say, "Fritz, why don't you come and help?" A man in the kitchen! But he came and he learned.

It was September and we had made plans to spend a lovely day at the World's Fair. Up bright and early, we bought the *New York Times* and were faced with shocking news: "Germany Invades Poland." Incredulous at first, we knew as it slowly sank in that war was upon us. As yet the United States was not involved, but Fritz had lived through World War I in Vienna; he had been dismissed from school for writing an antiwar composition, had suffered the postwar hunger. He knew the implication of the headline much more than I.

Settled into marriage I felt the need to stay in condition. I started ballet classes with Leon Fokine, who was teaching with his mother Alexandra Fedorova at 9 East 59th Street. The classes were enjoyable, but I knew that in order to support any dance activity, I would have to earn money. I found a studio in a ramshackle building on 65th Street and Broadway, the exact spot where Avery Fisher Hall now stands. The studio was an oasis where I could get away from my crowded home surroundings and be alone to practice and think. I would leave the apartment in late morning and return at dinner time.

Fritz had been conducting occasional out-of-town engagements (I even choreographed a short segment for one of them). He amazed me with his complete personality change on the podium. In normal life rather low-key, with an offbeat wit, but seemingly not too temperamental, he was a dynamo when he conducted. He did not indulge in theatrics, but used his baton to give exact beat and every cue. He had a special talent for making a moderately good orchestra sound much better because of his precision and stylistic acumen. I think I decided to marry him after I heard him conduct Mozart.

Meanwhile, the 92nd Street YMHA had initiated a dance series, as did Washington Irving High School. Engagements on these series encouraged me to continue in concert dance. On February 4, 1940, I gave a solo concert at the Y. Shortly after that concert, Fritz complained about his eyes. Since his vision was basically poor, I rushed with him to an ophthalmologist. Diagnosis: a detached retina. Dad had recently had the same problem and been operated on. Not able to tolerate the enforced immobility after the operation he had lost the sight of that eye.

More than anything else Fritz needed his eyesight if he was to continue as a conductor. At that time a retina operation was very serious. The retina had literally to be sewn back in place, and the healing process was crucial. For three days there had to be absolute immobility, and then six months of restricted activity—no violent movement, no lifting of any kind. Fritz had an iron will and made a perfect recovery. He was back conducting by the fall.

Then things began to improve for him. He was invited to teach advanced conducting and act as director of the opera department for the Juilliard School of Music summer session. This continued each summer until 1951. For us, it was recognition as well as a financial boon. At the same time, from October 1940 until September 1941, he became New York City director of music for the National Youth Administration, which involved many concerts and twenty-two world premieres of American compositions.

When in 1941 I was engaged by Joseph Mann for a concert on the Students' Dance Recital Series at Washington Irving, I was ready to choreograph again. My program included a satire called *Ballerina: Her Greatest Triumph*. It was a dance to Tchaikovsky, in which I pointed out the lack of credibility in some ballets when the heroine, after a brilliant technical tour de force, suddenly drops dead. The dance that explored a new style and medium was *Judgment Day*, to excerpts from James Weldon Johnson's poem, *God's Trombones* and Negro spirituals arranged by Harvey Brown. I spoke the text of the poem during the dance.

At last I felt that I was searching again after a hiatus of two years, but one performance a year was rather depressing. There were engagements at Wheaton College in 1942 and 1943, and the Students' Dance series moved to new quarters at the Central High School of Needle Trades in 1944. The season's series included Tamiris and Group, Martha Graham and Dance Company, Doris Humphrey and Charles Weidman, Mia Slavenska, and me.

For my program I created three new works, two of which lasted in my solo repertoire. *Out of This Sorrow*, again on the Spanish Civil War, started with a lament set to *cante jondo* music. The first section of the dance was done seated on a chair; the second moved in space, with only the castanets and heelwork as sound. My discovery of Carl Sandburg's *The Prairie*, lines of which I spoke, motivated the moods of the second new work. The costume was rust-orange, with an avocado green underskirt. I always loved the surprise of another color as the skirts swirled in sweeping leg movements and turns. These two works, added to my earlier *Lullaby to a Future Hero,* now became a suite of three dances called *Mothers of Men*: a Russian, a Spanish, and an American woman. The third new piece was *In Memoriam*, to a Shostakovich piano prelude. This activity kept me busy with dance. I worked daily no matter how sparse the performances. With excellent reviews in the periodicals, I was slowly regaining confidence.

As Fritz's activities were gathering impetus, the time seemed ripe for a change. The restricted quarters, the need to be discreet, were just too much. Playing the role of the traditional daughter-in-law, I declared that we had to have our own apartment. Consternation, but Fritz agreed with me. His mother and sister could continue to live together and he would contribute for his mother's share.

I found a beautiful apartment in the annex of the Chatsworth, on the southwest end of 72nd Street near the Hudson River, opposite the former Fokine site. We moved in spring 1941, and at last I had my own home. In a way, I felt that only now had our married life begun. My cooking is nothing to brag about, but I taught Fritz to live on a dancer's diet of broiled foods and lots of salads. No more fancy Viennese dishes with whipped cream desserts. He learned to like it, although he never lost his taste for good cooking or whipped cream when it was available.

Not long after we were installed in our new apartment we were sitting in the kitchen having one of my unpretentious dinners and listening to music on the radio. Suddenly the music stopped and a voice said, "We are interrupting this broadcast for an important announcement from the President of the United States." President Roosevelt's familiar voice solemnly informed that the Japanese had bombed Pearl Harbor. We looked at each other, stunned. Lives changed. We were warned and even on the East Coast we had to black out our windows.

During this time Fritz met Robert Russell Bennett, an arranger of leading Broadway shows, and a composer. The daily meeting place for Russell and his friends was a coffee shop near Radio City Music Hall, and Fritz became part of this group. Russell spoke of a new show he was doing, which he thought might interest Fritz. Light music was no stranger to Fritz. If the music was good, he felt the area was another challenge. *Lute Song* was an absolutely enchanting show, based on the Chinese play *Pi-Pa-Ki* and directed by John Houseman. Russell Bennett recommended Fritz to be engaged as conductor. Interestingly, the choreographer was Nimura, with Lisan Kay and Lisa Maslova as the lead dancers. Mary Martin, Yul Brynner in his Broadway lead debut,

Clarence Derwent, Augustine Duncan (Isadora's brother), and Mildred Dunnock headed the cast. Nimura choreographed some beautiful ballets, and the music was charming. It seemed a sure-fire hit, but in out-of-town tryouts *Lute Song* revealed insurmountable problems, and Fritz left before it opened in New York for a brief run. I thought it was too sensitive, too delicate for Broadway.

Being a symphony conductor required a permanent orchestra, and in the 1940s there were not many orchestras in the United States. Fritz had to rebuild his reputation. One of his most admirable qualities was that of hope. Even in the darkest days he would say, "You never know what the next telephone call or the next day's mail might bring." He was managed by Arthur Judson Concert Bureau, a division of Columbia Artists Management. Early in 1947 we heard that there was an opening in Erie, Pennsylvania. Fritz got the appointment. Now I really began to learn what it might mean to be a conductor's wife. My life became schizophrenic. For the winter season we rented a furnished apartment in a charming Victorian house, but we decided to keep the New York apartment since I was appearing as guest artist with the José Limón Company and Fritz had the Juilliard summer school. He stayed in Erie during the entire winter season and I commuted. I learned to give parties, more frightening for me than any performance. I attended rehearsals, checked acoustics, and discussed tempi.

Erie was bitter cold in winter. I rented the local dancing studio and trudged through heavy snow to practice as often as possible, but aside from the social life, there was little for me to do or see. Fritz was busy; I was bored and grateful to take the ten-hour train trip back to New York, where the pattern of my life was quite different. Fritz telephoned almost daily and never complained about my absence. Actually, I think the local ladies were delighted when I was away, so that they could have him more to themselves. We bought a car, a Pontiac, and learned to drive, but I insisted there be no radio because Fritz might listen more than he watched. However, I was in mortal fear when he drove alone, what with his poor eyesight and general lack of mechanical knowledge. He just drove slowly and carefully, and never had an accident.

For his concerts Fritz was able to attract leading soloists as guests because of his reputation as an excellent conductor. Jascha Heifetz was so impressed that after playing the Beethoven Violin Concerto and after numerous bows, he came out and said, "This is an exception to my rule," whereupon he played one of the Bach unaccompanied sonatas as an encore. Arthur Rubinstein was a well-loved visitor. He confided to Fritz, "I love the piano so much I would play for nothing, but don't tell anyone."

William Kapell agreed to accept an invitation, but only if he would be allowed to play the Mozart A Major Concerto, which was far from his usual repertoire. The Mozart rehearsal was a disaster. Fritz took Willy home, coached him in the Mozart style, and the concert was a huge success. The next day Willy arrived at our home with his book of Mozart sonatas. He kept Fritz busy all day until I insisted he leave so that Fritz could rest for that night's concert. The following summer Willy played the same Mozart concerto at his Lewisohn Stadium performance and received rave reviews. It came as a great shock when, on October 29, 1953, we heard a radio announcer say that there had been a fatal airplane crash near Australia. One of the passengers was William Kapell.

Early in spring 1953 we heard that there was an opening for music director and conductor of the Hartford Symphony. We met the board of directors; I did the talking because of Fritz's accent and his reticence. He got the appointment. I felt in a way this made up for my absences, which were now, with my work with the Limón company, becoming more frequent.

We rented a small furnished house in Wethersfield, Connecticut. Closer to New York and with a greater musical potential, Hartford was a positive change. From the beginning Fritz made it clear that he intended to make this a major orchestra, that his programming would be adventurous and on the highest level.

My social obligations increased. I learned to serve elegant dinners — they always required a "dress rehearsal" — and gave cocktail parties that became quite popular and provided a neutral territory for various factions to come together. It would take me a week to recover after one of these events. Everyone had a wonderful time, but I was a complete wreck.

After two seasons of renting a house, we decided we had to find an apartment in Hartford. Fritz, who was touring abroad, asked a friend to hunt. While I was preparing to perform in New London I received a note: "We have engaged an apartment right near Bushnell Auditorium. Come and look at it as soon as possible." It was beastly hot, but I drove to Hartford right away. When I walked in I thought, This must be a mistake; I must be in the wrong place. The agent assured me this was it. How could anyone have committed us to it? The building was an old loft studio-type building, with dark, dingy halls. The apartment had been totally neglected. The living room was filthy, the floor painted a crude brown, open steam pipes along the walls. I said it was impossible to have it livable within a month, but the deposit was already paid and the lease signed.

I drove back to New London and tried to put the apartment out of my mind. "Dance must come first, then you'll face this," but I could see no solution and was needled by the problem. By the end of the festival at New London, I was a nervous, dehydrated, physical mess, looking forward with diabolic glee to indulging in complete collapse. Instead, I had to plunge in directly and make the apartment a home before Fritz arrived at the end of September.

I got the landlord to agree to tear out the steam pipes and install radiators. I had the entire place painted off-white, then had carpenters build open wall shelves in a staggered wing shape on both sides of a fireplace and cupboards to hold Fritz's orchestra parts. The floors were repainted. After six weeks of running, shopping, hammering, pushing furniture, transporting things, it was ready. A complete metamorphosis, not only livable, but actually quite impressive. Fritz arrived, walked in, caught his breath. "It's stunning," he said.

I was bitter for quite a while. I would look at that apartment and think, There have gone ten years of my life—it took a long time to recover. Since I spent a good deal of time in New York I did not have much chance to enjoy it, but when I gave a cocktail party and people were astonished, coming in from the dowdy hallway, I was pleased and proud. It really became Fritz's home, where he worked, rehearsed guest artists, studied, and took the place for granted.

Fritz's programs in Hartford grew ambitious. He developed the Hartford Symphony Chorale, which enabled him to do major choral works, and began to introduce American audiences to the music of Gustav Mahler and Alban Berg. He even brought in the Limón company, with me as guest artist, for a full-evening concert with the orchestra—a rare occasion when a symphony conductor played our tempi perfectly. He began to make recordings with the orchestra. I had suggested to Fritz that it might be interesting if Aaron Copland orchestrated his Piano Variations, the music I used for a solo, *Cassandra*. Fritz agreed and wrote to Copland, who responded that he was just completing exactly that. It was a harsh, jagged work, interesting, but not easy to listen to.

Fritz did the first recording of Orchestral Variations for Vanguard.

When I was in Hartford I tried my best to make life as comfortable as possible for Fritz. What drove me to distraction was the state of crisis that working with Limón kept me in. We rehearsed the year round (for nothing). When I was not absolutely essential—and I always tried to arrange this during Fritz's rehearsals and major performances—I settled in to the rhythm of living in Hartford. Immediately, a Limón crisis seemed to arise, and I dashed back to New York as soon as I could (at my own expense), got through the rehearsal, and dashed back to Hartford. Sometimes I awoke not knowing where I was.

There were times I really wanted an extended stay in one place with Fritz, but my dedication to Limón and his reliance on me made it almost impossible. Once, in spring 1960 when our tour was cancelled, I was able to join Fritz in Norway for his concerts with the Oslo Philharmonic. Then we went on to Rome, where I was invited to return and stage my group work *Concertino* for the Accademia Nazionale di Danza. The next year Fritz was invited to conduct the Santiago de Chile Philharmonic, and I, having met Ernst Uthoff, director of the Chilean National Ballet, was invited to stage *Concertino* for that company. Fritz and I had a wonderful month together. From Chile, we traveled to Argentina, where Fritz conducted the Buenos Aires Philharmonic at the Teatro Colón, and I had an invitation to give a master course for the Argentine Association for Dance.

But traveling together was rare. More often, it was chance and sometimes unexpected crossings of our paths while we were on tour—a single day in Berlin, where he turned up sporting contact lenses; an extra day in Tokyo before traveling to Seoul. Therefore it was doubly precious, especially when Fritz had engagements in Copenhagen. There, he was on home ground. For me, just being with him, meeting his friends, was a special vacation.

During his tenure in Hartford from 1953 through 1964, Fritz developed a fine orchestra with an excellent reputation. Yet as the years passed, and the symphony board took the progress of the orchestra for granted, the usual power politics emerged. Factions began to pick on reasons to gain power: the programs were too adventurous, too modern, Fritz too strict with the players. Mainly, I think it was that Fritz was getting too much of the credit for the orchestra's achievement. By 1964 we saw the handwriting on the wall. The situation had become tense.

Newspapers took sides and untrue statements were casually printed. We consulted lawyers about libel, but were told that no one could win against a newspaper.

On May 6, 1964, Fritz gave his last concert with the Hartford Symphony. It was a masterful performance. He chose Benjamin Britten's *War Requiem*, a mammoth work for orchestra, chorus, three soloists, and a children's chorus—a first for Hartford. There were the usual silver-platter gifts, and many tears, particularly from the chorus, which was very devoted.

The board had planned a farewell reception at Bushnell Auditorium after the concert, but I said to Fritz, "We're not going. I refuse to be part of this hypocritical charade." We sent a note to those we knew were friends that we would receive them in the bar at the Hilton Hotel.

Now began a very difficult time for both of us. Fritz felt confident that with the reputation he had built with the Hartford orchestra, he would find another. So he tried to be cheerful, even though I could see he was deeply hurt. We had not noticed that the United States was undergoing a complete change of attitude concerning conductors. Youth was favored, as the pattern of new appointments made very clear. Fritz, who was sixty-three, realized that his chances of getting a permanent orchestra were dim. He decided to concentrate on guest appearances abroad. Although this meant prolonged separations, I encouraged him.

Now Fritz was abroad both winter and summer. He conducted in major cities in Europe, behind the Iron Curtain, and in the Far East. At intervals, depression—either his or mine—made for trying times. We were together less and less, yet our marriage held. I never let the thought of what his life was like while he was away enter my mind, nor did he pry into mine. We both knew we were busy working, and being fulfilled in our work was of primary importance.

In 1966–67, after some successful concerts in Tokyo, Fritz was invited by Tokyo University, through the Fulbright Commission, to teach opera conducting for a year. He hesitated, but I said, "You must accept. It is important. If you don't go, you will have regrets, be unhappy, and that would be of no help to me." He went. Fortunately, during that year I made a State Department-sponsored tour of Southeast Asia. Fritz arranged to conduct the Seoul Symphony Orchestra during the same two weeks I was to teach at Iwa University in Seoul; on my way home, I spent another week with him in Tokyo.

By this time I was teaching part-time at the North Carolina School of the Arts. I had started in 1965 when the school had just opened, and was commuting back and forth to New York, so life was hectic. Fritz had mentioned that he had suffered a slight heart attack while in Poland, but was all right. At times, when I was home with him, he complained of fatigue, and I noticed his speech sometimes slurred.

On December 5, 1968, I received a telephone call from London, where Fritz was preparing a broadcast concert with the London Philharmonia. A voice said, "This is Lily Sigal. I'm afraid I have some bad news. Fritz is in the hospital. It looks serious. You'd better come immediately!"

I called my brother, asked him to get me a ticket to London, and flew from Winston-Salem to New York that day. The following day I flew to London, and the moment I got to the airport I called Middlesex Hospital. "Mrs. Mahler," the voice at the other end said, "I'm afraid the news is not good. Your husband has had a massive stroke and has lost his speech."

I dashed to the hospital, and when I saw Fritz I knew it was bad. He knew me, but could not speak. His right side was paralyzed. Lily told me the full story. Evidently, during the night Fritz had not felt well. He found he could not move his arm. The next day was his final dress rehearsal for the concert. Not wanting to disturb Lily, he waited until morning, and then managed to call her. She immediately had an ambulance take him to the hospital. Fortunately, it was Middlesex, one of the best hospitals in London.

I sat with Fritz every afternoon. They started him on therapy, but no one could tell me how long it might be before he could tolerate the trip home. He was terribly depressed and really did not understand what had happened to him.

Life in its grimmest aspect was facing me, and I was not quite sure if I could handle it. I was alone, shattered, not knowing what the future would hold. I was constantly chilled to the bone, even though my hotel room had a little heat. The gray days, no spot of sunshine, the rain, all added to my own terrible depression. The two people who helped me hold on to my sanity were the dance notation expert, Ann Hutchinson, and her charming, dance-historian husband, Ivor Guest. Their home was an oasis, especially during the holiday season, a particularly bleak time.

Fritz showed some slight recovery. He wrote some words, hardly legible, with his left hand. A semblance of speech returned very slowly. He was in a large ward, but the doctors and nurses were gentle, efficient, and sympathetic. The doctors gave me a dismal picture of the future. My main thought was how to get Fritz home. Finally, the doctors said if a plane would take him, I could probably bring him home by January 2. I convinced BOAC that he was fit to travel. My brother arranged to have him admitted to Columbia Presbyterian Hospital, and would meet us at the airport with an ambulance.

When I tried to pay the bill at Middlesex Hospital they said that, since he had taken ill in their district, he was covered by socialized medicine. Even the doctors refused any money. I left gifts, deeply impressed by the integrity and dedication of these wonderful people.

The trip home was a nightmare. Fritz was totally disoriented; I tried to conceal from the attendants how ill he really was. We arrived late at night, and I waited until all the passengers left the plane. It was bitter cold. As I peered through the iced windows of the plane, I could not see the ambulance. People came in to clean the plane and left. The heat was cut off. It was freezing. Fritz was fading fast, and I was terribly frightened. I asked someone to call. I knew my brother could not have mistaken our arrival. After an hour, I heard some sound. Yes, an ambulance. Marvin rushed in. The motor had frozen on the way out and a second ambulance had to be sent. I was afraid Fritz could not survive this trip and the cold much longer. We raced to the hospital with the siren screaming, while I held Fritz's hand and hoped. Once Fritz was admitted and settled in, Marvin took me home, a physical and mental zero.

The change created a crisis for Fritz. He had hallucinations, and, when left unattended, fell out of bed. During my daily visits, he began to be belligerent. He thought he was in an asylum, and insisted he had to be taken out. He asked to see our personal doctor, Irving Solomon, who was an old friend. I was beside myself. Jean Gordon, publisher of *Dance Magazine*, came to our rescue. She suggested the Rusk Institute of Rehabilitation, a part of New York University Hospital, where Dr. Rusk admitted him the day of my call. I was comforted by the thoughtful treatment we had there, for with crisis after crisis, I was afraid that I, too, would end up in a hospital.

With Fritz installed, and after reassuring myself that at last he was in good hands, I could make plans to get back to work—for both psychological and financial reasons. I had to continue my part-time teaching at North Carolina School of the Arts, and since Fritz would have to stay for treatment and rehabilitation for quite some time, I could see him at the hospital on my New York time and know he was cared for while I was away.

As Fritz began to improve, he nagged me to take him home. When I tried to explain that there would be no one to tend him while I was away, he got furious and with what little speech he had accused me of not caring. It took all my power of reasoning to make him see that he still needed therapy and the doctors were not ready to release him. He had begun to handle a wheelchair, and work was being done to put a newly developed plastic brace on his leg and to teach him to walk with a cane. But always he wanted his home, his music, his privacy. This self-centeredness and illogic was typical of the illness. While at the school, I tried to block out this part of my life and concentrate on dance. It was my only therapy.

On May 28, 1969, Fritz was discharged, but had to return to the institute for therapy three times a week. Spring session was finished in North Carolina, and I engaged a woman to help take care of him while I spent two weeks in June setting my piece *Poème* on Linda Kent and George Faison of the Alvin Ailey company. After that I had accepted three weeks of summer-school teaching in July at North Carolina School of the Arts. It would be impossible to leave Fritz in stifling New York with unreliable help. I discussed it with Mom, and she suggested that he stay with her at the summer house on a lake near Otisville, seventy-five miles from the city. Fritz had always loved it there. I took him there with Merle, the attendant, knowing that Mom would take care of him on Merle's day off. I got Fritz installed in what had been Dad's room, and hoped things were solved for the moment. When I gave Merle fare to go to New York on her day off, she never returned. It was June 26—a dismal birthday for me—and I had to leave for Winston-Salem by July 1. A search for a temporary nursing home in the area turned up nothing, and finally Mom said, "Don't worry, he'll stay here and I'll take care of him. I'll try to find some help."

Poor Mom. After nine years of caring for Dad who had had a stroke and only two years of trying to recover from his death in December 1966, she was back in the same situation. I felt guilty and helpless. It was too late to cancel in North Carolina, and I needed the money to care for Fritz. I dashed back after three sweltering weeks of teaching. Although she had found a lovely Scandinavian masseuse to help, I could see Mom was having a difficult time. Twelve days later I was in New London to rehearse *Poème* for its performance in the festival. The piece went quite well, and I hurried back to our lake house, stopping first in New York to think through what my next move should be.

Trying to find responsible help in New York with my commuting would be impossible. It would be better to move Fritz to Winston-Salem and find help there. I piled him and his belongings in my car. Fritz was grateful and though the trip was hard on him he did not complain. He was happy that I was there. I found a maid, Ella-Mae, who was very pleasant, but who had four children with all the attendant crises. She would call me at 7:30 A.M. to say she could not come. I had to get Fritz up, give him his breakfast, and dash off to teach an 8:30 class. Back at 11 to give Fritz lunch, then off for a 2 P.M. class. Back for dinner, then off for a rehearsal at 6:30. One of the few bright moments I had had during Fritz's initial illness in London was a cable saying I had received one of the first choreography grants awarded by the National Endowment for the Arts. Now, in Winston-Salem, I had begun to choreograph. The only way I could survive this schedule and keep my sanity was to go back to New York on my time off, and Ella-Mae, fortunately, stayed with Fritz.

Fritz's personality changed again. He became very gentle and solicitous. I was practically his only relative—his mother and sister had died and we had lost contact with his niece. He recognized his dependence. I made an effort not to show how drained I was, but after a parade of housekeepers and another disastrous summer at the lake house, a drastic step was needed.

I had a serious talk with Fritz, whose speech had recovered enough so that I could easily understand him, and explained that I could no longer cope with the problem of adequate care for him. The best thing for him would be a nursing home, where I could visit him daily. It was hard to say this—he seemed so desolate, so helpless. I had to make him understand that I was not abandoning him. He was like the child we had agreed not to have. His own frustration at his helplessness brought on crying spells. We cried together.

His condition grew worse. I returned from visits to the nursing home in a state of desolation. It was hard to eat my simple dinner. I sank into bed exhausted, only to fall prey to nightmares. Waking was also a nightmare. Problems multiplied. I sold our beautiful Steinway piano and Fritz's books. His precious music library was sold to Isaac Stern. Pieces of my life were breaking away. Fritz gave up talking of recovery. The future seemed hopeless for both of us.

My personal doctor, aware of the state I was in, sent me to a Dr. Charles Winklestein, who I can say saved my life. He made me see that Fritz was no longer the man I had known. He forbade me to go to the nursing home daily, even to telephone daily (I did not stop the telephoning), and insisted that I accept an offer to go to Manila for three months. I took along as assistant Evelyn Shepard, a talented young dancer, and as comfort a Chihuahua I named Shutka II. We left for Manila on May 7, 1973.

On the morning of June 19, my brother called: "This is the call you have expected. Fritz died this morning, Monday, June 18." I took the next plane to Winston-Salem, and arrived after a thirty-hour trip. In the meantime Patricia Pence, a warm human being and superlative harpist, my dearest friend at the school, had taken care of all the preliminary arrangements.

Just before leaving for Manila, I had gone to say goodbye to Fritz and had taken some flowers and the dog with me. He had seen Shutka II a few times before and loved her. He was conscious for short spans of time. I kissed him and told him I would be back soon.

"Fritz," I asked, "do you remember the name of the doggie?" He smiled and whispered, "Shutka."

That was the last word I heard him say.

Kitty Doner and Television

"Why don't you get in touch with Kitty Doner," someone said. "She is interested in modern dancers for the Roxy shows." It was summer 1943. Still feeling that concert dance had very little future for me, I was searching for new possibilities in the dance field. The suggestion was offered in the dressing room of Ballet Arts at Carnegie Hall's Studio 61, that same studio with so many poignant memories. The school was now run by Nimura and Virginia Lee, with numerous guest teachers. From time to time I took a ballet class there with Edward Caton, who had a way of creating dance phrases that had a natural kinesthetic feel. Dressing room gossip is usually a good source, so I decided to contact Kitty Doner.

I had already had a fling at a nightclub act—very short-lived—with a vaudeville dancer named Joseph Hahn. It was not for me! People drinking, talking, noise. Choreographing for the Roxy theater, if it were possible, would certainly be more to my taste.

Kitty Doner had heard of me. We made an appointment to meet at the theater. Her voice on the phone was not the usual cold, dry voice I associated with "show biz"; it was warm and friendly. She sounded sincere and interested. Her voice in person was low and resonant with a typical New York twang. The woman was not at all what I expected. The smile seemed to start at her high forehead, descend into blue eyes that sparkled, past a small, straight nose to a wide, warm, smiling mouth. Her prominent teeth made the smile even broader. I could not help noticing her dainty ears, behind which short, brown hair was neatly tucked, and she had the trimmest ankles with the smallest feet I had ever seen.

Kitty dressed conservatively in tailored suits, but she had a flair for fashion, a way of tying a scarf, the color of a flower picking up the color of gloves. What Kitty had called in her youth "skinny legs," and had covered with trousers (in her performing days she had been a male impersonator to hide what she thought was her lack of beauty), are today's ideal: slender, with a racehorse quality of aliveness.

There was instant rapport; Kitty in her Broadway commercial theater vernacular and I with my concert dance aesthetics were thinking the same things. "Why don't I introduce you to Gae Foster, our producer. I'm sure she will be interested," and Kitty arranged an appointment. Gae, an imposing woman, her steel-gray hair in an elegant upsweep, had an air of authority that long years of experience had nurtured. They were planning a show featuring Ilona Massey, one of those flamboyant Hungarian beauties, and Gae thought it would be a good idea to surround her with some Hungarian numbers. Could I do something in that vein? Of course I could. I remembered the dance Fokine had taught us. I went home, chose some Brahms Hungarian Dances, choreographed a few phrases, and showed Gae my plan.

"It sounds good," she said. "We have a meeting with the production staff and the director, Mr. Partington." When asked to explain the dance number, I got up and demonstrated a few steps. "Why don't you dance in it yourself?" Partington said. "I'd love to!" I said. Contracts were signed. I decided to do a duet, and called in my nightclub partner, Joe Hahn. He was delighted. Kitty was thrilled and was there with her expert advice.

The picture on the bill for August 18, 1943, was *Heaven Can Wait*, featuring Gene Tierney. Here I was again—all day in makeup, four shows a day, five on Saturday, but a nice dressing room, with a couch where I could rest. I came down on stage at warning call to warm up, and learned that no one was allowed to sit down while in costume. If you did, you were fined.

The film was a great success and held over. Joe developed back trouble after two weeks and had to leave, so I picked a handsome young man from the chorus. He seemed far above the usual level. It was Alfredo Corvino, who had just arrived from South America, and this was his first job. The dance team of Veloz and Yolanda were also replaced, by Mary Raye and Naldi. Naldi was strong and did spectacular lifts, and if Mary missed he raised hell with her. The grueling routine left her black and blue.

Spending all day at the theater, I had a chance to meet and talk to Kitty often and watch her rehearse for the next show. She was assistant producer and choreographer of the Roxyettes (although the program never credited her), but she was interested in everything that was happening in the arts. Kitty's personality was irresistible. From playing leads in Al Jolson's shows, a headliner in her own act in vaudeville and at the Wintergarden, to the stock market crash she never lost her sense of humor. Here was this whimsical woman, a brilliant artist, who at one point had been reduced to selling eggs from her estate—the roof leaked but there was a bridle path and a rose garden. Now she could laugh about it. With a famous show biz career behind her, Kitty was still looking for new trends. Her taste was impeccable. A lively force behind the scenes, she was always scouting material and interesting talent.

The reviews of my Roxy performances were good, and I was offered another appearance beginning in April 1944. This one was with Paul Whiteman and His Orchestra. The show was built around Whiteman's specialty, the music of Gershwin, with Victor Borge playing an edited version of *Rhapsody in Blue*. I used my solo *It Ain't Necessarily So*, but expanded it with some dancers seated on side benches. They responded to my preaching with "revival meeting" gestures.

Kitty, ever on the alert for new directions, phoned one day: "Pauline, I just got a call from the William Morris Agency and I suggested that we both talk to them. A show has been suggested on Duke Ellington's music. They asked would we be interested, and what ideas did we have." The whole project petered out, but our suggestions must have had some impact because a few weeks later a young woman named Selma Lee called from William Morris to ask if we would be interested in a fifteen-minute dance slot for CBS television.

"That's it, P.K., that's the new thing. We have a chance to experiment, start at the beginning, and learn the idiom."

A meeting was arranged at CBS. We got so excited, we kept bubbling over with ideas. We made things sound so vivid. "We'll try it out for six shows," they said. The money was nothing, 300 dollars per show, from which we had to pay for dancers, costumes, props, a month's rehearsal studio, and musical accompaniment. But we felt it was worth it. In late summer 1945 there were as yet only 2,000 television sets in New York, and none were being commercially manufactured for sale. Programs were broadcast on what was called "closed circuit" to these 2,000 machines, with questionnaires sent out and a special viewing panel to evaluate the future of television. I was very excited and wanted to learn what that video camera could do, to get into the control room (which was quite primitive) and see how it all worked.

Kitty and I formed a production unit called "Choreotones"—Koner and Doner—it sounded like a vaudeville team. Kitty took care of all production elements; I did the choreography and performed. We worked out the ideas together, choosing very simple storylines or a mood for each ballet. We knew we would be reaching a nondance audience. Music was jazz, ballads, ethnic, or classical, depending on the idea. Professionalism was never compromised. We engaged some of the best dancers in the field, who rehearsed and performed for a pittance for the sake of the experience.

As I choreographed for television I visualized the camera frame, not a proscenium stage. Kitty and I coined the term "cameragraph," which meant the scenario contained specific shots for specific dance movements. We wanted an occasional closeup, to see the dancers' faces, their emotional quality. The movement was sometimes planned so that only the upper body or head was important. If the entire body was essential, we asked for a long shot. This awareness of camera framing had to be an integral part of the choreography. In one show the action started with the feet, transferred to the body, then concentrated on the head. We also had in mind certain scenic effects as part of our script.

Television equipment was still primitive and minimal. We could not depend on all the electronic tricks available today, but were forced to invent unusual effects by sheer ingenuity. Sometimes an accidental move created an unusual shot. I once swirled upstage center, then ran forward downstage. The camera man had pulled back, thinking I would come downstage first. Realizing his mistake, he dollied forward just as I was coming forward. What happened was very exciting: because we were moving in opposite directions simultaneously, depth and speed were added to the movement. We labeled this a "bellows shot." It was the high point of the dance and received special mention in *Television* magazine.

The CBS studio was in a small rectangular space in the Grand Central Building. There was no depth for the camera to pull back far enough to include the full moving body. The only solution was to use a corner for depth, so that our space became a triangle. We had two cameras with a single lens each. These cameras were on a wheeled base and could be turned side to side and tilted. There was no zoom or boom. Of course it was all black and white. Kitty and I plunged into this unknown realm of electronics with enthusiasm, verve, and energy.

Our first show was "Stardust Blues," broadcast on October 5, 1945. Taking a cue from the composer Hoagy Carmichael—who had just acted the role of a low-down piano player in a recent movie appearance and had composed a song called "Hong Kong"—we set the number in a Hong Kong nightspot. I choreographed a number for J. C. McCord, at the time a well-known modern dancer, as a character playing the piano. Then I did a solo to Carmichael's ballad, "Stardust." For contrast between East and West we invited Tei-ko, a Japanese dancer, to do an authentic Chinese dance to Chinese music. The director was Ben Feiner. The review in *Billboard* gave him credit for interesting use of camera shots.

For our part, Kitty and I learned our first and very important lesson about video dance. Because we were so detailed in our plans, friction often arose with the director or the scenic designer; everyone wanted to be the star of the show. We were not going to let anything or anybody stop us from creating what we envisioned—dance was the only star. James McNaughton, the scenic designer of "Stardust Blues," had created an elaborate decor for Tei-ko. The floor was painted in wild swirls and the background with highly ornamental pagodas, making it almost impossible to see Tei-ko in her ornate Chinese costume and long silk scarf. We suggested that the decor be simplified, but all the television people thought it was great—until they saw, or rather did not see, the dancer.

From then on we fought for simplicity in background. "Let the dancer's body create the design. Let the moving figure be visible without any conflicting lines, unless they specifically contribute," we urged. For one of our later shows, "Summertime," we pleaded with McNaughton: "Please, just give us a sky background, with maybe a few clouds. Just let us feel *space.*" After the usual hassle, he came up with one of his best designs. Lines on the floor converging to the corner, adding a sense of depth, with a log fence in the same perspective, and a sky with some clouds. It was the first time, I think, that a sky cyclorama was ever used on television.

On a small screen, dance design must be clear and very simple, and the groupings transparent. Four or six arms crossing each other in the shallow depth of a small studio can create a very confused image. We begged the cameramen not to frame the figures too tightly. They wanted to come in tight so the figures would look larger. Sometimes a foot or a hand would be chopped off. We fought this persistently. "Dance is performed in space," we said. "In order to give this sense of space, you must leave some air around the dancing; otherwise the figures look as if they are dancing in a box." They finally agreed we were right.

Each time we discovered a new element we had to argue with our director Paul Belanger. He had been a pianist, which helped for musical cueing, but he knew little about dance. Sometimes his suggestions were valid, but sometimes he refused to follow our cameragraphed script. This would cause a scene, and I would have to go to a "higher-up" for approval. It happened almost every show.

Our second program was broadcast November 2, 1945. It was called "Park Bench." Its theme was young love in London, Paris, and New York. A dancer played a London bobby, a French gendarme, and a New York policeman. The sets were charming: London Bridge, which split open to reveal the Eiffel Tower, and then New York's Central Park skyline, which slid in from two sides. The park bench was the static element that unified the sequences.

Kitty worked out the details of characterization and mime for the policemen, played by Joe Hahn. She also introduced innovative credits: they started with a closeup of a signpost to London Bridge; then the camera picked up the bobby strolling along, coming upon a fallen sign and picking it up; a closeup revealed the "Choreotones" title sign, which, turned over, read "Park Bench." The finale had all the girls on the bench. As the boys tilted the bench back, the girls' legs flew in the air, and the closing credits were revealed painted on the bottom of the bench.

CBS was thrilled. Its panel of fourteen evaluaters was enthusiastic. When our six shows were up, we were asked to do four more. Between October 1945 and May 1946 we did eight original shows, and had to repeat two. The one called "Summertime" was based on music from

Porgy and Bess. "Mississippi" was drawn from the music of Jerome Kern's *Showboat* and had a stellar cast: Bambi Linn and Robert Pagent, then dancing on Broadway in Agnes de Mille's *Carousel,* and Talley Beatty, who was in the revival of *Showboat.* I too performed, which saved on artists' fees. Even though that only amounted to $47.54 for my choreography and performing, I was getting invaluable experience in this newborn medium.

For our January 11, 1946, show, we decided to adapt some of my solos for specific camera shots. We named the show "Sketches." I chose "It Might As Well Be Spring," "Love Song," with a text from Langston Hughes, "Passing Love," and "Jitterbug Sketches," a work on contemporary youth. The show opened with an artist sketching a young girl, as a narrator explained the motif. Then the camera dissolved to the dancer. Between each dance the camera cut back to the drawing board, always dissolving to the next solo.

All these shows were live—instantaneous transmission. Rehearsals had to be most carefully prepared. Once we went on the air we were giving a vital live performance, without retakes. Any mistakes, mechanical or performing, were there. The little red light on the two cameras was our audience. At that time there were no recording devices, no kinescopes, no videotape, so we have no record of our work.

Since our premise for doing these shows was to learn about television, we had consciously formed theories about how dance and television should be approached. There were already three television magazines in circulation (even though television was not yet public): *Telescreen, Televisor,* and *Television.* We were invited to do a regular column, "Tele-Dance," for *Telescreen.* We also wrote a sort of primer for dancers on television dance, which was published in the January 1949 *Dance Observer* and reprinted in Anatole Chujoy's *Dance Encyclopedia.* One of the things we foresaw was the importance of dance for commercials, since dance is essentially a visual art, highly mobile in an imaginative way.

At the end of the season the Television Broadcasters Association gave an award to our director for one of the best series of 1945–46. Since we were credited only as choreographers and producers, nobody but those on the inside really knew what we had contributed.

By 1946 the war was over. Television sets were coming out on the market. After a year of struggling and earning nothing (Kitty still had her job) we came to the conclusion that the moment television went commercial our personal tastes would not be considered; sponsors would have the say. Up to now we had had the precious commodity of time. We could make mistakes, explore, and dream of the future. Time was going to become too expensive for the detail of artistry. Slowly our hopes for a new dance art form specifically for television were fading.

In 1947, after six years at the Roxy, Kitty decided to leave when they refused to increase her salary of $43.80 a week. Gae Foster had often staged the *Holiday on Ice* shows, and sometimes Kitty assisted her. Now Gae had retired from the ice shows, so Kitty was asked to contribute. We worked so well together that Kitty said, "Pauline, I know you can choreograph some specialty numbers." I knew nothing about ice skating, except that the movement and flow ice skaters could achieve always made dancers jealous. Still, I would try. As Kitty put it, "We're going from a hot box to an ice field."

Inside edges, outside edges, spread eagles, double axels—I had to learn an entirely new vocabulary. Ideas were created for each skater's specialty: speed, comedy, or pair dancing. We did two shows. The 1947 show was an experiment for me, and I did only a few numbers. By now I was involved with the Limón Company, but my schedule was still quite light. For the 1948 *Holiday on Ice*, Kitty and I staged all the specialty numbers. For "Ballet School," a ballet barre was brought out. The costumes were elegant pink tutus with small black ribbons worn around the throat. A ballet master gave a ballet barre to the skaters, and the gauche, impossible "enfant terrible" was the comedienne.

By now my ego had reaffirmed itself. Concert dance was again my priority. Still, strange as it may seem considering our many controversies, Paul Belanger kept coming back to me for special television events. *Through the Crystal Ball*, sponsored by Ford in 1949, was a series of ballet programs. Paul asked me to do one. I suggested "Alice in Wonderland." Kitty had already moved out of New York to a place where she could concentrate on writing her autobiography: "I know you can do it on your own," she said. I was not at all sure. I missed her advice, her critical eye, and her input, but I had learned much from her. Now I would have to face the problems myself, a step forward in my own growth.

I suggested to the set designer that he adapt the original John Tenniel drawings of *Alice*. I had the idea of using a child's slide as a chute for the White Rabbit to go underground, oversize sets to make Alice look small, and little sets when she grew tall. I had seen a film with Esther

Williams doing an underwater ballet sequence in which she appeared from various corners of the frame. "This is television," I said. "There are no side wings. You can enter from above, the corners, or beneath." It was a revelation. I put a ladder outside of the camera focus. A dancer jumped from the top and entered from the top of the screen, with a magical effect.

The music was a collage of excerpts from works like Prokofiev's Fifth Symphony and Richard Strauss's *Le Bourgeois Gentilhomme*. I also asked Irma Jurist to write a song for the Dormouse to sing and dance at the Mad Hatter's tea party. At the Queen's party, live dancers rolled as croquet balls. The cast was stellar: Bambi Linn, Herbert Ross, Duncan Noble, Stuart Hodes, J. C. McCord, Nelle Fisher, Lavina Nielson, and Arthur Treacher.

In just these three years television had made great strides. The studio this time was large enough to divide into separate areas of action, with appropriate sets. The lighting was vastly improved. Technicians, cameras, and electronics had improved enormously. I was excited about this show. A thirty-minute segment was not easy for *Alice*, but I picked key moments, and condensed the continuity. Kinescope had been introduced, but the actual show was still a live performance. Unfortunately the only kinescope, which the director had, has been lost.

In 1955, Paul Belanger, my controversial director, again called: "Pauline, I know you'll be surprised, but I want you, as a special favor, to work with me."

"Well, Paul, you know how we always end. I don't know if I can go through it."

"Don't worry," he said. "I promise this time it will be fine. Somehow whenever I work with you I have success. This is special. RCA is about to try the first televised remote show and commercial. It will be done in Florida at the Fontainebleau Hotel. I want it to be inventive and good entertainment, and you can take along the dancers. You will stage the musical number and the commercial."

I would be adequately paid and housed at the Fontainebleau for three days. Again a challenge and again an adventure I could not resist. I engaged two or three dancers, and then asked Carmen de Lavallade and Geoffrey Holder, who were dancing in the Broadway show *House of Flowers*, if they would be interested. "Perfect," they said. "We're going to be married, and the date in Miami will be a honeymoon."

I did a moment of them emerging from the ocean onto the beach.

Polly Bergen was to do a number in a living room set. I gave her movement, using the set, making the song more visual, while highlighting the song phrases. She was a joy to work with. I draped pretty models over RCA-TV receivers, arranged simple movement for the commercial —and not one unpleasant moment with Belanger. We finally made it, I thought, after ten years!

Kitty Doner's intrinsic artistry led me into a realm of theater sensitivity I had not known. Perhaps the most important thing was the friendship we had grown into. She became an artistic mentor for me, and my first outside eye. As I rehearsed she would say, "P.K., you're working too hard. Hold back a little. Too much energy negates itself. Contain the movement. This is not a theater, where everything must be larger than life. Your audience, every one of them, is sitting in a front row." Kitty's eagle eye did not let me get away with anything—not only me, but everyone. Dear Kitty, I thank you.

With Doris Humphrey

Dead end! I felt shriveled after an escape into commercial dance, a year of television, ice shows. Now the need returned to do what I really loved—serious dance, meaningful dance. I returned to solo dance, but ideas did not come. It was a time of doubting and uncertainty. I was tired of looking for answers all alone. I ached for someone to tell me what to do, but there had never been anyone in the concert field I could relate to on a personal level.

On March 18, 1945, I had participated in a concert at the 92nd Street YMHA. Doris Humphrey, who had recently become director of its Dance Education Department, was there. Afterward I received a letter from her:

> Thank you very much for the invitation to your concert. It's a pleasure to see such sure technical facility, even virtuosity. The one I like best was to the Shostakovich. Here I thought you were most eloquent and I liked the way you spoke and danced the spirituals. To venture a little criticism in the others, I thought that your versatility was sometimes your handicap . . . since you can do everything, you

do, and I would have liked a little less—more restraint. On the other hand, I have never seen faster or more cleancut pantomime and movement than in your last dance. . . .

Here was a leader in the dance world who had taken the time to write a very perceptive criticism, encouraging and, I felt, very true. My versatility *was* a drawback since it kept me from defining my personal area in dance. I called Doris to ask if she would be interested in working with me. "Anything you like," I said. "Either choreograph a dance or guide me in the choreographic process by working on a solo together." She agreed enthusiastically.

We discussed a minimal financial arrangement that I thought I could afford. In exchange, Doris would have another body with which to experiment. Now I had hope. There would be someone to tell me It's good or It's bad, someone honestly interested in the result. This is what I needed. After fifteen years of working alone and from instinct, I would have a director, a great choreographer, an outside eye.

I trembled in anticipation of our first session. We were to meet at the Dance Players' Studio in midtown. Doris had to climb a steep flight of stairs, a difficulty for her because of the developing arthritis in her hips. I had a chair ready for her when she walked in. Her glowing light auburn hair was caught in a snood hanging low over the back of her neck, the exquisite bone structure of her face, with the taut skin defining the shape, was like a piece of sculpture. She sat down, opened her purse, and produced a narrow length of cloth and a piece of music.

"This is a score for baritone and piano that Lukas Foss has sent me. It is called *Song of Anguish*. The text is from Isaiah. I thought it might make a particularly interesting solo. And I brought this piece of cloth. Try pinning it to your leotard and holding the ends in your hands." I pinned the cloth to the front neckline of my leotard and grasped it at arm's length. The rest hung loose from my hands. "Now play around with it," Doris said.

That was all I needed. My arms reached back, stretching the cloth. It framed my face. I wound my arms in it and whipped the ends. It became a lash. I let it hang loose, then lifted the ends to my eyes —tears. The tautness, the limpness, the whipping sound created a fascinating new kind of movement, new shapes, new dynamics. Although the text from the Old Testament guided us, the first thing

Doris impressed on me was, "Never be literal. Text," she said, "can be used as a point of departure or you may approach it metaphorically. If it is used literally, why bother? It speaks for itself."

I was like a sponge. All the old excitement of creating was surging back. Our work together was a continuous revelation. I responded to each of Doris's suggestions and could see that she too was excited. In our two sessions per week, we were building a dance that had three uninterrupted sections: Accusation, Lamentation, and Denunciation. The text and the music demanded different moods. The text was the voice of the prophet; I was the antagonist, the iniquitous one. Between sessions I explored new movement from her verbal images. Creating movement always came easily, and one of her first criticisms was, "Pauline, you're too prolific. You create enough movement for one idea to suffice for three dances. You must learn to develop your material. Choose the most pertinent movement, stemming from your motivation [just as with Fokine, motivation was a key word], and extend it phrase-wise, theme-wise, and put it into form." Taking a single movement, she showed me how to extend, vary, invent, forming a long sequence that came from the seminal movement.

In the "Lamentation," there was a phrase, ". . . and the earth reeled." Marvelous! Here was a chance to turn, spin, be brilliant. Then, Doris's quiet voice said, "Let's stop a moment. The earth is heavy, the earth is large, and it moves on its axis. Why don't you take a shape that makes you feel the weight, the largeness?" I raised my arms to make one simple, downward arc. She said, "Now, without moving from your spot, feel as though you are rolling on an axis." Without changing my arms, I swayed and tilted slowly. Immediately I felt a sense of tremendous weight, of boundless space. At that moment I became the earth. The quiet voice said, ". . . and the earth reeled."

This was my turning point. It burned into my consciousness. I discovered an essential truth, Doris's truth in choreography: dig for the seed of an idea and then realize it in movement honed to its essence —the difference between working from within and working from without. Simplicity and honesty made Doris Humphrey's works stand apart. That rehearsal, that moment of insight, served as a beacon for me. Now I would find myself, my own movement.

Doris did not deny technical brilliance; she demanded it when the motivation for it was valid. She had a way of challenging dancers to get the best out of them technically. "I'm not sure this is possible," she would say, "but I see something like this." The something like this could be almost devilish to achieve. I would never admit that anything was impossible. That would be saying I was an incompetent dancer.

The first time Doris challenged me this way was for a passage of the "Denunciation" section. She wanted a violent movement. "I see you starting very high and crossing the stage on a diagonal, descending gradually into a low crawl, then backing up the reverse way to the high position." I began to experiment and thought that maybe it was possible. After many hours I finally created an exciting passage. Flailing the ends of the scarf wound around my arms, I started from a *demi-pointe* on one foot, and, as I traveled forward, descended until I was traveling in a knee crawl. I finished with a lashing, beating movement against the verbal prophecy, then traveled back from the crawl to my starting position. The dance demanded that this passage be repeated twice, but during the time of discovering and technically achieving it, I had to repeat it many times. This was probably the cause of a torn Achilles' tendon sometime later, but it was not impossible!

I designed the costume, a black bodice with a skirt of terra cotta and black panels trimmed with turquoise fringe. The scarf was greenish yellow. To me, the costume felt biblical. When the work was near completion, Fritz found an excellent baritone, who sang the musical text backstage. I presented the work at the Students' Dance Recitals concert on November 30, 1946. The program credit read, "Choreographic Direction by Doris Humphrey." The piece went well, but dramatically something was missing. Since the protagonist, the baritone, was offstage, I seemed to lose the sense of true conflict.

I discussed this with Doris. "What if I were to costume the singer and give him simple dramatic movement? With him on stage my own dancing would seem more dramatically valid."

"I like that," Doris said. "Why not work on it?"

Fritz found another young baritone, Robert Walton, who was interested in the challenge of moving while singing an operatic vocal line. I restaged the work, changing the title to *Voice in the Wilderness*, retaining all my own dance material, and choreographing very simple movement for him as The Prophet. Now I had a focal point, a live dynamic relationship. This change made a tremendous difference.

The new version premiered at Jacob's Pillow on July 30 and 31, 1948. This time it had real impact. I performed it again at Connecticut

College in New London on August 18, 1948, the year the Bennington Dance Festival became the American Dance Festival. After the revision I asked Doris if she approved. She did. So did John Martin in the *New York Times* of August 20, 1948: "Miss Koner's *Voice in the Wilderness* . . . is a dramatic and beautifully made piece along unusual lines. The singer . . . actually plays the role of The Prophet to Miss Koner's dancing of the role of The Iniquitous One, and there is constant dramatic interchange between them. . . . Mr. Walton moves well, and . . . Miss Koner's performance is a marvelous one, both technically and emotionally."

In a way this was a rebirth—a conscious knowing for the first time how and what I was creating, rather than instinct or trial and error. Doris helped me discover my true identity. In the year and a half between the first and second versions of the solo, an entire new perspective in my dance awareness was molded.

Early in our association Doris had said, "Pauline, I choreographed a duet called *The Story of Mankind* for José Limón and Beatrice Seckler at the Bennington summer festival. It's a satire based on a cartoon by Carl Rose that I saw in *The New Yorker*. Bea has just left me. I have seen you do comedy and I think you would be perfect for the part. Would you like to do it with José?"

This was so unexpected that I held my breath for a moment. I had once asked José if he would work with me, but he had been committed to the Humphrey-Weidman Company. When I found my voice I said, "Yes, Doris. Oh, yes. It sounds wonderful."

True to Doris's philosophy of involvement with the human condition, *The Story of Mankind* was a funny, biting comment on the superficialities of civilization, man striving to achieve, and woman pushing him on to bigger and better things, only to end in self-destruction. Humorous works, which any repertoire needs, are the most difficult to create, and *Story* was hilarious. It was divided into episodes tracing man-and-woman's progress from primitive cave to Greek palace to medieval castle to Victorian brownstone, to modern penthouse. And back they go to the cave. It had an interesting set designed by Michael Czaja, which served as a Greek couch, a medieval dining table, a Victorian parlor, and finally, upended, a penthouse. The commissioned piano score by Lionel Nowak was charming.

Rehearsals began. First, Doris explained her idea of the characters. This gave me the point of departure on how to play the role. In each period of civilization the female character was the activist, prodding the lazy man to better conditions of living, finer manners, nicer homes, more comfort.

Now that Doris was taking a second look at the work, she decided to make some changes. She gave me images. "In the primitive," she said, "you're furious with him. He uses you as a pillow to sleep on. He sits and fiddles around with two sticks, getting nowhere. You want to wring his neck and tear his eyes out." Then she let me find movement that suited my sense of satire and timing. She was sympathetic to bits of detail I would suggest, so that I found this a creative as well as joyous experience.

Working with José was exciting. He was tireless and so was I. We found that we had exactly the same sense of breath and timing, and that physically our bodies blended perfectly. Dancing with another person after fifteen years of aloneness was exhilarating.

Actually José hated doing comedy. As Doris put it, "Comedy is something he endures. This particular piece has a bitter message, which sweetens it for him." Yet in relaxed social surroundings he could be wonderfully humorous. He did not realize how comic he was in *Story*, as, lying on his couch, he devoured clusters of grapes in the Greek scene, or gluttonously pawed his food at our medieval dining table. In the primitive scene, he carefully balanced two crossed poles on my head, placed my hands to hold them, laid a fur piece on the top, and, having created a roof for himself, sat beneath it, hugged my leg, and fell asleep. Sometimes I found it difficult not to break into laughter when I looked at him. *He* never believed he was really funny.

In the *New York Times* of Sunday, January 12, 1947, John Martin did a feature on the Limón company, "The Dance: A Major Force Enters the Field": "*The Story of Mankind* . . . is both hilarious and underlyingly serious. A . . . break with precedent is the presence of Pauline Koner as guest artist in the company. Long a solo artist of reputation, Miss Koner is the first of the independents to feel the necessity of working under a great creative director. It must have required courage to take such a step, but the result has obviously justified it; she is dancing admirably and according to her own testimony loving it."

The Story of Mankind was always a success, but even rave reviews never made José comfortable in the work. I always enjoyed performing it, finding new details to introduce at each performance. My personal success in this work was for me the final healing after years of depression.

I think that for Doris and me 1946 was a year of crucial, positive change. Doris had come alive again, functioning at top level after facing the fact that arthritis forced her to stop dancing. Now she had discovered that her own body was not essential to continue her career. We were there, bodies for her to use in ways she might never have demanded of herself. The most important change for me was psychological. One of the greatest choreographers and innovators in the dance believed in me, encouraged me. I had found a focus, a way of integrating all my dance experience into a single line of development. I no longer had to ask How or What. I had opened the door a crack when I had approached Doris. Now it swung wide open.

Although Doris's technique was based on certain key principles, it never was codified. There was a constant search for new movement, dictated by the subject matter of each work. Even a pure dance work was always filled with new, challenging ideas. Sitting on her chair facing us in the studio with a purse-sized ashtray beside her, a cigarette always between her fingers, she was able to be objective about her creations. Dancing in one's own works makes that almost impossible.

It was wonderful to watch her penetrating blue eyes sparkle with enthusiasm when she saw something she had imagined in her mind come to life. If she hit a snag, we took a break. Doris retreated into herself, able to block out her surroundings, and eventually came up with a solution. Sometimes she tried several variations of an idea until she found exactly what she wanted. This was for me a kind of choreographic schooling. Often I watched her work on dances I was not in, simply to learn. This was as fascinating as dancing in her pieces, for then I too could see with objectivity. We shared a sensitivity to rhythm, dynamics, and musical phrasing (a sensitivity that Fritz had refined for me). Often, if she felt a tempo was wrong, she would check with me because watching a movement felt different from doing it.

Not only was Doris a great choreographer, she was also a true director. The two are not necessarily synonymous. She had insight into the hidden potential of each dancer she worked with and was able to realize it. She developed polished artists from relatively raw material. Her mania for perfection of detail kept the Limón Company at peak level. Phrasing, dynamics, purity, simplicity, mannerisms—nothing escaped those ever-watchful eyes. At dress rehearsals, with everyone's nerves frazzled and bodies exhausted, with crises in technical production, Doris sat in the theater making corrections, solving problems, often staying up until 4 A.M. to achieve a lighting effect. She never complained and never lost her temper. Her face would become more drawn. The cigarette butts would pile up. She would release the dancers, but *she* remained until she had what she wanted. She was a great director, a rare director.

Doris also climbed up rickety stairs to some god-forsaken loft to see some unknown young dancer who had asked her to look at a dance. She felt it her duty to give young dancers the benefit of the doubt. She went to every performance of modern dance she was physically able to get to.

Doris Hering wrote in the October 1952 *Dance Magazine*:

> Doris Humphrey knows how to make people dance. She enables them to find the hidden spring within themselves that produces those enticing alternations of action and repose that are true dance. She involves them in chain reactions of neuro-muscular impulse that go from one body to the next, that make one body move smoothly and sedately while the next one is set afire and swirls out into a Dionysian variation, only to be reabsorbed into the moving mass until the chain reaction takes place somewhere else. As the emphasis upon style becomes more pronounced, one realizes that Doris Humphrey, Artistic Director of the José Limón Company, has always been aware of good style.

Shortly after the company's debut in 1947, I tore my Achilles' tendon. I was upset that during my recuperation Doris rarely called or showed personal warmth or concern. She was so involved in herself and her work that almost nothing else existed—especially since I was a newcomer. Still, I wanted to keep in contact. Occasionally I called, and she was politely sympathetic. I knew I wanted to continue the relationship, so I buried my hurt feelings by apologizing for her: she is too busy, she is ill, she is worried about personal problems. When I was off crutches and able to hobble along on a cane, I called Doris and asked if I could watch a rehearsal. "Of course," said Doris. "Please come."

Doris had been thinking of a new work and wanted music by an American composer. She had asked Fritz if he could suggest something, and he had proposed Aaron Copland's Piano Sonata. Doris fell in love with it, and began to set what was finally called *Day on Earth*—a work about simple people, a day, a lifetime, with Doris's inherent philosophy, There will be a new, a better time.

I sat there and watched this extraordinary woman create what is one of the masterpieces of the modern repertoire. The cast was Letitia Ide (The Mother), Miriam Pandor (A Young Love), Melisa Nicolaides (The Child), and José Limón (The Man). José was not at this rehearsal. It was enthralling to see how Doris, indicating movement ideas with a stream of verbal imagery, drew from the three dancers movement and emotional qualities that left me in tears. I was amazed at how she could make the ten-year-old Melisa, a thin, coltish child, create a sense of wonder. It was based on a free improvisational quality. Doris said, "I want you to have stars in your eyes." Letitia, one of the finest artists I have ever encountered, was superb. When the child leaves the stage—a symbol of leaving life—Letitia was that mother, all mothers, as she walked back and forth beating her arms in a helpless little gesture.

In March 1948 Doris began a work to Bartók's Sonata for Two Pianos and Percussion, a fascinating, but devilishly difficult piece of music. She titled the work *Corybantic*. It dealt with the conflict of our time, with aggression, with defense, with destruction, and with renewal. There was hope in her resolution, but it would not come without difficulty.

Our early rehearsals revealed Doris's wonderful feeling for patterns and interesting foot movements. She found novel and unusual dance effects, but working to the Bartók was wild. Doris set everything to counts, with no reference to the music; she liked it that way. I found it extremely trying and longed for some unity with the music. Totally focused on counting, we grew unaware of the music; it was just sound. That was frustrating, but a good experience. In the end, Doris was right.

This was the first time I worked with Doris from the beginning of one of her pieces. She came to the studio with very definite ideas blocked in her mind; the space design was planned before specific movement was created. Doris moved us around in this design, sometimes just asking us to walk the space. Then she began searching for the precise movement out of her motivations.

The program listed three movements: (Agon) Beyond the edge of the known lies the terror of the unknown—the enemy. In the contest with him, all reason is engulfed by passion; (Pathos) Ritual of survival and communion; (Satyric) Discovery of the unknown and celebration. Having ended the first movement in total destruction, we were all scattered on the floor on our backs. To start the second movement Doris said, "Very slowly, start to raise your right arm and think of it as if a root is growing from deep within the earth, weaving its way around obstacles until it is above earth. Then let your bodies rise slowly, constantly with the sense that you are growing high into the space."

At the premiere on August 18, 1948, midway through the first American Dance Festival, the feeling I had doing this in the greenish-blue light was an awareness of being born, of discovering life, of finding a strange peace. I was told by those who saw it that the effect was eerie, mystical, unworldly—survival! In another section she grouped three of us in a pool of light stage left, standing in a conversation of understanding and communion. Again, the timing was extempore—rising, reaching, giving, receiving, slowly, up and down in the single light.

Doris revised the last movement the following year for the second New London season. She also simplified the program notes: Maelstrom of panic, Resurrection, and Carnival of unreason. It became "a vision of our time; the dilemma of the man of good will beset by fear and panic." This was much more to the point, and even more apt in appraising how prophetic her vision was. Sadly the work did not stay long in the repertoire. Audiences found it difficult to comprehend. Although not entirely clear in its tonality, I found it one of Doris's most fascinating works, full of original movement and sections that were inspired with beauty and simplicity. It was way ahead of its time.

Even though I had never studied with Doris, I was learning by association, listening, watching, absorbing. The most important thing I learned from *Corybantic* was how she approached music. She had an unerring instinct for tempo, for the subtlest dynamics. Doris had several basic theories, foremost among them: Do not be slavish to the music, beat for beat or phrase for phrase. She consciously counterpointed slow music with fast movement and vice versa. Sometimes she paralleled a phrase or accent, sometimes deliberately delayed it. If a section was uncountable, she worked without the music and set movement on what she called "dramatic phrasing" or "breath timing." Then she would say, "Let's play the music and see what happens." Invariably the movement fitted perfectly, and we found key notes as signals to keep us together. I had allowed musical instinct to guide me; this approach was another step forward in conscious knowledge.

In fall 1948, between the two performances of *Corybantic*, I asked Doris if she would consent to be my artistic adviser for a group work. I was really afraid of choreographing for a group, but having watched

Doris, I felt I would like to try. Her gracious acceptance gave me the courage I needed. I had found a beautiful recording of Carl Philip Emmanuel Bach's Concerto in D Major in our collection at home. It had an exquisite slow movement for the solo English horn — slow movements always condition my choice of music, at least of baroque or classical. To keep the work chamber-music size, I decided to use three women and two men. Afraid to face others and be blank, I first worked alone with Doris, finding thematic material that could be developed.

She began by warning me not to let my musical knowledge control the dance phrases, if the movement demanded it to work beyond the musical phrase. I thought that the structure of baroque music especially should be respected, but I was learning. I showed Doris the material I had prepared and her only suggestion was to alter the arm pattern, which in turn gave a fresh approach to the movement. Much of the movement came from the initial motivation — a robust greeting, an invitation. We talked about transition in movement and about the pull of gravity. She said I used rebound instinctively, but should use it consciously.

As the work progressed Doris helped to clarify the manipulation of the group as a whole. The first thing was always to plan the space design in advance, and to think one pattern ahead because the present one was determined by what followed. Focus was an all-important element, a center of concentration that linked the dancers. Added to this was what she called ground base — as in music, the sustained theme underlying the changing movements. She cautioned against using too many countermovements and counterlines.

When I felt confident enough to proceed, I contacted dancers I knew and asked if they would be willing to rehearse with the idea that when the work was completed, it would be offered for performance. I was lucky to get Nelle Fisher, who had been in Martha Graham's company, Lidija Franklin, who had danced a lead in *Brigadoon*, Robert Herget, who later choreographed for Broadway, and Glen Tetley, who had studied with Hanya Holm. This was quite a cast for one's first group dance, and I was terrified when I had to face them the first day. Things seemed to go well, my material pleased the dancers, my confidence grew, and soon I was totally immersed in the excitement of seeing the dance take shape. The music was a great help; it set the style, and the tempos of its three movements gave me an architectural shape. As I finished each movement, I asked Doris to look at it. At the end of the piece, Doris said, "I think it's excellent." It pleased her! I went home from that rehearsal with my head in the clouds.

Now I was able to offer it to Theatre Dance, Inc., a series that presented new works by various choreographers at the 92nd Street YMHA. We performed *Concerto in D* in the Dance Center there on Sunday afternoon, March 27, 1949. It was a milestone for me.

With my commitment to the Limón company, working on my own could be done only when I had free time. My own works were spaced haphazardly, yet each new project gave me more insight. Knowing I could always come to Doris for advice and criticism gave me security I had never before felt. I also learned a lesson from the Bach work: if performances are few, it is impossible to retain the same cast and more time is spent rehearsing replacements than on new choreography.

During fall 1949, I wanted to try a work diametrically opposed to *Concerto in D*. I asked Doris and José if they would mind my working with company dancers, provided schedules did not conflict and the dancers were interested. That way I was sure to have dancers who had the same schedule I did. Doris and José agreed.

A theme had long been brewing in my mind: Fearing the violence of her emotions, a woman breaks with her lover. He marries her sister. A year passes and the couple arrives for the first visit. I called the work *The Visit*.

I asked Lucas Hoving and Betty Jones if they would be interested in being the lover and the sister. I took the role of the woman, and I also wanted a character depicting the inner self of the woman. Ruth Currier agreed to do the role. In the 1949–50 season our engagements were sparse, so all three agreed to work with me. I chose a piano sonata by Ernest Bloch. It was not the best possible music for my idea, but I had to get going. I asked a friend, William Cecil, to design a set that would be mobile and suggest the exterior as well as the interior of a Victorian House. I saw it as a Victorian theater piece. He devised the framework of a doorway, with the typical fan-shaped arch over it. A length of frame extended on both diagonals to downstage pillars on either side of the stage. The pillars were on rollers, and as the scenes changed the dancers moved them, changing the shape. I like sets for dance that are functional.

The work was divided into three sections: The Waiting, The Arrival; The Walk in the Garden at Night; and The Departure. The first movement was the exterior; in the second we moved the pillars to center stage. We were in two separate rooms, the man and the woman, knowing there was only a wall between us—longing to touch, with our emotions revealed. Then, both pillars were moved to one side, framing the garden at night. Finally, at the departure, we were back to the exterior of the house. In the moments when I had to be formal and restrained, Ruth, in another area of the stage, revealed my inner self, my true feelings of love, frustration, and despair.

It was hard to find movement for some of the passages, this being my first attempt at narrative subject matter. One of these moments was a sequence during the "Walk in the Garden." My idea was to depict a conversation between Lucas and me, hiding old memories by being extremely formal. How could I suggest this conversation without mimetic movement? I was stuck. I asked Doris for help. She came to the studio and watched. Then she said, "Pauline, what happens in conversation?"

"Well, one talks and the other listens," I said.

"And then what happens?" she asked.

"The listener responds and the speaker listens," I answered.

"One person is dominant," Doris said, "the speaker. The listener is the receiver. Why don't you progress on a diagonal. The speaker standing, the listener in a low crawl. In answering, the roles are reversed."

We tried several versions. Lucas took walking steps, focusing on me as he bent his upper body toward me and used an arm gesture, while I, holding his arm, did a low forward crawl, focusing on him. Then I stood up, doing Lucas's movement, as he dipped into a crawl. Yes! We definitely felt a give and take, and this made for an extremely unusual movement passage. It was the first time I understood how Doris analyzed a realistic situation, digging for the inner reactions, then stylizing these into movement. This was dance, not mime.

The Visit was first presented on a Choreographers' Workshop program at the YMHA on March 26, 1950. Its theatricality made it an audience success, but I thought that the compromise with the music weakened the development, that I had not fully realized my intentions dramatically. Still, it was a step forward for me. Moreover, Doris was pleased, and that was important.

While I was preparing *Concerto* and *The Visit*, Doris had created *Invention*, which the Limón company presented at the American Dance Festival in August 1949. A trio for José, Betty, and Ruth, with commissioned music by Norman Lloyd, it was a charming pure dance work, remarkably innovative in movement and beautifully performed. On the same program was José's greatest work, *The Moor's Pavane*, which completely overshadowed *Invention*. Doris, who did not seem to mind, started to look for a new, contrasting idea. Another humorous work would help the repertoire.

We were never quite clear what her premise was. Perhaps she had not crystallized it herself. When she started, she said this would be a backstage scene, with the light battens lowered and visible to the audience. I would be sitting at a makeup table, getting ready. She had no music yet. She also tried bits and pieces of other ideas with Lucas, Betty, and Ruth. Somehow, none of us could find humor in any of the suggestions, and no matter how hard we tried, rehearsals bogged down so that we dreaded them.

We were afraid Doris might be making a terrible mistake and wanted to spare her the embarrassment. The four of us talked it over and decided we ought to discuss this with her. Since I was the senior member, I was chosen to do the talking. I explained that we could not seem to catch the humor she was aiming at—trying to be tactful—but I could see the shock and hurt in her eyes. She was extremely quiet, puffed hard at her cigarette—a scrim dropped between us.

"If that's how you all feel, well . . ."

Though this had been a group decision, somehow Doris's hurt was directed at me. I was the one who had spoken privately to her, to save her from having to face the rest of the group. I wondered if we were right in confronting Doris at such an early stage. Perhaps we should have let her develop her idea. Perhaps we had made the mistake.

I think that Doris never forgot that incident, and I have been haunted by a sense of guilt. Although she respected me, and always helped when I asked her for advice, she never was warm or really close in the thirteen years we worked together. But then, emotionally Doris was reserved to the point of remoteness—except at rehearsals, when her involvement would break through the reserve. Emotional passages in her works were deeply touching, though contained.

Had I ruined a relationship that was essential for my own artistic growth? I tried to put it out of my mind, but when Doris announced that she was planning a new work with no part for me, I was even more apprehensive. She envisaged this work as a vehicle for José and Ruth, with Betty and Lucas in subsidiary roles; I do not think the incident had anything to do with the casting.

The new work was based on visions of a dreamer; it had a hypnotic quality. Presented as *Quartet* on August 16, 1951, at the American Dance Festival, it was enthusiastically received by the audience. In the next morning's *New York Times*, John Martin savaged it: "Miss Humphrey's . . . ambitious work, set to the highly interesting music of an English composer, Priaulx Rainier . . . had a touch of nostalgia about it, for it tended to recall the early Laban-Wigman period of modern dance which concerned itself so largely with obsessions and hallucinations. . . ."

Doris was shocked. We simply could not understand his reaction, when all the other reviews were glowing. She tried to hide how deeply she was hurt and disappointed, but determined to prove her point she kept the work in the repertoire. On tour it was retitled *Illusion*, and the next Juilliard season in December 1952, it was presented with barely any changes under its final title, *Night Spell*. John Martin had the courage to admit his mistake by giving it a rave notice.

All this time my life was hectic—commuting to Pennsylvania to be with Fritz, rehearsing on my own, working with José and with Doris, and spending summers at the American Dance Festival at Connecticut College. During the first years, I was resident there only for rehearsing and performing. In 1952 I was invited to teach two technique classes. In the heat of a New London summer the schedule ran from early morning to late at night, when the whole company was available to rehearse. One of Doris's problems was transporting her cat, Monahan, to New London. Monahan was an enormous gray animal with a very domineering personality. He was an important member of Doris's family, and often took precedence over more urgent matters. One summer I offered to drive Doris to New London. Monahan hated cars. He whined and carried on the entire trip. Doris was so uncomfortable that thereafter she hired a limousine each summer. Remote as she was with people, she was absolutely devoted to the cat.

Meanwhile, my choreographic pendulum swung me toward a light work, a humorous work if possible. "I'd like to attempt a satire," I said to Doris, "but I don't know exactly what angle to pursue." "Why don't you look at Abner Dean's drawings?" Doris answered. "If you're looking for an idea, you might find something in his book." Doris was always generous with ideas or music she found interesting.

Some months later, I came upon a book called *It's a Long Way to Heaven*, full of lost little people caught in the tragicomedy of life. The artist's stylized nude figures wondered endlessly at the insanities, the complexities, and the hilarities of living. I looked for the artist's name —Abner Dean! His figures were full of movement ideas, and his strange world haunted me. I decided to contact him. We met, and he turned out to be a charming, warm man, a dance enthusiast. I asked his permission to do a dance work based on some of his drawings. He suggested doing an original work, which he would sketch and outline, and we could combine our various ideas.

Working with Abner was a joy. We met often. He triggered my mind as I did his, and finally what evolved was a ballet, *Amorous Adventure*. In it were five characters, four men (three of them were played by the same dancer) and a woman. It took me about two years to crystallize the characters. I was obsessed by their antic behavior.

The story dealt with a husband and wife; transparent bags over their heads kept them blissfully unaware of who they really were. The set consisted of three various-sized wishbones (a Dean signature). As the Woman passed through each one, she met a man. I asked Doris if she thought Charles Weidman would be interested, and she said, "Why not?" I approached Charles with trepidation. After all, he was a senior member in the hierarchy of modern dance. Charles accepted, and I was thrilled. For the other man I invited Lucas Hoving, and Doris strongly recommended that he do it. Freda Miller was commissioned to write a piano score. The characters were A Kind of Wife (me); A Sort of Husband (Charles); A Trio of Variations from the Norm: A Man with a Predictable Future, A Man with an Inevitable Present, A Man with a Contrived Past (Lucas). Abner wrote the program note: "This is the story of a girl with amatory hiccups, an unbalanced equation and several men who have peripheral influence on her personal mathematics. The dance resolves no world problems, and its conclusion 'X' still represents the unknown."

The dance began with one of my feet neatly tied to my husband's with a blue ribbon. We were on the floor reading a book. When boredom got to be too much, we decided to remove the bags and have a better look at each other. He was enamored; I was appalled. This was not my dream man. Whereupon I untied our knot and took off on a journey to find my ideal. Passing through the first wishbone, I encountered the man in love with himself. Abner drew a marvelous cartoon of Lucas, which Remy Charlip painted on white China silk squares. These were attached to the shirt of Lucas's costume. I made no impression on this man, and he wandered off. Charles, in a similar costume with his own portraits on his shirt, tried to imitate Lucas. On to the next wishbone. There I met a man with a rope tied around his waist and extending offstage into the wings—the umbilical cord. This relationship did not work either. Charles entered, but his piece of rope dangled behind him. Finally through the third wishbone, to meet the man with many conquests—hearts and medals all over his chest. He was so aggressive that Charles had to save me. Then, tying both my legs together, he dragged me offstage, back to our original life pattern.

Doris often came to our rehearsals at the old Humphrey-Weidman Studio Theatre on West 16th Street. She offered wonderful solutions whenever we hit a snag. Often what struck us as ridiculous one day would die the next, and finally one never can tell what will be really funny until the audience response is there—or isn't.

Amorous Adventure premiered at the American Dance Festival on August 19, 1951. It went fairly well, but I was not too happy. I had been in Europe with Fritz in the early spring and we had had a falling out, which made me tense, nervous, and impatient. Most likely, I had no objective feeling about the piece. After the first performance I could feel where it needed tightening, highlighting, and cutting. It had all the right ingredients, but like all humor, it needed time and performing and, I also felt, another musical approach. After the New London performance, I soured, despite some excellent reviews, like Winthrop Palmer's in the October 1951 *Dance News*: "Pauline Koner's *Amorous Adventure* . . . was a delightful spoofing of the comic eugenics and the battle of the sexes with never a moment of social significance, for which it deserves a gold medal. . . ."

Early in spring 1952 Doris announced she would do a new, pure dance work using the company. She asked Simon Sadoff, our musical director, to find some interesting Mozart. Doris used the music's titles, Fantasy and Fugue in C Major and the Fugue in C Minor, to name her work. For decor, she used three narrow scrims. Two hung upstage right, with an opening between them, which allowed for unusual entrances; the third hung farther downstage and left, with a narrow twelve-inch platform directly behind it. These scrims broke up the stage area and became part of the dance design. For the costumes, Pauline Lawrence Limón used shades of red, from orange-red to mauve, the girls in tights and leotards, with long tulle skirts, the men in tights. The Mozart was visually as well as choreographically a beautiful work.

José opened the piece, standing in the entrance between the two scrims, one leg extended, head held high. The first movement was a quartet for José, Betty, Lucas, and Lavina Nielsen, Lucas's wife, who had joined the company. It was a bright dance full of movement—the four dancers singly, in pairs, and together entering and exiting in weaving designs—and Doris's unusual treatment of the music. The second movement was set for Ruth in mauve and me in crimson. Doris said, "Pauline, you make your entrance between the panels. Standing in that entrance, give me the sense of walking and exploring the space with your hands. Start with small movement and then increase it till you finally come forward."

I started by raising my back leg in a small, low *attitude*, alternating legs as though traveling, and used small hand gestures, touching and feeling the air in front of me. I loved this entrance. It always gave me the sense of hovering in the air. "Do one of your skimming walks around the stage," Doris said, "and then invite Ruth to join you." A light came up behind the platform scrim, revealing Ruth on the platform. She came toward me on this very narrow ledge with a dreamlike walk, stepped down, joined me in the open area. Doris gave us slow, ritual movement, sculptural, sustained, peaceful, against the multifaceted sound of the fugue.

Doris Hering, in her review, called this second movement a "rite of passage." I think this caught its quality. On opening night, August 24, 1952, at the American Dance Festival, Pauline Limón had Ruth and me wear long, open-paneled robes over our costumes, which we then removed for the last movement. The consensus was that we were too heavily costumed; we both felt hampered. For the second performance, off went the tulle skirts, and we wore the robes over our leotards and tights. It felt much better, but gave us only about fifteen counts of fast music to get out of the robes and into the skirts for the third movement.

Doris treated the third movement as a real fugue. It was an exuberant finale, with intricate patterns in space and movement for the six of us. Ruth and I were always panic-stricken that we would miss our entrances. It required an effort to pull ourselves together after the quick change of costume and of emotional pace.

Besides the Mozart premiere, Doris decided to revive "Variations and Conclusion" from *New Dance*. José was the only one who had ever performed this 1935 work. The rest of us found the movement style quite different from Doris's present approach; it was more angular, and the body coordinations seemed alien and uncomfortable. It took hard work to make the movement feel natural, and it was technically extremely demanding. Jumps and turns had unusual juxtapositions of arms. José had Charles Weidman's part; I had Doris's. José preferred his original part, which Lucas was now doing. When he heard that Doris might change the solo, he asked if he could do the original. It is easy to understand that anything created for José's body would hardly be right for Lucas, and José was more comfortable in what was his. Doris agreed. It was fortunate for me that my part kept me at floor level during the finale, so that I did not have to do Doris's famous turning, 4/4 rhythm sequence on one of the boxes that formed a pyramid.

For spring 1953 the Bethsabee de Rothschild Foundation was planning a season of American dance at the Alvin Theatre, to include performances by the leading modern dance companies and some soloists. The Foundation commissioned Doris to create a new work for the season.

"I think this will surprise you," Doris said, with a mischievous twinkle in her eye and a lift of the chin. "I'm going to do a Spanish piece." Surprise was hardly the word. We were excited. This would be a whole new Doris. She explained that she did not mean authentic Spanish, but a work that would convey its temperament and flavor, with a basic comment about men and women.

The music, specially written by Carlos Surinach, was *Rítmo Jondo* (Deep rhythm) based on Spanish gypsy songs and dances. The first section was for José and three additional men: Ray Harrison, Charles Czarny, and Crandall Diehl; the second for the company women; the third for the men and women. The set, designed by Jean Rosenthal, was made of painted mesh and gave the effect of a clump of trees, through which the men entered.

The men's dance was brilliant and technically very demanding, with stamping foot patterns, leaps, and lifts. It was like nothing she had ever done before. For the women's dance, Doris gave me four long branches and said, "You have sixteen bars of music after the entrance of the three girls. I want you to enter from the trees and come downstage left, holding the branches with the quality of ritual. Then you will give a branch to each of the girls." The mood was a spring ritual, slow, simple, the femininity a wonderful contrast to the virility of the men's dance.

At one point Betty, Ruth, Lavina, and I were in a row upstage. Doris set a slow promenade traveling downstage and added a progression of arm movements. "I want your arms to feel like branches of a tree," she said. It was an illuminating moment. Ever since, I have used the shape of tree branches to create arm design. The source has infinite variety, as opposed to the codified arm positions of ballet and other techniques.

For the third section, a dance of celebration developed, with hints of folk dance in chain design and couple dancing. The men unwound the brightly colored sashes they wore and the girls used them, swinging and twirling them in space. José and I did a short, wild, abandoned duet, where I could let loose my Spanish flair. This was my brief big moment; for the rest I considered my part a fill-in.

Doris ended the work on a very strange note. José called to the men; they bowed farewell to the women and left them suddenly, lost and alone. We followed toward their exit on our knees, supplicating. We rose—they were out of sight—we wilted to the floor, desolate. I interpreted it as a universal comment: the men went off to their work, the women waited patiently, the men returned for brief moments to enjoy, celebrate, and then went off again, always leaving the women to wait.

John Martin's review appeared in the April 16, 1953, *New York Times*:

> The amazing Miss Humphrey has given us here a piece which, except for its musical sensitiveness, its choreographic resourcefulness, and its general excellence, is utterly unlike anything she has done before. It is a suite . . . related by a substantial though nonrepresentational dramatic unity. Its actual material is not that of the Spanish dance, but its spirit is completely Spanish with an artist's perspective to give its values.
>
> Out of the music . . . she captured the underlying tensions, which make them even when they are gay, full of passion and forebodings. The [three sections] build a superbly moody and high-mettled drama in abstraction.

After the success of *Rítmo Jondo*, Doris (unwilling to rest, which she always felt was a waste of time) announced her plans for the upcoming American Dance Festival. Again a surprise was in store for us. This time she found her source in Stephen Spender's poem "The Fates," from his collection *Ruins and Visions*. Out of it Doris wove a dance drama that was different, but in a direct line of evolution from *Corybantic*, which dealt in abstract terms with a world problem, through *Day on Earth*, which depicted in a simple way real people living out universal themes, to this new work, which faced the problem of the not-so-simple life: what is reality, what illusion. Her premise was the poem:

Oh, which are the actors which the audience
Both, both, vowing the real is unreal.

She divided the work into two parts: Scenes in a garden, a theater, and a street; The storm rises, The walls fall tearing down, The fragile life of the interior. The music was an inspired choice, the first movement of Benjamin Britten's String Quartet No. 1 and his entire String Quartet No. 2. I was cast as The Mother; Lucas was The Son; Lavina, The Actress (doubling as The Bride); José, The Actor; Crandall Diehl, An Actor (doubling as A Young Man); Charles Czarny, Newsboy; and Betty and Ruth, Two Girls. Lucas and I had the opening scene, set to the eerie, high string sound of the first Quartet's first movement.

"You will start this seated in a garden swing, facing each other. It will be a real swing that will move back and forth, so remember that what you do will be in relation to the swaying. You, Pauline, are a possessive mother—probably from New England—whose aim is to shelter her son from all the anxieties and problems of life. You, Lucas, having been brought up this way, have no concept of what life is like outside this protected garden world that your mother has built. Occasionally, there is a moment of disquiet for you, but your mother is always there to still your questions and your fears."

Lucas and I placed two straight-backed chairs facing each other and sat down. "I want you to have a conversation. You both are very calm, secure. The son adores his mother. She worships him." We began tilting back and forth to simulate the swaying, and built a sequence. Lucas at one point lifted me high and seated me on the back of the chair as though on a pedestal.

"Now, Pauline, you get out of the swing, and I want you to do some movement traveling around the edges of the stage, giving the sense of, This is your world—enclosed—your garden, your life." I worked out this sequence. "Good," Doris said. "Now, Lucas, you have a solo section that has some agitation, a need to break away. Then, Pauline, calm him with a quieting gesture. Tell him there is no need to worry. You are there to protect him."

As rehearsals went on we became more and more fascinated. We had to develop dance movement from gesture and, above all, believe who we were. One day, Lucas and I were discussing this. How could I, five-foot-one, Semitic, dark-haired, dark-eyed, believe that this blond, six-foot-two Dutchman was my son? "I have it," said Lucas. "My father emigrated to the West Indies, and married there." Somehow, that seemed necessary for us. Yes, I certainly could be his mother, but to make it even more plausible, Pauline Limón said to me, "You know, I think we'll work a small strand of blond hair into your hairdo to link the two of you."

In the second scene, which took place in a theater, Lucas and I sat on the stage apron in a simulated theater box, with our backs to the audience while we watched the drama on stage. José, The Actor, finds his mistress with a lover. Furious, he knifes the man and, after a macabre duet with The Mistress, chokes her. This was performed as high melodrama, and the choking scene was handled in a most inventive way, with José lifting the front of Lavina's skirt to wrap her head, holding her around the neck and chest off the floor, revealing her spasmodic leg movements in death throes. It had a Goya-like effect. This drama never touched the two of us. We were insulated, knowing this was unreal. After politely applauding, we left the theater and slowly, calmly, promenaded home. During this promenade I held my skirts, not to be contaminated by the frenetic newsboy or the two sleazy girls cavorting in the street. We were above this gutter life. Doris's casting brought out unseen potential in Betty and Ruth. Betty played a wild, raucous gamine; Ruth, a slinky, blowsy, sexy vamp. It was hard to believe these were the lyric, exquisite dancers we normally knew. Their scene with The Newsboy was a highlight of *Ruins and Visions*.

Then José had a solo—a lament. Was it still part of the play or of his real life? At this point, José merged the two. Again the scene changed. War stepped in to snatch the son from his mother and his young bride.

"You are shattered," Doris instructed me. "You scream as you see your son taken from you. You are bereft." When The Son is returned, dead, the drama of life has become a reality for which the sheltered are unprepared. "Suddenly you realize that death in life, or death in the theater, are one." The Actor appears to comfort the two grieving women. I had a wonderful duet with José, in which he helped me to understand and accept life on its own terms. The Actor, perhaps representing all art, became the catalyst.

Doris ended the work by having all of us drop our dramatic characters, merging in a ritual procession of collective humanity. We walked very slowly downstage, our arms rising with serenity and hope as the lights faded. Who, at some moment of crisis, has not said, "This can't be happening to me. It's not real." In the drama of life, the real is the reality beyond all realities. At that moment, we do not know if we are actors in some illusory drama on stage or if we are living the moment. The dividing line disappears.

Just as in *Rítmo Jondo*, I thought my part was quite unimportant. It had almost no real dancing except for the duet with José, who had the central role. Mine was a wonderful acting part. I had to create a three-dimensional character and show how the drama of life changed her from an arrogant, withdrawn, domineering woman into a compassionate one who discovers the anguish of reality and must live with it.

The technical rehearsals on the stage of Palmer Auditorium at Connecticut College were a nightmare. The swing, suspended about ten inches above the floor, was hung from battens. It was a heavy prop made of solid wood. The battens interfered with the velour borders. When this was solved and we were able to swing, Lucas and I did so with great difficulty for, not only did it sway, but the battens swayed as well. We had to keep it moving within a minimum of space, and I was always apprehensive lest we get stuck. There was also the challenge of my stepping off and onto it again. After days of effort we finally got it to work, though we kept our fingers crossed. For this reason *Ruins and Visions* was rarely toured, and sadly was not seen enough.

I was astonished when the reviews singled out my performance. The major newspapers and periodicals gave the work rave notices. An article in *The Saturday Review* of April 16, 1955, by Norma Stahl took me completely by surprise:

An interesting, perhaps significant departure ... is seen in Miss Humphrey's recent *Ruins and Visions* [the premiere had been August 20, 1953]. For the first time ... her work is built not around Limón's talents, but rather around those of Pauline Koner, who is one of the finest female dramatic dancers on the stage, and who appears with the company as guest artist.

Miss Koner's intensity as The Mother expresses to perfection the double sense of the adjective in Spender's line, "O—mask of weeded motherhood." She is the mateless mother who has rooted everything out, save her obsession for her son.

If this was so, it was not Doris's intention. I did have the easier role because it was clear-cut. José's, with its duality of actor/person, was

Above: *In Memoriam* (1944). Photo, Gerda Peterich. Opposite, top: With Fritz Mahler, 1939. Bottom: Fritz Mahler at the piano, ca. 1955. Photo, Marvin Koner.

Opposite page: Kitty Doner at the Lido (night-club in Montreal), 1935. Left: *It Ain't Necessarily So* (1940). Photo, Gerda Peter-ich. Below: With Robert Pagent in *It's a Date*, CBS-TV, 1945.

With José Limón in Humphrey's "Caveman Era" from *The Story of Mankind* (1946).
Photo, Morris Gordon (Dance Collection, The New York Public Library).

Above: José Limón and Doris Humphrey in Humphrey's *Chorale Preludes*, J. S. Bach (1942). Photo, Marcus Blechman, courtesy of Charles Woodford. Below: With Robert Walton in *Voice in the Wilderness* (1945), Jacob's Pillow, 1948. Photo, John Lindquist.

Opposite: "Improvisation" (1955). Photo © Peter Basch. This page: *Cassandra* (1953). Photo © Peter Basch.

José Limon, Pauline Koner, Lucas Hoving : "La Malinche"

Opposite, top: Lucy Venable and Koner in *Concertino* (1955). Photo, Matthew Wysocki.
Opposite, bottom: With Lucas Hoving in Humphrey's *Ruins and Visions* (1953). Photo ©
Peter Basch. This page: José Limón, Lucas Hoving, and Koner in Limón's *La Malinche*
(1947). Photo, Serge Lido, © Irène Lidova, courtesy Irène Lidova.

Above: Lucas Hoving, Betty Jones, José Limón, and Koner in Limón's *Moor's Pavane* (1949). Photo, Serge Lido, © Irène Lidova, courtesy Irène Lidova. Opposite page, top: *The Shining Dark* (1958). Photo © Peter Basch. Below: With José Limón in rehearsal of his *Visitation* (1952). Photo, Robert Perry (Dance Collection, The New York Public Library).

Opposite: José Limón American Dance Company on their South American tour, 1960. (Front: Lenore Lattimer, Betty Jones, Pauline Koner, José Limón, Pauline Limón, Ann Vachon; behind: Chester Wolenski, Lucas Hoving, Chuck Tomlinson, Harlan McCallum, Simon Sadoff.) Above: Members of the Limón Company with President and Mrs. Lyndon B. Johnson, following a performance of *The Moor's Pavane* in the East Room of the White House, 1967. (Lucas Hoving, Lady Bird Johnson, Pauline Koner, Betty Jones, President Johnson, and José Limón.)

ambiguous. He was used as a symbol of Art more than as a true character.

Since *Ruins and Visions* did not demand too much of my time at New London, I thought this might be an opportunity to do something on my own, something I could be free to work on whenever possible. The character of Cassandra had always appealed to me. She was a symbol of people's blindness, never recognizing the truth that stares at them with diabolical eyes. What with the hysteria the House Committee on Un-American Activities and Senator Joseph McCarthy were whipping up, it seemed the right moment to make her come alive again. I chose Aaron Copland's fiendishly complex, harsh Piano Variations. It dated from 1930, when he was exploring strange sonorities and rhythms.

I set the time of the action after the fall of Troy. I read everything I could find, but Aeschylus' *Agamemnon* gave me the material I needed. The dance had four sections: brooding about the destruction she saw, dead children in the streets, rivulets of blood, the city in flames; a short moment of lamentation; then frenzy, and finally recognition of her fate. She foresaw all this, prophesied it, and no one believed her. Cassandra was never crazy; she was hysterical with the frustration of knowing.

I used as a set two small platforms, one about two-and-a-half feet square and ten inches high, and behind it and slightly to the left, a higher cube. Behind this hung a narrow length of black cloth. The piece opened with me on the cube in a striking red, black, and gold costume. The hanging cloth gave the impression of a pillar. I was standing at the entrance of the temple, a red glow like flames lighting me. Doris always said a good beginning and good end are half the success of a work. I memorized every note of each variation and worked with and against them. Since Cassandra is a character from Greek legend, the movement had to be highly stylized and the qualities larger than life.

Set for a premiere at the festival, I used every spare moment of that summer to work on this solo. Things were going well until I got to the "Frenzy" section. Showing Doris what I had done, I said, "Now what? I'm stuck."

She thought a while and then said, "You say she is frustrated, and hysterical as a result. Well, what happens to people when they are hysterical?" I had been hysterical at times in my life, but never analyzed it. "Well," she said, "you lose your sense of proportion, don't you? Coordination becomes confused. There is a lack of control, you tremble. Why don't you experiment with these ideas and see what happens?"

That week the Limón company traveled to Jacob's Pillow for a week's engagement. I took my record player and music with me, found studio space, and worked daily. Then it started coming—isolated head and arm movements flying in different directions developed from a trembling, shuddering basic movement. The trembling was transferred to foot rhythms, which then traveled in space, turns were added, until it ended—after a side-kicking, shrieking gesture—in sudden limpness. It was nerve-wracking to rehearse over and over until I set exactly what I wanted. Back at New London, I said, "Doris, please come and see." It was either very good, or very bad. I could not tell which.

When I finished there was absolute silence. Then Doris looked at me with a kind of wonder. "It's terrific. It's the best piece of choreography and dancing you've ever done. It's original, brilliant, and dramatically overwhelming." I went home and cried with relief. Doris did not praise easily.

I knew what I wanted for the end: complete destruction. The frenzy finished with a wild circling of the stage, a jump onto the platforms, a reach up for the cloth, and then I tore it down so that it enveloped me. I took its entire fifteen-yard length and, with a slow walk, fed it to the downstage diagonal, throwing an end to be caught in the wing. The other end had been anchored in the downstage right wing. Now, as two helpers stretched it taut, the cloth became an image of doom, of Fate, of tears. I worked under it, manipulating and learning to handle this tremendous length of cloth, working it into the symbolic shapes I needed. At the final chords, standing center stage, I pulled it violently over my head. As the helpers released it, the whole length of cloth flew in from the wings—a black cloud of Fate enshrouding me.

To work out the last section, I had to use the stage as often as possible, so I sacrificed my lunch hour until I made this image work. Needless to say, the cloth never fell the same way twice. Part of the training was to learn to handle it, no matter what. Thomas Skelton devised a dramatic light effect, with a diagonal shaft of light on the cyclorama.

The first performance was August 20, 1953. The program note quoted from Aeschylus—"The cup of agony / Whereof I chant, foams with a draught for me"—and described the character: Cassandra, prophetess of Troy, doomed by the gods never to be believed, stands amid the destruction she foretold, and foresees her inevitable doom.

As I sat that night in the dressing room, preparing for this violent role—my first solo in many years—nerves drawn to a fine edge, I had to block out the fact that, with only a fifteen-minute intermission, I would have to change character from the doomed Cassandra to the contained, elegant mother of *Ruins and Visions*. As luck would have it, both works had their premieres that night. It was one of the most difficult performing moments to date in my dance career. I think it took some kind of self-hypnotism, but I survived, and both works were reviewed enthusiastically. From Walter Terry in the August 22, 1953, *Herald Tribune*:

> *Cassandra* is a tremendously powerful characterization of the classical seeress. . . . In movement style it constantly recalls the movement idiom of Martha Graham [a compliment, but it was Doris's influence]. . . . Miss Koner remains a distinct personality with a distinct rhythmic attack on phrasing and with a highly individual use of gesture. *Cassandra* is an enormously stirring piece, the finest solo Miss Koner has ever created and indeed, one of the best solos in the repertory of contemporary dance. . . . Miss Koner danced it with brilliance of action and a dynamic intensity that seemed to fill the theater with an unseen urgency, with an inexorable rush of demoniac lamentation.

During this period, I could not help noticing that Doris's limp was getting much worse. Although she never complained, the pain she endured was plainly visible. Then she told us she would be away from rehearsals for a while. "I have decided to have this new hip operation," she announced. "It's the one Arthur Godfrey has had, and the doctors feel I have a good chance for recovery." As soon as she was able, she appeared on crutches for rehearsals and seemed much encouraged. When she graduated to a cane we felt that she was well on her way, but evidently there was setback. Also, she was beginning to have trouble with the other hip.

With her typical reserve, Doris did not say much about it, but it was a bitter time for her. As always, her escape was in dance, and she began to plan a new work for the American Dance Festival. She had come upon the true story of Felipe, a Spanish gypsy, who had been invited by Diaghilev to coach Léonide Massine and the Ballets Russes for *Le Tricorne*. They proved artistically incompatible, and the resulting clash seemed to unbalance his mind. He became known as "Felipe the Mad."

For the work, *Felipe el Loco*, Doris made a collage of guitar music played by Vincente Gomez, Carlos Montoya, and Andrés Segovia. By occasionally altering the playing speeds of the records she created a strange musical background. The sections were "The Arrival," "The Lesson," and "The Madness." People dressed in misty gray under cold blue light communicated the cold welcome given to a foreigner. The Spaniard, chilled and frustrated by the ballet dancers' inflexibility, goes mad, and in the last scene he sits alone, lost, dreaming of his sweetheart.

My role was the Imaginary Dancer. Doris asked me to use castanets, and I played a rhythm sequence from behind the black curtain at the back of the stage before entering from the center. She then asked me to set a dance. I used the castanets and heelwork without musical accompaniment. José joined me in a duet. Then I disappeared, leaving him to his madness. Since José had never been a Spanish dancer, Doris choreographed modern movement with a Spanish flavor. I, on the other hand, used authentic style, so there was a discrepancy. I think her idea in asking me to do the authentic was to make his dream of his native roots believable and to show the contrast. This would have worked if José's movement had been more Spanish.

On the night of the premiere, August 22, 1954, Doris sat in her usual place in the hallway backstage at Palmer Auditorium. She looked anxious. All of us felt uncertain about the work, but as always before a performance, Doris encouraged us, told us we were wonderful. We depended on her moral support at all performances. She sat there like the Oracle at Delphi. Because we were all so anxious, there seemed to be a special electricity in the theater that night. At the end of *Felipe el Loco* there was a standing ovation. Actually, the work was not very successful because of the stylistic differences, even though Doris later improved José's role, and never got that kind of audience response again. Doris was disappointed, but as she once said to me, "One must constantly choreograph, so that the percentage of success will overcome the percentage of failure. One cannot create a masterpiece every time."

Established in Hartford and with a studio available, any free time I had was spent on my own work. A virtue of solo dance is the chance to work on it wherever you are. I had been discussing another dance idea with Abner Dean, something a little zany as an antidote to the violent *Cassandra*. Abner's idea had to do with an angel who, in her life on earth, had been jilted by her lover. She now decides to return and get even. For *Interlude for Angelica* I used a six-foot ladder, the top of which was heaven. Small wings were sewn to a tiny coral-colored vest over the basic coral leotard and tights and a stylized halo decorated my head. The male antagonist was constructed, life-size, of yellow balloons—a round one for the head, a watermelon-shaped one for the body, and long narrow ones for the arms and legs. He was suspended by fishline from a batten. Since I used this image as a live character, manipulating his arms in an embrace, the dance at times felt like a duet.

To segments from Handel's suite *The Faithful Shepherd*, I started on the top of the ladder, lying on my stomach doing a flying sequence. Looking down, I saw my lover and decided to confront him. Descending the ladder steps from heaven to earth, I took off my wings and hung them on the side of the ladder, thus absolving heaven from whatever might happen. There was a tricky technical sequence on earth, very dancey, some coy moments with my balloon man. Since there was no response, I pulled a sequined hatpin from my halo and pierced his inflated ego, balloon by balloon, to a wonderful musical accompaniment. Beholding the limp nothing dangling helplessly, I blithely put on my wings, and quite happily ascended the ladder to continue my flight.

Tharon Musser was technical director for the Limón company. She helped me with the lighting and the construction of the balloon man. I bought balloons wholesale by the gross and carried a foot-pedal devise for blowing them up. Doris, as my artistic adviser, guided me from time to time. This was not a guffaw-type of humor; it was a gay, light, dancey piece. It also a made a point about male-female relations, a point that satisfied me, a gleeful vengeance of my own for some past incidents in my life. During the Limón tour in spring 1955, it was included on the program as an antidote to the repertoire of principally serious and heavy works.

About this time Doris was persuaded after much urging to move to an elevator building. As much as she hated living uptown, she moved to the Ruxton, an apartment hotel on 72nd Street and Columbus Avenue, which was closer and more convenient for her Juilliard activities. Of course, I was delighted because I lived only three blocks west. This meant I could stop by, see her, help her if needed. One day Doris called and asked me to come over. I knocked at her door and heard a muffled, "Come in, it's unlocked."

I stopped short in the doorway. There was Doris on her hands and knees on the floor, her crutches lying beside her. My first thought was that she had fallen. "Oh, no," she said. "Monahan is sick. He's hiding under the bookcase and I can't get him." I got Monahan out, helped Doris up, and said, "Doris, what if I had not come. How could you have gotten up?" She answered, "I really hadn't thought about that. You see, I just had to get him out."

Doris finally got to the reason for asking me to come over. "I have a favor to ask," she said. "I was scheduled to give a lecture on choreography for the dance section of the American Association for Health, Physical Education and Recreation. I'm simply not up to it, but I don't want to cancel. I would like you to stand in for me. I know you can do it. I've heard you speak before."

"But, Doris," I said, "I know nothing theoretical about choreography, have never studied it. What could I say? I'd love to help, but I don't feel qualified."

"Don't worry. Just come tomorrow and bring a notebook. I will brief you, and we'll work out an outline." The following day I had a complete course in choreography in a three-hour session.

This was the first time Doris told me about her four categories of gesture: social, functional, ritual, emotional. Then she explained her theory of stylization of gesture into movement, which she eventually crystallized in her book, *The Art of Making Dances*. She also talked about basic form. We chose parts of her works, my works, and José's for me to demonstrate. "There," she said, "now I know you'll be fine."

The lecture was held in a very large room at Teachers College, Columbia University. I stood surrounded by a curtain of faces attached to bodies seated in chairs. Pencils and pads were much in evidence. Either I'll bomb, or I'll be terrific, I thought. At that moment, my mouth was so parched that my lips stuck together. "You've got to be good for Doris's sake," I told myself. "She sent you as a replacement for herself. You can't let her down." Once I got going, I enjoyed it. I could see the expressions on these faces. They were agreeing, they were nodding, pencils were scribbling. Then I thought, This too is a performance. You must apply the principles you teach.

When I finished, there was resounding applause. I was surrounded by the teachers and they were excited, asking questions, congratulating me. I had lived up to Doris's expectations. The experience was also a discovery: I could lecture on dance. The words came easily once I began to talk, but the preparation—research; shaping the lecture; making numerous outlines, first fleshed out, then diminishing until all the material had been integrated until I could speak without the notes —was hard work. Lecturing was as demanding as a stage performance, perhaps more so, since the audience was not as removed. Keeping the audience involved, whether in performance or at a lecture, was the key.

Bethsabee de Rothschild sponsored another season of modern dance in spring 1955, this time at the ANTA Theatre in New York. Doris decided to revive *Lament for Ignacio Sánchez Mejías* and asked if I would like to do the role previously taken by an actress. This meant speaking the lines, with minimal movement. I loved the idea; I had always wanted a chance to do it. Doris coached me and allowed me a little more movement. The season also included the first New York performance of *Felipe el Loco*, and I performed my solos *Cassandra* and *Angelica*.

The night before the performance of *Felipe*, I heard the disturbing news that Doris was in the hospital with acute appendicitis. We were numbed—who would be out there with the moral support we needed? The operation was successful, and a few days later I visited her. Knowing she loved beautiful lingerie, I brought her an exquisite peignoir of lavender layered over pink, which made her hair glow. Doris was delighted. This frail woman, who constantly drove herself, was beset with more than her share of illness. When she recovered from the appendicitis, she had serious dental problems, and what very few people knew is that she had a hearing problem in one ear. She would say, "Sit on my good side, so I can hear you." Yet each time she had a physical setback, she seemed more than ever determined to go on with her work, pushing herself harder than ever. She was continually seeking new directions, ideas, music, sets, lighting. Everything concerned her.

One day, browsing through Fritz's record collection, I came upon a group of charming concertini by Pergolesi. The more I listened, the more enchanted I became. I knew that Doris was not planning to use me, although José was, for the 1955 summer festival, so I began to think of doing a piece of my own. I asked Lucy Venable, who was assisting me in classes at New London, and Elizabeth Harris, a student, if they would like to work with me; both of them were excited.

I named the new work *Concertino in A Major*. Set in the Renaissance, a lady and her ladies-in-waiting are first at court—elegant, formal, conversational. For the second movement, a solo, the girls slowly pulled aside the background black velvet curtains to reveal a sky-blue cyclorama, like the large window of my private bedroom. Uncoiling my hair,

I revealed the woman behind the elegant façade—fragile, feminine, dreaming, praying, reminiscing, to a haunting *andante* melody. The third movement we called, for a working name (one always has working names that are more true than the titles), "the picnic." It was a gay, bright dance in 6/8 time, bouncy, laughing. Out of doors, with our hair loose and skirts tucked up, we forgot the wear and tear of court formality.

As I finished each movement I showed it to Doris, always nervous, but she simply said, "Just keep on." When I completed it, Doris gave me her blessing. "It's absolutely lovely," she said. She herself was working on a baroque piece, *Airs and Graces*, to music by Locatelli, for Betty, Ruth, Lucas, and Lavina.

With Doris as an adviser, I had become more confident in creating small group works, assured she was there if I needed her. I was working totally on my own, as was José, and we showed her our works for criticism and advice. *Concertino* was a satisfying piece to work on; I loved the music, and the movement, and style came easily. I had no intention of creating a major work. It had a slight theme: the necessity to maintain the social façade, but the inner need to know oneself. I was doing this to satisfy *my* inner need for movement, for lyricism, and the satisfaction of moving to beautiful sound.

The premiere of *Concertino* was on a full Limón program at the American Dance Festival, August 20, 1955, and I was delighted that John Martin gave it an excellent review. What bowled me over was reading his summation of the festival the following Sunday: "In the recent series, there were four new works of major proportions. . . . The best of [them] was Pauline Koner's *Concertino in A Major* . . . a simple composition for three dancers, without program, and yet, not a mere "visualization" of the score. . . . The choreography has both the bounce and the flavor of the old court dances, without bothering with authentic forms, and its invention is charming and musical. So indeed is Miss Koner's performance."

I was torn between elation and embarrassment. José had done two works, *Scherzo* and *Symphony for Strings*, and Doris one, *Airs and Graces*. How could my work be chosen above the others? I felt a little uncomfortable on the surface, but how could I not be proud of my success? Through the years I have staged *Concertino* in Italy, in Chile, for the Dayton Ballet (the first American company other than my own to do it), the Atlanta Ballet, and in Manila. It transformed from three to five people, yet nothing but the numbers and costumes changed, and it still survives.

On a Sunday in September I was thrown back to the time after my solo debut, when Dad yelled up to me, "Pauline, read this!" The headline in the *New York Times* dance section stared up at me: "Koner: Some Grateful Thoughts on a Gifted Artist," by John Martin.

In the years since she has been appearing as guest artist with José Limón's company she has arrived at her true fulfillment; and part of that fulfillment indeed lies in the very fact of her alliance with that company. For an independent solo artist of rank voluntarily to join forces with another artist was an unheard-of proceeding when she did it. Far from being a gesture of defeat, however, it was an act of high artistic insight. . . . To work with other dancers of quality, especially under the direction of a master choreographer such as Mr. Limón's Artistic Director, Doris Humphrey, is to find widening dimensions and deepening channels for art. The proof is clearly seen in the fact that though Miss Koner in the old days on her own was recognized as an artist of talent, now she ranks easily among the most distinguished dancers in the field.

Miss Koner is that rarest of all current phenomena, a well-educated dancer. Though she is in every sense a modern dancer, she has knowledge of many other styles. . . . But she is no synthetic; she knows the values of creative movement in the modern dance and invokes them consistently, calling into use her craft skills in other media only when they are required for special purposes. . . .

She has established no "school" of her own, paid no attention to nurturing her personal idiosyncrasies of movement, attempted no synthesizing of everything she knows into one master method. Rather does she seem to have concentrated her efforts upon becoming an artist with the result that she has become a singularly broad, able, and individual one.

I think this growth and recognition would not have come about if Doris had not been so supportive, if both she and José had not allowed me the freedom of doing things my own way in my special roles. Doris demanded that all her dancers be people, not mechanical dance specimens. She stressed that we must retain our individuality, and she was able to blend that individuality into a whole. She assigned a particular part to me and said, "Why don't you go off in a corner and work on it?" She told me what she needed, gave me the music, and off I went to diddle, thinking, I'll show her this material, and then she'll make something of it. What usually happened was, "Fine, that will do perfectly."

Since I thought it could be better, I went off again to set and polish the diddling until I felt right about it before Doris integrated it into the rest of the piece. I always seemed to be waiting, hoping Doris would take the time to set something for me. The nearest I came was for her to make specific suggestions, and then while she watched I would find some movement that pleased her. This was an invaluable challenge, for I had to live up to the entire concept of her piece so that it retained the sense of the whole. I think Doris recognized that I had a specific way of phrasing, of sharpness and attack. This kind of freedom was a spark that helped me to maintain and even to develop individuality, with none of the binding strings often attached to working within a company.

Despite her physical difficulties, Doris was busier than ever. Classes at Juilliard, directing the Juilliard Dance Theatre, creating works for the Limón company was a day and night job. Preparing for the April 1956 Juilliard Festival of American Music and Dance was definitely pressured. Since the Limón company was leaving on tour in February, she had to start early in the fall with us.

She called her new work *Theatre Piece No. 2*. Subtitled "A Concerto for Light, Movement, Sound and Voices," it was a coordination of various elements of theater in juxtaposition—a harbinger of mixed-media theater. The music was a commissioned score by Otto Luening for electronic tape and orchestra and Tharon Musser did the innovative lighting.

Part I was "In the Beginning." It was performed by José, Lucas, Betty, Ruth, Lavina, and me, with Otto's wife Ethel singing the vocal line. It dealt with the discovery of light. At one point the dancers were grouped in a tight clump, center stage. A down spot slowly faded in, and Doris said, "I want you to sense the light, reach up to it, embrace it, sense it with your whole body." It felt like a discovery not only of light, but of life itself.

Part II, "Ritual," was based on primitive movement, and was performed by José and six men. Part III, "Satires from the Theatre," consisted of three sections. Lucas and I, dressed in evening clothes, sat on two chairs and had a conversation, a takeoff on a Noël Coward drawing-room comedy. We spoke lines in exaggerated voices, Doris's aim being to make us and the scene look as artificial and inane as possible. At the end, the chairs, which were attached to ropes, were visibly pulled away, and the scene totally disintegrated. We had no dance movement at all. The second section had Betty manipulate an elastic loop until she got so wound up in it she was immobilized. The third section was a takeoff on a diva singing an aria, with Lavina in a spotlight miming the exaggerated, hammy, clichéd movement that some singers affect.

Part IV, "Poem of Praise," had a soprano voice and a narrator, and consisted of a duet for José and Ruth, then a final section for the six of us who had opened the piece. I think that here Doris was true to her basic theory of hope, and an affirmation of her belief in mankind.

The piece did not have much success. Doris was tired, and some of the movement lacked the usual spontaneity. Furthermore, there was no consistency of style, and though there were brilliant moments in each section, the work as a whole lacked the continuous thread of an idea.

About this time I was approached by a member of the UNESCO staff to help organize a presentation as a finale to a month-long conference on Asian-American cultural relations. Asian cultural leaders, university professors, cabinet officers, and a member of the Cambodian Royal Council were to meet with Americans in six cities to discuss and define common cultural interests and to identify misunderstandings. The conference was to culminate in Washington, D.C., where the program, to be presented by the American Council of Learned Societies, would take place at Lisner Auditorium of George Washington University.

What was needed was some sort of concert highlighting the common cultural interests. My suggestion was to present "Drama of Dance as a Universal Language." The only requirement was that at least two Asian countries had to be represented on the program, along with the United States. I had a choice of Burma, Cambodia, Ceylon, India, Indonesia, Laos, Pakistan, the Philippines, Thailand, and Vietnam. I knew I could get East Indian dancers, but finding a second group from one of the participating nations was a saga. After running around to various embassies, I discovered that two young Javanese men, studying at Columbia University, were excellent dancers. I met them, and they showed me a "fighting" dance and a "mask of love" dance. From what they said in their broken English, I hoped that they had agreed to participate by coming to Washington. For the Indian dancers, I contacted Bhaskar, who had recently come to the United States, and he in turn suggested his friend Bhanumathi to dance with him.

Having found the cast, I now had to structure the evening. For the first half, I asked Doris if she would speak on gesture. Each nationality would then demonstrate that gesture, weeping for example, in their particular dance style, and the similarities would be recognizable no matter how different the style. Doris was excited about it. We rehearsed once in New York, and Pauline Limón outfitted her in a flattering gossamer dress and jacket. My part of the program was a performance of *Concertino*, with Lucy Venable and Elizabeth Harris, and *Cassandra*.

Pulling this event together had been more of a challenge than I had anticipated, and I was terrified. I never thought it would happen until we were all together on stage. The audience was filled with conferees and embassy dignitaries, many of whom had not seen American modern dance. In the first half Doris was seated on a chair, looking absolutely stunning. We dancers stood in three groups, and as Doris spoke we demonstrated the same gesture, one after the other, in our own styles. The second half was devoted to each unit performing two works. The audience was enthusiastic, and I was later told that at an evaluation of the conference our performance was considered the highlight.

Since Doris and José had done works for the 1956 Juilliard Dance Theatre spring season, they decided to take a breather from choreography, and Doris concentrated on her classes. This was for me an unexpected bubble of free time, a time to follow through on germinating ideas.

For a long time I had been thinking about Helen Keller, whose only medium of communication was movement—the manual alphabet. I had the cast for it and now had the time, so I dug in and learned the manual alphabet. This all happened before the Broadway production of *The Miracle Worker*. I read everything available and saw a documentary of Keller's activities. From these I chose the pertinent moments of her life as a sequence, and concentrated on the two important women who helped her to become and to be: Annie Sullivan, whom she called Teacher, and Polly Thomson, who continued when Annie became too ill. When I told Doris about my idea and the way I planned to realize it, she was encouraging. "It's a wonderful idea for a dance work," she said, "but you will have to handle it very carefully." I did not name the characters, calling them instead One in Silence and Darkness (me), One Who Comes to Teach (Lucy Venable), and One Who Comes to Help (Elizabeth Harris). I set the work, which I named *The Shining Dark*, to Leon Kirchner's Quartet No. 1.

The first section, "World of Nothingness," was a solo for me. I used a transparent length of gray gauze hung on a bar about eight feet high, center stage. The cloth, stretched on the floor downstage and upstage, created a kind of tent. I did the entire section within this tent area, which to me was a symbol of Helen's isolation from the world. I used strange isolated head rolls, body jerks, inarticulate movement for her lack of understanding and her efforts to communicate.

The second movement, "World of Awakening," dealt with her first consciousness of language, associating water with the letters of the manual alphabet spelled into her hand by Annie. We used those letters as a movement theme, and as Helen's consciousness and thought grew, the scrim was drawn up and disappeared. She was liberated from her prison of deaf-blindness.

The third movement was "Panic of Loss." When Teacher died, Helen wrote that she felt as if she were deaf and blind again, and fell into a deep depression. When I first choreographed it, it was a duet with the One Who Comes to Help. The fourth movement was "Remembered Image." Here the teacher returns as a memory, and Helen realizes she must continue her life, which is so important to the rest of the world.

As I worked, I showed the sections to Doris. She particularly liked the opening and the closing, and made suggestions for the other sections. The work had its premiere at the American Dance Festival on August 16, 1956. It went well, but I felt something was not quite right. After the performance, Doris said, "You know, Pauline, now that I have seen it from the house, I think the 'Panic of Loss' section is too sentimental. It gets bogged down. Why don't you try another approach?"

She was absolutely right: it needed an intensity and starkness that was lacking. Helen's own words about being back where she began were my clue. I devised a miniature of the opening "tent" by sewing similar fabric to a cap. This was concealed near the back curtain. I was able, in movement, to get this on my head so that my body became encased in the transparent cloth. I did a strange solo which had a sense of isolation, blindness, inarticulateness, and desperation. It is one of the most difficult things I ever attempted. When Doris saw this version, she said, "Pauline, you've done it. That solo gives the work the focus it needed, as well as the dynamic range it lacked."

I presented this version July 1 through 5, 1958, at Jacob's Pillow. This time it really jelled. I felt it the moment we finished the first performance. It was also part of that summer's season at the American Dance Festival. Later in the fall we performed it on CBS-TV's "Look Up and Live," with an accompanying narration written by Walter Sorell. The reviews were excellent.

Only when a work is performed for an audience can one really know its essence. Only from the electric current of response can one feel what is right and what is wrong. With the few opportunities to perform my own works, a good bit of time often elapsed before I could make the revisions I felt were needed. Above all, I was grateful to Doris for pointing out weaknesses. It was this kind of honest advice that gave me the courage to dare.

During the 1956 summer session at Connecticut College I had remarked to Doris that the curriculum emphasized technique, choreography, stagecraft, and music, at the expense of the art of performing. I believed there should be a course specifically aimed at the elements of performing. Doris thought that was a wonderful idea, and suggested that I work on a plan to submit at our final meeting.

At the end of each season Dr. Rosemary Park, the president of Connecticut College and a staunch supporter of the summer dance school and festival, gave a wonderful buffet dinner (she certainly knew dancers and their appetites, especially when all the dancing was behind them). An evaluation meeting followed, and I brought up the subject of a performance course to be called "Elements of Performing," to consist of two major sections: the art—motivation, emotion, focus, and dynamics; the craft—stage props, hand props, fabric, costume, lights, sound, and curtain calls.

Doris firmly supported it, and the others agreed. The course was scheduled for the following summer season. From then on it was part of the regular curriculum and in demand all over the world because it remained unique. Teaching this course became much more satisfying for me than teaching technique, and I still discover new elements. I am sometimes stopped in the street by someone who says, "You don't remember me, but I took your Elements course twenty years ago, and I have never forgotten it." This is the most fulfilling thing a teacher can hear.

In 1957, with an upcoming European tour sponsored by the President's Special International Program for Cultural Presentations, we were all excited, but first we had to get through the festival. New London summers were invariably hot and humid, and festival time always seemed a cue for the hottest days of the summer. There were classes to teach—and added to mine the start of my Elements of Performing course—and rehearsals, endless rehearsals. Doris knew we needed a bright opening work for our otherwise weighty programs. She completed *Dance Overture*, to music by Paul Creston, for an August 15 premiere. It was a sunny piece, full of interesting space design and fast movement, with individuals darting out of the group for solos and duets. I was paired with Lucas. It fulfilled its purpose and put the audience in a receptive mood. The audience cheered in sheer delight to see the company bright and gay, dancing lightly, brilliantly—even though we were dead tired. There was barely time to get home after the festival and pack before we left the following week for London.

I do not think Doris realized the problems she had set for herself on this tour. Six of her works were scheduled: *Dance Overture, Variations and Conclusion from New Dance, Rítmo Jondo, Night Spell, Day on Earth, Lament for Ignacio Sánchez Mejías,* and *Ruins and Visions.* The last three had intrinsic problems. Because of child labor laws we could not take a child on tour. This meant that in each city Doris had to audition, teach, and rehearse a child. This, plus the normal performance and rehearsal load, was nerve-wracking for both Doris and José. As for *Lament,* it was thought that the American English Letitia and I spoke would be a hindrance in London. They decided to have the text read by an English actress in the pit. Nothing could have been more artificial. Finally *Ruins and Visions* always presented the problem of hanging the swing. Doris's three major works suffered the worst performances. The press was icy. This was a terrible blow to Doris. It was decided to drop *Lament* (I was grateful for that), but José insisted that *Day on Earth* continue. It lasted through the Paris and Berlin engagements, and then it too was dropped. This at least guaranteed Doris's and José's physical survival.

Doris was terribly shocked to discover that the press preferred José's works to hers. The London press was bad, the Paris, worse. Fortunately, Doris's husband Leo had joined us the week after we left, and after our Berlin Festival performances he and Doris traveled to Paris and southern Spain, while we went off to Poland. This took her mind off the disappointment and frustration of the tour, at least for a short time. She joined us when we returned to Bonn and Leo had left for home.

The first time I saw her standing alone at the station, with her fur coat and makeup bag in one hand, cane in the other—just standing, waiting—I winced. The young members of our company were too excited about Europe to think of anyone but themselves. José and Pauline were immediately surrounded by welcoming committees and disappeared. I, the outsider, also stood there. I made up my mind that, from that moment on, I would always be with Doris on arrivals and departures. She would not ask for help unless it was unavoidable. I carried her things as well as my own, got the porters and taxis. We were invariably the last to arrive at hotels. Hotel arrangements seemed badly handled. Instead of reserved rooms waiting for us, it was always first-come, first-served, except for José. No one ever thought of reserving a special room for Doris, who ended up with the poorest accommodations. José's thoughtlessness shocked me. Doris never said a word.

No one greeted her as the very great artist that she was; no one cared to interview her—she stood there on the sidelines, isolated and unrecognized. I was embarrassed for her, felt her humiliation, and watched her slow fading as this went on. I think this experience did what no physical handicap or artistic problems had ever done before—it broke her spirit. We were not close, but the sadness that enveloped her was very hard for me to bear. The light had gone out, and there was bitterness in her words.

After the tour I dashed to Hartford to be with Fritz. I had been away too long. Weeks later, the first thing I did when I got back to New York was to visit Doris. "You know," she said, "José is working on a new piece inspired by his Polish visit, *Missa Brevis*. He rarely talks to me about it, and when I saw a rehearsal he didn't even ask my opinion. I think it's too long, but he hasn't asked and so I will not say so." When I could not hide my surprise, she said, "You know, José is a lone eagle flying in the sky. No one can touch him."

Her face was drawn, her lips pressed tight, the ever-present smoke from her cigarette clouded her eyes. I never saw Doris cry. There were tears, invisible tears. This rejection after the European experience seemed to shatter her. "I don't want to do a new work this summer," she said. "I've decided to concentrate on my book. I've chosen a title —*The Art of Making Dances*. It says exactly what the book is. How do you like it?"

I told her it was just right, and how essential it was for her to write the book. "I need it. Others need it. There is so little valid information on choreography, Doris. It is the most important thing you can do." I meant it, and I have used the book as a text for years. It is a precious legacy.

Doris used all her time outside her classes during the 1958 New London summer session to work on the book. Leo, a ship's officer whose leaves were short and sporadic, was there the latter part of

August, and I think she needed him desperately. Although she never mentioned how she felt, she did not look well. Once she said to me, "I think I must be gaining weight; all my clothes are too tight in the waistline." One of her assistants had to let out the seams for her. Otherwise, she said nothing.

She came home, and Leo had to leave. When I could not reach her by phone one day, I called José. "Doris is in the hospital," he said. "She has to be operated on. They're not sure what's wrong." When I called again, I was told she had complications. With all the medical talk I had heard from Dad's associates, I suspected that she had cancer. She was told only that she needed rest. The Limóns took an apartment in the Ruxton; with the agonizing truth facing them, they devoted themselves to caring for her. Leo came back. Doris simply took all of this as one of her transitory illnesses. I dropped in quite often, and Doris, actress that she was, seemed cheerful. We talked shop. One of her main concerns was that new trends in modern dance were destroying its humanity. It was becoming arid. She said vehemently, "Pauline, we must not let them take over. You must fight, keep the spark of the human being in everything you do. Don't give in."

One day I walked in on Leo, sitting with a tape recorder surrounded by reels of tape. "Leo, what in the world have you got there?" "Well," he said, "I taped Doris's classes this summer. It seemed important." I often wonder what happened to those tapes.

Another time Leo said to me, "You know, Doris is a great artist, and I feel it is my mission in life to care for her." When Leo had to return to work, a nurse was hired. I came as often as possible to visit, bring goodies, and talk dance. She would be propped up in bed, wearing the lavender peignoir I had given her, her hair carefully groomed, eager to talk about her activities. The book had been delivered to the publisher. She was working on a new piece for the Juilliard Company, the *Brandenburg Concerto No. 4*. "Ruth comes here. I block out the material, then she teaches it to the company. It works very well." One day she said, "I'm so delighted I have almost finished the Bach piece. I plan to see a run-through shortly, early in January."

Then there were complications. Gangrene developed in her leg, amputation was considered. When José told me this, I shuddered. Why put her through further agony? I had received a Christmas card from her, and looked forward to giving her some special gift, perhaps some new lingerie. The day before Christmas, she was taken to the hospital.

José's voice was grim. Pauline had chewed her fingernails to the quick. I waited for news. On December 29, 1958, José called. "Pauline, Doris has died."

Even though I knew it was inevitable, the reality was a shock. I broke down. I felt as though I had fallen into an abyss. The sense of emptiness frightened me. I could no longer call and say, "Doris, I need your advice." Leo could not be reached in time; he arrived the next day. I waited to hear further news. Would there be a service? Could we make our farewells? Nothing. Silence. It was as though she had evaporated. After a few days, I called Leo. He was desolate. "Leo, would you like to come over and talk, or just be quiet? Please come." He did. I gave him a large glass of scotch to dull the misery in his eyes. I took one myself. We sat together quietly and listened to the *adagio* of Bach's Toccata, Adagio, and Fugue in C Major.

With José Limón

He walked into the studio dressed in his practice clothes, this broad-shouldered, six-foot-tall man. His head was a sculptor's dream—a high forehead sloped toward receding black hair, piercing black eyes, set deep within their sockets and shielded by remoteness, olive skin drawn tight over high cheekbones, the nose with a slight Mayan curve. His handsome face had now matured. It was strikingly beautiful, revealing his Spanish-Indian heritage. The whole person exuded a vitality that filled the studio.

"Pauline, I'm delighted. It's an honor to have you working with us. I cannot tell you how happy I was when Doris told me you had accepted," he said in his staccato style of speaking.

Before that rehearsal for *The Story of Mankind*, Doris had said, "Pauline, I think I ought to warn you. Some people find José's manner a little strange, overdone. He is extremely baroque, almost overpolite, but you'll get used to it." I found it charming.

We were both tentative. This was the man I had once approached to dance with me. Then, it was impossible; now, I stood there as Doris and he showed me what to do. Would it work? Dancing with a partner demands a rapport in timing, emotional quality, and physical adaptability. I was five feet tall, small-boned; he, enormous—more so by comparison. My training was entirely different. Oh, I hoped it would work! I wanted to dance with José Limón.

By the end of that first rehearsal, there was no doubt. Doris was visibly delighted. She made changes that fit the two of us, and we both discovered that we were enjoying every moment. We capitalized on our size difference so that some of the phrases seemed funnier. My speed, sharpness, and attack highlighted his magnificent, larger, slower speed. José was so strong that I trusted him completely and participated in the lifts without hesitation—it felt as if we had worked together for years. What a wonderful newness for me to have another person to focus on, play against.

We had to stop; studio time had run out. "I'll see you tomorrow," he said. "Have a good rest." Rest! I was so excited that when I got home I must have worn Fritz out with my nonstop chatter about the rehearsal.

José's company was just getting started in fall 1946. It had grown out of the trio he had formed the year before with Beatrice Seckler and Dorothy Bird when he was released from the army. Dorothy eventually left to appear in a musical. Bea and José continued to work with Doris, who choreographed *The Story of Mankind* for them during the 1946 season at Bennington, and Bea left shortly thereafter. Doris also created *Lament for Ignacio Sánchez Mejías* for him, using the actress Ellen Love and Letitia Ide—an incomparable artist, a goddess whose movement exemplified the essence of Doris's style. With an expanded repertoire available to him, José decided to form his own company. Miriam Pandor, a student of José's, was brought in to replace Dorothy. Doris accepted the invitation to be artistic director. Planning for a New York company debut—to include *Story* and *Lament* with José's *Vivaldi Concerto* and his solo *Chaconne* to Bach—was in progress. That was when I came in; I was asked to do *Story* and the Vivaldi.

In October rehearsals were in high gear for out-of-town tryout dates on November 22, 26, and December 9. There was tension, but we were all exhilarated at the prospect of the birth of the company. As I watched rehearsals I saw that this company was akin to a sensitive chamber-music ensemble, each person an individual of top calibre. José and I would warm up together before rehearsal. He had to work hard to keep limber, not having a naturally elastic body, but once he was moving, there was a transformation: every part of him was alive. He had learned to contain his energy so that the inner force was felt rather than seen. He took over space and made it come alive as he shaped it. There seemed to be a reach beyond himself that made his body sinuous with an animal litheness. He had a quality of nobility and elegance in everything he did. His presence and intensity of movement were unmatched.

Every dancer in town was at the Belasco Theatre on January 5, 1947. At that time dance concerts were few and far between, and this was a special event. A new company with two New York premieres by Doris Humphrey was important. The audience response was stupendous, and the press followed with glowing reviews. John Martin wrote in the January 6 *New York Times*:

> If the shape of things to come in the dance world during 1947 is in any way indicated by the first event of the New Year, it should be a banner year. For José Limón brought his little company to the Belasco Theatre . . . and covered himself with glory. [*The Story of Mankind*] is marvelously danced and mugged by Mr. Limón and Pauline Koner, who has joined the company as guest artist and what an excellent dancer and comedian she is! Her technique is tremendous, but she has also a wonderful theatrical sense—timing, style, and comment.

This was the first time Martin had written about me since the 1939 debacle. He had not seen my solo concerts, which were in off-Broadway houses. Now I was surprised and thrilled. The wound began to heal. I had made the right decision; I could look forward again with hope.

I could not see José objectively in the works we danced together, but sitting in the studio or watching from the wings was a revelation. I think the role of the Bullfighter in *Lament*, with Doris's unusual movement as a metaphor for memories inspired by the Lorca poetry, revealed in some way the core of José's personality. The dedication, the danger, the fight for survival and the inevitable challenge were all there. It could only have been done by José. The nobility of his entrance—the fighting, his bare torso gleaming with sweat that highlighted every muscle—his encounter with the figure of Fate—the goring, a solo where he stood on his head, with legs waving in the air to symbolize his reeling—the passage with the constant foot beat that indicated heartbeat. At the end, standing on a small platform, he revolved slowly, while the mourning woman chanted the lines:

But I sing of you
I sing for a later time,
Of your elegance and your grace . . .
Your appetite for death and the taste of his mouth
And the sadness lying beneath your valiant joy.
I sing his elegance in words that tremble
And remember a sad wind through the olive trees.

The Bullfighter was not dead. He lived on in the memory of those who saw him, in the memory of his beloved. This was Lorca's statement about immortality.

Following our successful New York debut, we did a performance at Vassar College on February 11 and at the High School for Needle Trades on February 22. When I came home after that concert, I was extremely tired and my left foot was stiff and slightly swollen. I mentioned it to Fritz, worried because we had a matinee at the 92nd Street YMHA the next afternoon. Husbands of dancers are accustomed to complaints about aches and pains. They develop a kind of reflex response. "Don't worry," Fritz told me. "Soak the foot in hot water, rest it, and you'll be fine by tomorrow morning."

I was not fine the next morning. It still ached and responded strangely when I tried to move it. "It's just stiff from overwork," I told myself. "I'll get to the theater very early and do a slow warmup." I got to the Y about noon, put on my makeup, did my hair, had everything ready so that I could keep moving and then just slip into costume for the opening *Vivaldi Concerto*. This dance had a fast third movement in which I had some light, buoyant, airy solo moments. I was just beginning, when I heard what sounded like a loud pop as I jumped off my left foot. I landed on the right and knew something had happened. My reflex was to put the left foot down and see if I could go on. I felt no floor. I was near the downstage right wing. Taking a long step offstage on the right leg, I grabbed hold of a light stand, while José and Miriam somehow finished the third movement without me. *Lament* was performed. Then an announcement was made that, because of an injury, *The Story of Mankind* would be cancelled.

Meanwhile, a house doctor was called who knew very little about such matters; the best he could do was tape the foot. Something felt very wrong. I could not move my foot, and there was no sensation. I insisted on calling Paul Lapidus, my orthopedist and a family friend.

His answering service took a message, while I sat waiting in the dressing room, numb with fear. Finally, the phone rang. "Pauline. What's wrong?" I told him what had happened. "I was going on a picnic with my boys, but I'll be right there."

I heaved a sigh of relief. He walked in soon after, still dressed in blue jeans and a checked lumber jacket. He ripped off the tape, saying "This should never have been done." After a few minutes of testing, he said, "You've torn your Achilles' tendon. I'm calling the hospital. I'll have to operate as soon as possible." My things were packed, and I was taken to the hospital.

It took two hours to be admitted. It felt like two years. The next morning I woke up very sick, my leg suspended and in a cast. I still had my theater makeup on, lashes and all. My parents were there, very upset that they had missed that performance and were not present to help. I was in a state of semi-shock. The doctor said I was lucky he did not have to graft skin and was able to sew all the strands together. How serious way my injury? No one would say. I had not heard of such an injury before. There were not as many torn Achilles' tendons as there are now, with the advance of dance technique taking a heavy toll.

I was told the cast would have to stay on eight weeks, and then we would know more. I lay on my back creating all kinds of exercises to keep the rest of me in shape, became adept with crutches, but when the cast came off all my hopes were shattered. My foot was atrophied—a club foot. Life's seesaw had taken a macabre tilt, just when everything had looked so bright. Massage and soaking in hot water every two hours were prescribed. The first time I could even wiggle a toe was a major event. I could not let this be the end. I would make that foot work. I *would* dance again. Slowly, as the foot began to move a little more, I devised exercises that seemed to help. I was determined, and Dad was smart—he never told me that the doctor had said I had less than a fifty-fifty chance of dancing again.

It was very disturbing that after the first few telephone calls from José and Doris there was a ghastly silence. Had they written me off? José's student, Betty Jones, was replacing me in the *Vivaldi* and *Story of Mankind* was shelved. Through the years I discovered this was the pattern: the interest existed only if you could participate—if you were needed. All their involvement with humanity on a universal level did not seem to filter down to the personal level.

My friend Kitty Doner made up for the lack of moral support with her firm Christian Science philosophy. "Of course you'll dance again, even better than before. You'd better start getting into condition as soon as possible for that first performance." Dear Kitty, I believed her and never gave up hope. Although I was still using a cane, I was able to work with her on the *Holiday on Ice* specialty numbers.

Miracle of miracles, the foot was working again. The Achilles' had grown back almost twice as thick because of scar tissue and needed more warmup time, but it was strong, and slowly I was able to rehearse all my solo dances. The Limóns and Doris were surprised and delighted when I came to a rehearsal of *Story of Mankind* and whizzed through it with no problems. I trembled with the joy of it.

On December 10, 1947, I performed for the first time in the Philadelphia Art Alliance concert, and on December 21 we gave a concert at the New York City Center. Betty appeared with Miriam in *Vivaldi Concerto* and *Day on Earth* was added to the program. Walter Terry, making note of my injury, said in his review that nevertheless I had "raced with wit, vigor, and virtuosity" through *Story* and that José and I had developed our parts considerably. At the end of January 1948 I was able to give a complete solo recital at the State Teachers College in Fredonia, New York.

A sense of physical and mental renewal after having survived a trial gave me new insights. I learned that strength of movement does not grow with increase of energy. The power of a movement depends on inner intensity and containment of that energy. Control, rather than wild physical abandon, was the secret of performing with a variety of nuance. This added subtlety I had not known before.

I spent as much time as possible in New York to rehearse with Doris and José, and got used to José's habitual greeting, "Pauline, my dear, how are you? Have you slept well?" The answer did not matter; if you came back for an evening rehearsal, the greeting would be the same. His voice was always warm, gracious, sounding as if he was truly concerned. After daily hearing the same intonation, the same intensity, I realized it was a reflex manner of greeting, rather than a meaningful involvement. When one of us asked him, "How are you?" he always said, "Don't ask. I might tell you."

Since everyone had a different schedule, the usual pattern was individual rehearsals for special parts in the afternoon between his classes. The evenings were reserved for full company rehearsal, running from eight until ten or later. Between these, on off days, I squeezed in rehearsals for my personal works. There was very little time for anything else except dancing, but at that time I wanted very little else.

That first summer at Connecticut College in 1948 was a revelation. This high-powered concentration on dance was a new world. Technique classes, composition (both Louis Horst and Doris taught composition), music for dancers, and much more. Everybody ate, breathed, and almost slept dance. Wherever you went—on the green, in the corridors, in the rooms—there were bodies moving, preparing their assignments, practicing technique, stretching, or massaging aching muscles, and when not moving, they were talking dance. It was stimulating that first year. In later years, as it expanded, there were times when it became overpowering.

In the beginning, company engagements were few and far between, which made it difficult to hold on to a pianist. Genevieve Pitot was one of the leading modern dance musicians, but was not always available. By some good fortune José heard of Simon Sadoff, a concert pianist whom I had met at Jacob's Pillow. Early in spring 1948 Simon joined us and eventually became a very important member of the José Limón Company, first as pianist, then as adviser, arranger, and musical director. Simon had a talent for languages, a rich baritone singing voice, a wealth of anecdotes, and a laugh that could be heard everywhere. His laughter helped us through many trying times.

One day in 1948 José said to me, "You know, I have an idea I have wanted to use for a dance for a long time. It is a Mexican legend about a woman called La Malinche. I have a book I will give you that tells the story. You would be perfect for the part. Would you be interested in working with me?"

"José, I would love to. When would you want to start?"

"Well," he said, "there is one problem. I see this work for three characters: Malinche; the Indian, which I would do; and Cortés. I need to find another man."

Somewhere or other, I had seen Lucas Hoving. He had danced in the Jooss Ballet, and when they were stranded in South America during World War II, he decided to settle in the United States. However, he felt he had to join the Dutch army. When he was released, he returned to the United States. Kitty mentioned that he had worked at the Roxy. Lucas was very blond, six-foot-two, mostly legs, and extremely thin, the exact opposite of José.

"Do you know Lucas Hoving?" I asked José. "If he is interested, I think he would be perfect for the part." José said they had met at a ballet class they both took. "I'll speak to him. I think that's a good idea." A few days later José said he had talked to Lucas, who was very interested. José explained his plan. "I want it very simple, seen with the mind of a naïve peasant. We are strolling players, going from village to village, acting out the story."

The legend had it that when Cortés arrived in Mexico he was thought to be the Golden God who had been predicted. An Indian princess named Malantzin was given to him as a gift. She was evidently very clever and mastered enough of the Spanish language to act as interpreter. She fell in love with Cortés and was his mistress. She became a great lady, was baptized Doña Marina, and eventually married one of the Spanish courtiers. After her death, her repentant spirit lamented the betrayal of her Indian heritage. During the struggles for freedom from Spanish rule, she expiated her sin by returning as the wild Malinche to lead her people to victory.

José intended to have music written, so we started setting the piece in silence. There was a little entrance march to the village square—I between tall men. I held a rose, the symbol of Mexico. With a few short solo phrases we established our characters, and the play began. First, my duet with Lucas, who carried a wooden sword, the hilt making it symbolic of the cross. In attaching the rose to the sword, I gave him Mexico. The duet culminated in Lucas fastening around my waist a huge black felt skirt, trimmed in gold. I was a great lady. We did a short, stately sequence, which ended when he walked over me toward El Indio (José), crouching downstage right, and walked over him. The conquest was complete.

The second section was a lament. I now realized the betrayal of my people—time was telescoped. Somehow, there seemed to be an instinctive understanding among us that, as a choreographer, I could save time and know what was best for my body by working on my solos alone. I used a yellow silk kerchief attached to the skirt to symbolize my tears, and found the desired quality in pictures of the very primitive carved saint figures in Mexican churches. I decided to be utterly simple, stark. I chose a stilted walk as my ground base and relied on an occasional hand gesture, with or without the handkerchief, and added head movement to create a lament. It was a plea to El Indio. Each time he pulled away from my touch, the walk and the gestures became more intense with inner agony, until with final strength he finally pushed me away. At this point I slowly walked upstage, discarding the symbolic skirt and becoming again the Indian. José's solo built in violence to a tremendous peak—the uprising and revolt of the peons. I joined in behind him—La Malinche goading him on, leading him to victory.

That duet was completed in a burst of creativity. On a Sunday afternoon, early in March 1949, we rented a studio from 2 until 4 P.M. José sang some Mexican trumpet calls used in the revolt against Spain, which he wanted as the themes for the duet. We started with foot patterns, an antiphonal conversation. Then we both moved in space. I introduced hand-clapping rhythms; José started embellishing these into movement. We had a marvelous way of working together. His movement would trigger a reaction on my part and mine on his. We went through those two hours singing the trumpet calls at the top of our voices and by 4 P.M. we had blocked the entire duet. At the end of the piece, I reached for the rose on the sword (which Lucas held as he lay in the downstage corner), plucked it, and offered it to José, giving Mexico back to him. We finished center stage, the rose in our joined hands as we slowly pulled away, counterbalancing each other, our eyes seeing the future.

At this point the play was finished. We resumed our little entrance march, joined by Lucas, circled the stage, made our bow to the audience, and went off to the next village.

The dance was completely set. José had asked a friend to compose the music. On a Wednesday in April, exactly one week before we were to try out the work at a Boston concert, the composer admitted he could not handle it. The work had been announced, so in desperation José called Norman Lloyd, who was very fond of José and Doris. Norman described vividly what happened in an article for the Spring 1961 issue of *The Juilliard Review*:

> José Limón's *La Malinche* was written in exactly thirty-six hours. . . . I went downtown to the dance studio where José was rehearsing. I took with me a big batch of manuscript paper. The dancers . . . performed the work for me. I took in the general quality of the piece. Next we worked phrase-by-phrase. I drew bar lines on manuscript paper, notated accents, cadences and any important dance rhythms. José sang the trumpet calls. . . .
>
> To simplify matters, I decided to use a "village band" sound of trumpets, drums, and piano. From there it was easy to identify the

trumpet with the Spaniard, the drums with the Mexican, and a soprano voice with La Malinche. Contrapuntal or harmonic subtleties were out. There was no time to write much music.

A gay little Mexican folk tune served as the basis of the beginning and ending of the work. . . . I sat down and wrote for thirty-six hours, filling up the paper with the stipulated amount of music. After a short nap, I took the sketches into the rehearsal studio. We "tried on" the music. With a few minor adjustments it fit, thanks to the great musical understanding and absolute rhythmic precision of the three dancers.

We had a memorable two-hour rehearsal with the sound. After weeks of working in silence or making our own sounds, it seemed totally alien. The music was charming, but not yet in our ears. Later, for major concerts of *La Malinche*, we had the orchestration. For tours Simon made a piano arrangement. Betty, who had a lovely soprano voice, sang the solo and Simon joined her in the duet.

The premiere of *La Malinche* was at the Ziegfeld Theatre on April 1, 1949, during a three-day Limón company season in which we also performed *Corybantic* for the first time in New York. *Malinche* was heralded as an important addition to the repertoire, although it was inevitably compared to Martha Graham's *El Penitente*. Its subject matter, however, was based on sociological rather than religious history, and the choreographic material and music had a more Mexican flavor. In the October *Dance Magazine*, Doris Hering observed that this was one of my most grateful roles, that it was thrilling to see how I had grown from a technician into a dance actress. Doris Humphrey later said, "You know, Pauline, when I watch you and José in the closing duet of *Malinche* I never think of you as smaller. Somehow you give the impression by the largeness of your movement of being the same size as José." *Malinche* has always been one of my favorite Limón roles.

We had a few out-of-town dates that turned out to be pleasurable adventures. If it was an overnight trip, Pauline Limón (who stayed home) booked roomettes on the train. Letitia arrived with a hamper of goodies, from canapés to roast turkey slices, plus the requisite drink to go with the canapés. José, Simon, Letitia, and I would spend the time in her roomette, demolishing with great relish the banquet she had provided. She had that precious faculty of creating an ambience of joyous warmth wherever she was, very relaxing before the inevitable anxieties of performance. José and Letitia would tell anecdotes of early Humphrey-Weidman days. Triggered by a martini, José would revert to, as Doris put it, his "hearty, Rabelaisian humor." Simon, with his rich baritone laugh, added an obbligato. So we, the more mature members, had a great time thanks to Letitia, whom I grew to love.

The summer session at New London loomed, and the talk of a new work became dominant. José mentioned doing one based on *Othello* —not a literal piece, but using the play as a point of departure. The idea had been suggested by a friend, Betts Dooley. It would use only four characters—Othello, Desdemona, Iago, and Emilia—and be set in the period of the High Renaissance. The motivation was the theme of jealousy—how it can totally destroy rational thinking. José used only the central plot device of the handkerchief to establish Iago's malicious planning to "prove" Desdemona's infidelity. We were very excited when he said he wanted Lucas for Iago, Betty for Desdemona, and me for Emilia.

With the dance idea crystallized, José was still having trouble finding the right music. He wrote about it in a tenth-anniversary letter to the cast: "I despaired of finding the right music for it. I searched for weeks. I listened, hoping to find suitable music in Monteverdi, in Bartók, in Schoenberg, and many others. No success. Again, Doris came to the rescue. She found *The Gordian Knot Untied* and *Abdelazer Suite* by Purcell. It was relatively simple to select sections which fitted our dance." Simon Sadoff was delegated to arrange the music for piano.

I found in my library a copy of *Othello* and began to study my character. Emilia was the most elusive of all to define, and I decided to dig and create a psychological background from the few speeches she has in the play. Who? Why? How? were the questions to resolve in order to make her three-dimensional.

Usually, works for the summer dance festival were started in the spring in New York. Just as José was beginning to block his ideas and experiment with movement, it was time for me to go to Erie to be with Fritz for the conclusion of the symphony season. Ruth Currier, a lovely young student of José's, had just joined the company. I suggested that Ruth could stand in for me in the unison sections, and then later we could work on my special parts. José agreed. He planned the work in a most fascinating way: a suite of formal court dances, broken by incidents that revealed character and plot. Instead of *Othello*, he called it *The Moor's Pavane*.

When I arrived in New London he showed me what he had already blocked. What I saw did not convince me dramatically—the handkerchief motif was not clearly defined. "What do you think?" he asked. "Well, José, I'd love to talk about it, if you like, after rehearsal." That evening we sat on a large rock at the entrance driveway to the college.

"The way it is now, I don't think I could feel that Emilia is Iago's pawn. The use of the handkerchief does not visually prove it." As we sat there, we traced a series of dance moves to create a consistently dramatic sequence:

1. Betty drops the handkerchief during one of the formal dances and I find it.
2. I do a short solo, highlighting the handkerchief, bringing it into sharp focus.
3. A duet with Lucas follows; I show him the handkerchief, teasing him, flirting, until he snatches it away.
4. Now he has the proof he needs to show to José (Emilia never sees the duplicity).
5. In a duet with José, Lucas produces the handkerchief and convinces Othello of Desdemona's infidelity.
6. When Emilia accuses Othello of murder, he shows her the handkerchief.
7. Finally realizing that Iago is the source of the villainy, Emilia denounces him.

Now, even in this capsule version, *Pavane* was logical and convincing, and could motivate the dramatic climax needed to make the ballet credible. I took the handkerchief speech from the play as the key to my character and began to work on my solo.

As in other pieces, I created my own solo and duet parts, while José choreographed the remainder of the work, but his was the only credit that ever appeared on a program. There were experiments, discussions among us about our characters, and always changes. Finally, we were near the end of the piece. José was suffering from the usual summer-session fatigue, the studio was stifling, perspiration ran in buckets, inspiration had run dry, and time was running out. At this point, Doris to the rescue. We needed an ending that would be unusual. Doris came up with a brilliant solution.

The murder would not be visible. Othello pushes Desdemona to the ground, while Iago and Emilia travel toward each other facing the audience center stage. Iago spreads Emilia's skirt as a screen to hide the act. Wheeling about, Emilia discovers Desdemona dead.

I always got gooseflesh performing these final moments: José showing me the handkerchief—my taking it and burying my face in it—the realization—the accusation of Iago—a final moment of lament over the body of Desdemona—then the sudden whirling away of Lucas and me to opposite downstage corners (another suggestion by Doris)—to be drawn back with a gesture faintly reminiscent of prayer to the prostrate figures of José and Betty—the quick drop of head and hand to chest—a sob, the inner anguish—then the slow reaching forward of the arm with open palm to the audience.

While we were rehearsing, Pauline was designing the costumes. They were to be Renaissance: José in burgundy, Betty in white, Lucas in greenish-yellow-gold, I in tangerine orange. All were in fine velvet except for Betty's, which was chiffon. Pauline never drew designs. She had a mental image of what she was after, then captured us and created the costumes on our body, trying different lines and ideas. It was tiring, but worth it.

My costume was the last she got to, barely one week before the premiere. The bare-shouldered, fitted bodice of orange velvet had reddish-orange net pleated across the bosom. This was outlined by gold braid, which then hooked halter-fashion behind my neck. The whale-boned bodice suspended on half-inch gold braid was all that held the costume on my body. Long, tight sleeves with a high puff were pulled on separately. Over a very full orange organdy petticoat she placed an enormous orange circular velvet skirt, cartridge-pleated in front at my waist, which hung to my insteps and tapered to a ten-inch length on the floor beyond my heels. As the velvet overskirt was being pinned on, I assumed she meant to cut the back even with the front. A day before dress rehearsal she gave me the dress.

"Here, Pauline, why don't you work in it a while?" she said. I put it on and was appalled. "But Pauline, you forgot to trim the skirt." "I know," came the answer, "but it looks so terrific, I couldn't bear to cut it. Anyway, you can handle anything, so why don't you and Lucas work with it tonight?"

That was a nightmare night. We worked in the old gym until 4 A.M. Lucas learned how to avoid stepping on the train, and I devised a whole set of movements specifically designed for clearing my legs. I was panic-stricken. What if I got caught in the yards of organdy and velvet, unable to move?

We stood there on the darkened Palmer Auditorium stage, nervous, intense, in a tight cluster—a breathless moment—the center spot coming up on our joined hands, slowly reaching upward. *The Moor's Pavane* had begun.

There was electricity in the air—on stage—in the audience. The final chord, two arms reaching forward, palms open, the quivering silence crying, This is the tragedy of the Moor. Fadeout. A dead hush, then thunderous applause. Bravos. *The Moor's Pavane* was born. Until that moment, we had no idea if the piece was good or bad; we had worked feverishly until the last moment. We stood there, slightly stunned, dripping wet. It was a hot night on August 17, 1949. As we stood there taking bow after bow, my one thought was, Thank God, no costume disaster.

The Moor's Pavane is very dear to me. Each successive performance from 1949 to 1967 was an artistic challenge. What nuance could I add, how further enrich the character?

With the creation of *Pavane*, José was recognized as a choreographer of the first rank, for which he received the 1950 *Dance Magazine* Award. Watching the strides he had made in three years under the direction of Doris Humphrey was to see the transition from potential to full maturity. The Limón company now became, along with Martha Graham's company, one of the leading modern dance groups. Added to an occasional New York performance and the American Dance Festival, short fall and spring tours became the usual pattern.

Though we were a young, small company, we played major cities and campuses—Chicago, Detroit, Washington, D.C., Louisville, Miami, University of Wisconsin, University of Indiana. For many in our audiences, dance was a new experience. Mostly they were sympathetic and the critics tried to understand. In cities like Chicago, critics such as Ann Barzel and Claudia Cassidy really gave us welcome.

In early spring 1950 José sprang a surprise. "Guess what? Ruth Page called and asked if I would be interested in cooperating on her project to take a company to Paris for a month. I said I'd let her know. I had to discuss it with you first. Her idea is to take a company she is now assembling with Bentley Stone, and she would like to add *The Moor's Pavane* and *La Malinche* with the original cast to the repertoire. She'll pay transportation and a small salary. There is, however, a condition —each one of us must participate in one of her works. Well, what?"

Paris in May, to dance at the Théâtre des Champs-Elysées—who would say no? I had not been in Paris since the early 1930s, and I had never danced there.

Page's company was called Les Ballets Américains. I was in *Billy Sunday*, José and Lucas in *The Bells*, and Betty was a Salvation Army girl in *Frankie and Johnny*. Pauline Limón was billed as assistant to José and Simon as our music director. By the last week in April the excitement was high.

Springtime Paris—the delicate scent of tiny lilies of the valley sold in small bunches in the streets was already in my nostrils. Ruth Page and her husband, Tom Fisher, had chartered a plane. I was delighted when they said there was some extra space and invited Fritz, who had a concert date in Europe, to come along. The flight took twelve hours, incredible compared to six-day steamer trips.

The Théâtre des Champs-Elysées was lovely, with a good-sized stage. Rehearsals went well. I was having knee trouble, José back trouble, but the theater had a resident masseur, available at all times. Things like this were taken for granted in Europe.

Opening night. Everyone on edge, which was good. The house was sold out, but the audience seemed unresponsive. We thought it must be because the sound was dampened backstage. However, after *Frankie and Johnny*, we could not be mistaken. It was loud and clear, shouts of "Boo! Boo!"—plenty of response. Had something happened?

The next day the reviews were devastating. No one understood Ruth's *Frankie and Johnny* as a kind of American folklore piece. They took it straight. As for the Limón company, the best the French critics could come up with, never having seen modern dance before, was to compare us to Kabuki and mime. The incident was called "La Scandale." Ruth Page stuck to her guns. We stayed and completed the entire engagement. Privately, many actors, painters, and sculptors came to talk. The actors from the Comédie Française said we did more for *Othello* in twenty minutes than they did in an entire evening. Ruth had the last laugh: when she returned to Paris with her ballet *Revenge*, which she staged for Les Ballets des Champs-Elysées, she became the rage of Paris.

On our return we immediately plunged into preparations for the American Dance Festival. José had two works in mind. One was to be pure dance to Bach's Preludes and Fugues for the standard company of five (Bach was one of the great musical loves of Doris and José). The other was to be a dramatic duet for José and Letitia, dealing with Adam and Eve's expulsion from Eden, set to Arnold Schoenberg's Second Chamber Symphony.

For the modern dance of those years the Bach seemed revolutionary. Simon was seated at the piano in a spotlight (a novelty); José, Lucas, Betty, Ruth, and I were grouped around the piano, listening as he played. We exited and the piece, which was a suite of dances, proceeded. There were trios, duets, solos, and a final quartet. José and I opened with a duet. José also assigned the D-major Prelude as a solo for me, and as usual asked if I could work on it alone. He always seemed very happy when I agreed to this; he knew my personal style would offer variety.

Pauline dressed the work in formal black and white, with everyone wearing ballet slippers. Because of the costume and the shoes it had a semi-balletic quality. Some of the reviews were critical of this. In fact, I had started to rehearse in ballet shoes because my feet (all bones and no flesh) were battered from years of working barefoot. José soon followed suit. Always, if a piece demanded shoes for stylistic reasons, we had two pairs: one with regular leather soles for sticky floors and one with a thin layer of rubber for slippery floors. Sometimes even the rubber did not help, and the stage was washed with Coca-Cola, sticky enough to give traction.

The Bach piece was called *Concert*, and it certainly surprised the New London audience as well as the critics. I was embarrassed, knowing the solo was totally mine, to read the reviews. From Nik Krevitsky in the August–September 1950 *Dance Observer*: "Mr. Limón has provided his company with charming and sometimes uninteresting balletic movement. The most beautiful section is the solo Pauline Koner performs in a style befitting Markova . . . ," and Doris Hering in the October *Dance Magazine*: "He has been so entranced with the nobility of Bach's music that he has ignored the fact that it is also fleet, detailed, and exceedingly lively. All of the dances, with the exception of Pauline Koner's ballet-flavored solo, were Wagnerian rather than Bachian." José simply glossed over the tributes.

José's real success that season was *The Exiles*, a truly inventive and poetic duet based on a diagonal progression from upstage left to downstage right. As performed by the fabulous Letitia and José, it was a monumental yet simple work, heroic, with a sense of biblical truth and intensity. Letitia had a warmth and weight to her movement that made the space come alive, vibrate. Costumed in a long, narrow beige gown, her Eve was a mature earthwoman. José, in earth-toned trousers, his chest bare, complemented this mature concept of Adam and Eve. The first section had a rich, flowing movement. The second was more dynamic, as the music demanded. When Letitia retired from the company, José rechoreographed the role for Ruth. It took on a completely new dimension, younger, more sensuous, and Pauline costumed Ruth in a flesh-colored leotard that accented the physical rather than the emotional qualities of the Letitia version.

A young dance student on scholarship in New London was assigned to the stage crew. While I rehearsed on stage, I noticed that he seemed very adept at lighting. I thought, The boy shows talent, and pigeonholed it for some future emergency. Toward the end of the festival season, I heard Pauline murmuring to herself. She often did this when there was a problem. "I don't know what we're going to do about a lighting person for our tour. Tharon Musser can't go. I can't find anyone.

Although I rarely gave advice in this department, I said, "Have you noticed Tom Skelton? He's on the tech crew. Why don't you talk to him?"

"Well, I'll see," she said. And that was that. The next thing I heard was, "We're taking Tom Skelton on tour with us." That was the beginning of his outstanding career.

Pauline had the reputation of being difficult. I was not too aware of it, but perhaps by the time I entered the scene she had mellowed. Although she acted as all-round company manager, our bookings were handled by Musical Artists, run by Susan Pimsleur. However, without Pauline's contribution to the company, I doubt if it could have achieved what it did. Foremost, her costumes were superb, sometimes quite daring. She did all the designs for the company, as she had done for Humphrey-Weidman. I learned a great deal from her. Furthermore, she had an instinct for what was good, passable, or bad. Although she was evidently afraid to voice her opinions to Doris or José, I could see her chewing her fingernails or shaking her head, and could not help overhearing some of her muttered criticisms.

She also had a definite idiom of her own. If something was going on that was not to her liking, she would say, "Well, I'll tell you, it's a *thing*." Her opinion of those around her was that they were either "People Persons" or "Not a People Person." She had a biting sarcasm and was a fantastic mimic. Sometimes at parties she told, with demonstration, stories about the Denishawn trip to the Orient that were so hilarious she had us all shrieking with laughter. Even Doris, who knew those stories, could not help breaking up.

I got along quite well with Pauline. We had differences about the line or style of a costume—short as I was, certain lines were taboo for my body—but such differences were rare and always resolved. I respected and became fond of her. I knew she did not have an easy job worrying about José, the company, Doris, and most of all money for studio rental, pianist, costumes, tours. In these early company days, she and José lived very frugally in one room at the Wellington Hotel and on weekends in an old barn they had bought in Stockton, New Jersey. All their income went to the dance. There was never much left for them or the company members. With a minimal wardrobe, José could still look elegant; Pauline's clothes were threadbare. José never complained, but only when the Juilliard Dance Department began in 1951 could he rely on a steady income. Government grants were unheard of, and commissioned work from Juilliard or the American Dance Festival was rare.

It was difficult for me, too. As the years went on, hotels, food, and commuting fares increased, but whenever I hinted that I would like a small increase in my performing fee of fifty dollars, I was told it was impossible. Performing became an expensive luxury for me. Throughout my marriage I paid for all my dance expenses and my own clothing; it was the least I could contribute. Still, I kept on. What else could I do? I could not live without dance. Guest teaching helped, and I knew we were all facing the same financial problems. It was not easy, yet the company held together because of its quality and growing reputation.

Fall 1950 brought an unexpected invitation to perform at the Palacio de Bellas Artes in Mexico City from September 19 to October 1. The invitation had come from Miguel Covarrubias, the director of the dance department. We arrived a full week in advance to rehearse and adjust to the altitude. We were installed in a charming hotel right in the middle of the city. It was a former convent, two tiers of rooms built around an open courtyard that served as the hotel restaurant, with colored umbrellas shielding the tables from the sun. It was called the Hotel des Cortes.

Mexico City was very exotic—the wonderful Indian people, with sparkling, luminous dark eyes, shiny jet-black hair, vibrant personalities—for us quite a different world. Among the many things I found exciting, the color struck me the most. The intense blue of the sky, that special pink we call Mexican pink, the blue of the turquoise stone used in their jewelry, the multistriped serapes, the reds and greens, all startlingly juxtaposed. I became drunk with color.

Miguel's wife Rosa, an artist in her own right, immediately offered her services and advice. The first thing she said when she saw my Malinche costume in the two tones of blue was, "That's all wrong. It's not Mexican. We have to make a new costume in Mexican pink. The bodice fitted, slightly lighter in color, with short puffed sleeves; the skirt, in darker pink, must have a ruffle. Without the ruffle at the bottom, it won't be Mexican." Presto! In two days I was in a pink costume, and with my long black braids entwined with gold ribbons I looked more Mexican than the Mexicans. After what I had seen in the little back streets of the city, I knew Rosa was right. The critic Salvador Novo compared *La Malinche* to an Orozco painting.

Our reception both professionally and socially was tremendous. José had come home. He was theirs, and they were proud of him, as well they should have been. José and Betty gave classes at the National School of Dance. We made friends with many dancers who had their own companies. We were wined and dined by the composer Carlos Chavez, director general of the National Institute of Fine Arts, by the architect Luis Barragán, by Miguel and Rosa. The newspapers carried full-page stories and pictures. What a difference from Paris!

Mexico was a wonderful experience for us all, but I think for José it must have been a rebirth, a finding of his roots. He had left Mexico as a child; he returned as a prince. He was now the peer of Chavez and Covarrubias. There was a new dignity and a pride in his heritage, which led him to seek new sources for dance from the history of Mexico. *Tonantzintla*, to music by Antonio Soler, was a charming dance based on a legend about the birthday celebration of Santa Maria Tonantzintla, done in the style of Mexican baroque art. Another was *Dialogues*, with music by Norman Lloyd. José and Lucas danced two parallel sections, one concerning Cortés and Montezuma, the other Maximilian and Juárez. Neither work remained in the repertoire.

José was invited by the Mexican government to remain and rehabilitate the dance in Mexico along modern lines. Working there, with all the artistic resources he needed—sets, costumes, orchestra—was surely exciting and satisfying for him, but how could he continue to grow without replenishment? For this he needed Doris, the New York dance scene, the company, which for him was always a stimulant. He refused the offer, but did return the following year to teach and choreograph.

One of my most exciting artistic experiences with José was working on *The Visitation*. It told the story of the Annunciation, in which, as José described it, the lives of two lowly human beings are transfigured utterly after a visit by a celestial messenger. It tells of omnipotence and the great mystery of faith. "He hath put down the mighty from their seat and hath exalted the humble and the meek." He saw it as a simple tale, without affectation or pompous religious overtones. The cast was a man (José), his wife (me), and The Stranger (Lucas). We three always worked well together.

In early spring, before we began to work, I had the opportunity to go to Florence with Fritz. I spent all my time haunting the Uffizi Gallery, absorbing the religious paintings, many of the Annunciation. I was searching for the quality of this young girl, and for a specific style. I returned saturated with the mysticism and glow of the paintings. When we started to work on the piece in New London, I felt ready. I had become that young Mary. The only props we used were a small bench and a plank. The plank became a symbol of the man's work as a carpenter, then a bed, and finally I stretched along it as José held it horizontally. Holding me against the plank, he lifted it to a vertical position, which seemed to predict the Crucifixion. This ending was an inspired image. I trembled, transfigured, as I hung there in the air, braced by José's strong arms.

The choreographic material was fresh and inventive. It opened with me sitting on the bench, quietly weaving, as José did a work solo. There was a duet in which we lived our humble life. Then the plank, resting on the diagonal from the edge of the bench to the floor, became our bed. I was awakened by the entrance of The Stranger, the angel of the Annunciation. We did a duet. When he left, I was aware of an uncanny change. This was a solo. Since the music, Schoenberg's Three Pieces for piano, was somewhat short, I decided I would create the solo in silence. This somehow lent it an added strength and mystery, and left me free to create what I really felt. Following was the man's realization of the woman's condition. Not understanding, there was anger, condemnation, but when The Stranger returned, realization and a final duet of acceptance.

Pauline costumed us in El Greco blues and greens. I was in a high-waisted gown, and Lucas wore a tunic with wide, bell-shaped sleeves that faintly suggested angel wings. José wore trousers and a loose-sleeved shirt. Pauline wanted the waistline of my gown to start just under the bosom. "But, Pauline," I said, "it will hide all the movement every time I bend forward. There will just be a blob of fabric rather than the shape I intended." "But that's the style," she said. After several rather tense fittings she agreed to add some rows of stitching that would hold the width of the dress to the line of my body until slightly above the normal waistline, and we were both satisfied.

The Visitation, at its premiere at the American Dance Festival on August 23, 1952, was an instant success. It was the kind of piece that left a deep impression on the audience. To this day, those who saw it say they cannot forget it. How sad that, aside from a few photographs, there is no record of this work, one of José's finest and most touching from what I call his chamber-dance period.

Not all of José's works reached such nobility. For the 1953 festival he prepared a group piece about which he himself later commented that he had fallen flat on his face with *Don Juan Fantasia*. It was built on Franz Liszt's prankish paraphrase of motifs from Mozart's *Don Giovanni*. José felt he had committed a still more tasteless prank.

No such trouble occurred the following summer, when he did *The Traitor*, a Connecticut College commission. This was the first time the college had commissioned a work from José. Aside from the tribute, it meant less worry about the expenses of production. Since I was not involved in it, I know little of the inner problems of its creation, but found the finished work an overwhelming experience.

For *The Traitor* José used an unprecedented six male dancers. The opportunity to work with men created a new dimension in his choreography. He now had the chance to expand his movement, which was so distinctly masculine, heroic in line and concept. With the assurance that years had brought to his choreographic imagination, this work triggered a desire to enlarge the company. It stimulated a new direction—in some ways to advantage; in others perhaps a loss.

Fall 1954 was a season of honor for José and his company. Congress, under President Eisenhower, had just passed a law allowing the State Department in collaboration with ANTA to send American artists abroad. Eager to implement the program, the State Department consulted José, and without advance preparation it was announced that the Limón company was being sent to South America.

Excitement! Repertoire had to be chosen, costumes repaired. It was impossible to drag the unwieldly *Story of Mankind* prop, so a lightweight collapsible one had to be created and built. (When it was finished, they discovered it would not fit through the plane cargo doors and again it had to be adjusted.) *Variations and Conclusion from New Dance* had a series of boxes on which the dancers performed. After much discussion, it was decided to construct a new set there. We were to leave by mid-November, so out came the summer clothes since it would be warm in most places. In addition to *Story* and *Variations* we took almost all our major works. Besides the extended company, the group included a child for *Day on Earth* (and her mother for chaperone), Tharon Musser for lighting and stage management, and Simon Sadoff.

Having loved the color and exoticism of Mexico, I looked forward to South America, but was disappointed as it was not nearly so colorful. We arrived in Rio de Janeiro, settled at the Ambassador Hotel, and most of what I saw of the city was on my walks to and from the Teatro Municipal. The city's architecture ranged from baroque to ultramodern. I particularly liked some façades done in mosaic with brightly colored tiles, which seemed truly Brazilian. In the distance I could catch a glimpse of the famous Christ figure standing high up on a mountaintop against the sky. We discovered that it was not wise for women to walk alone in the street after dark, so Letitia and I always arranged to be together.

There was much to tie up in a week's time. We knew we had a tremendous responsibility as the first cultural representatives officially sent by the United States. Here we were, a modern dance group, appearing where modern American dance had almost never been seen. The Jooss Ballet had traveled through South America, but our style was quite different, so we were apprehensive. We opened on November 23, and to our amazement it was an absolutely smashing success. José wrote to Doris:

> . . . there was a brilliant sophisticated audience and a magnificent stage, good lights, good orchestra. The boxes for the Variations made here looked stunning against the most beautiful blue cyclorama I ever saw, at great depth, lit like a dream. . . . The dancers were at high pitch. The response was enthusiastic and long.

Backstage came the most impressive collection of flowers and people from the American Embassy (who were very pleased and relieved . . .) and Brazilians, Argentinians and other elegant and distinguished foreigners. Much photographing of me with bigwigs from the embassy and the arts. . . . I think we can chalk up a considerable triumph for the American Dance.

The first night was Doris's evening, except for *The Moor's Pavane*. The Latins were much more responsive to the quality of Doris's work than the Europeans were on our later tour. I think they were less jaded, more honest in their emotional responses, and respected the content of a work, not just the trimmings. The day after, we did a lecture-demonstration at the Museum of Modern Art, and the following night again a performance, with a program that had three of my major roles: *Ruins and Visions*, *Malinche*, and *Story of Mankind*. During the final movement of *Mankind* José and I were on the tiny six-foot-high platform, when he jerked his head unexpectedly as I leaned over him. I never knew a head could be that hard. His cranium smashed against my left eye and I was stunned for a moment. When I reached the dressing room my left eyelid was swelling and I had a lump the size of an almond. For the remainder of our engagement, I needed all my makeup skills to cover a black, blue, purple, and green bruise.

Our next stop was São Paulo, an industrial city. As José said in another letter to Doris, "Dull, stuffy, a bad copy of Detroit, with all of its vices and none of its virtues." With poor publicity and in the wrong season, the audience was small, but enthusiastic. However, we had a little more time to shop for gifts and to gorge on the famous Brazilian beef done on charcoal and brought sizzling on enormous skewers.

At last we arrived in Montevideo, where an international conference of UNESCO was in full swing. We were to be part of the cultural presentation sponsored by the American delegation. We stayed at a beautiful old hotel, the Victoria Plaza. The Teatro Solis, where we performed December 7–10, was a lovely old-world theater. Again there was constant rehearsal for three different programs. The weather was warm and sunny, but I had little chance to appreciate it. Except for a short ride along the seashore one afternoon, all I remember is dashing through the handsome lobby of the hotel to and from rehearsal. Since the performances started at 10 P.M., our entire schedule was askew. The hotel dining room did not open until 8 P.M., so special arrangements were made to serve our dinner earlier. Trying to whip up performance pitch so late was a trial, but we knew we had a unique audience—sophisticated, international. It was culturally and politically important to make a strong impression.

This was the climax of our trip. The advance press and reviews were exceptional and the audience enthusiastic. After the opening-night performance, the American delegation came backstage to congratulate us. Much handshaking, photographs. I could see the faces beaming with enthusiasm and relief. Montevideo really took us to its heart. Ten o'clock performances suddenly became a pleasure.

There was one free day after the last concert that Letitia and I used to dash around buying gifts. On government tours we received a weekly salary, more than I ever earned before or after with the Limón company. Buenos Aires, originally on our schedule, cancelled because it was the wrong season and they were totally unprepared. So plans were made to return directly home.

There is no doubt that this trip added glamor and prestige to the Limón company. José was particularly happy that South America as well as Mexico had now accepted him, and the fact that he spoke Spanish brought him close to the people and the press. Doris's works had been well received, and this gave her an enhanced sense of achievement.

Upon our return, José mentioned that he would like to do a pure dance for the upcoming summer festival, so I lent him the recording of William Schuman's recent *Symphony for Strings*, and it had instant appeal. All through my years with Doris and José, we often fed each other musical ideas. Schuman's work was complicated, but José conceived some fascinating choreographic moments, quite different from anything he had done before.

"Pauline, you know that fabulous leap I've seen in one of your pictures? I want you to enter with that leap over my body." Well, this was no simple matter—a profile leap, front knee bent, back leg arched high in back, head thrown back. How would I know if I cleared him? What if I landed on his back? It could finish him as a dancer. Evidently he trusted me, and therefore I dared, because that was my entrance on August 19, 1955, at the American Dance Festival. Nevertheless, the butterflies were there every time I had to fly out from that upstage left wing. Wherever we did that piece, I paced the stage to set how many steps it would take to clear José center stage.

The second movement had a slow, lyric quality. Pauline decided she wanted us glamorous—José in gold lamé trousers; the women in silver lamé leotards. I had a long blue partial skirt—long things made me look taller. Doris Hering described the performance in the October *Dance Magazine*:

> Mr. Limón started the heroic introductory theme of the dance and was soon joined by Pauline Koner, Lucas Hoving, Lavina Nielsen, Ruth Currier and Betty Jones. They leapt a course in circles with each man guiding two women.
>
> Three girls were left gazing diagonally upstage. They sank to the floor in contractions and Lucas Hoving wove slowly among their still forms. Mr. Limón entered, carrying Pauline Koner. He set her tenderly upon the ground as the music sang and there began a series of lovely, almost worshipful lifts. All massed for a robust finale.
>
> One of the most satisfying aspects of *Symphony for Strings* was the opportunity it gave various members of the company for virtuoso dancing. Pauline Koner was like some fiery primitive bacchante as she tore through leaps and sharp shifts in direction. One is so accustomed to thinking of her as a dramatic dancer, that it always a revelation to see how dazzling a technician she is.

Although it was what one may call a pure dance, it had many emotional overtones. We toured the work, and did it at the Juilliard spring season in 1956, but it did not stay long in the repertoire.

In this first decade of the company's existence it had grown in renown and prestige, if not in size. The annual pattern of tours and New London residencies were sometimes broken by exciting events, such as the New York City Dance theatre in 1949—a program put together by the publicists Isadora Bennett and Richard Pleasant that united the major modern dance companies and soloists for a season at the City Center—and the two Bethsabee de Rothschild Foundation "American Dance" series. Everyone danced better in these series than ever before; the stages were large, the accompaniment a live orchestra (conducted by our own Simon Sadoff), and Jean Rosenthal magically created inspired new lighting.

The American Dance Festival was the summer ritual. I knew I had to plan for six weeks of teaching, rehearsing, and sweating in ninety-degree temperatures with no air-conditioning. With this in view, I rented a faculty apartment in a house opposite the college. José and

Pauline stayed directly below. Within two weeks I would be nervous, pressured, tense, and could not understand how José, with much greater responsibilities, could whistle some little ditty every morning as he went in and out of his house before his first 10 A.M. class. Sometimes he whistled Bach; at other times an unrecognizable tune floated up to my window. He whistled on for all the years that I was at New London with the company. Although I did not know it at the time, José was an insomniac. He suffered strange torments—terrors in the night—throughout his life. He worked at least twelve hours a day, and the circles under his eyes signaled the fatigue, as his drawn face signaled the dehydration, but in the mornings I would hear the blithe whistling.

Tours were a necessary evil. I no longer enjoyed touring—the exhaustion, the too-frequent illnesses and injuries, the need and determination to perform at all costs. On one-night stands I would lose track of where we were. It was always the same—the station, the hotel, the theater. Hotel rooms were usually shabby and meals, such as they were, something to get through. If Letitia was along it was bearable. The company had sort of paired off: Betty and Ruth, Simon and Lucas, and of course Pauline and José.

For the first couple of years Pauline came along as company manager as well as light designer and technical manager. Privately, all may have been well, but I once witnessed José explode at her during a technical rehearsal. Soon a specialized light designer traveled with us and José himself briefed us on itinerary. Blessed with an infallible memory for places and dates, he was very good at this.

After performance we all went to the only open restaurant—if there was one. At our university dates there was always the small reception, with punch and pink or green cookies, much too sweet. A bar was a chance to gulp beer that quenched thirst and replenished our salt-starved bodies. Then it was back to the hotel for the apple and cheese in our valise. Occasionally, there was the oasis of an ex-dancer's or a friend's home, or an understanding board member who arranged an intimate party with real food for the dancers. We could relax, have a drink, nourish ourselves. José regaled us with stories; Simon sang or played. These were bright moments of relief.

Sometimes the others preferred to go directly to the hotel, so José and I would find a restaurant. I watched him order steak and potatoes, finish it off with relish, then order another. He had a prodigious capacity for food, after all the energy he expended. Usually, he was in every work on the program, often giving a master class during the day and rehearsing before the evening performance.

Whenever I think of those tours I am overcome by the aroma of oranges. José always carried at least a dozen in a paper bag and from time to time through the entire trip hand-peeled and ate his way through them. His desire for oranges seemed insatiable. We both discovered that if we took swigs of honey between dances we could sustain energy. I carried a small jar upright in my makeup case. José carried his with his shoes in one of the blue denim drawstring bags Pauline had made for each of us. One afternoon José dashed into my dressing room: "Pauline, my jar of honey has spilled. Everything is a mess. May I borrow some of your honey tonight?" After that, he decided that we would buy a jar in each place, and if we shared it at a performance, that polished it off.

One winter tour I missed altogether. I came down with a sudden fever. The doctors diagnosed a mild case of mononucleosis. "No tour," they said. "You'll never make it. The fever may last quite a while, and even when it's gone you'll suffer from constant fatigue." I was desperate. No understudy. What to do? Betty came to my home and from bed I taught her *Story of Mankind*. Ruth was coached in *The Visitation*. I heard that Pauline immediately altered the costume to her original high-waisted version. From José came an unusual letter: "I miss you very, very much and all your fire and artistry and your superb command of the stage, your incredible powers of projection. The babies are doing nobly, even heroically and expertly, too. I am quite proud of them. They have really risen to the occasion—but they are not you."

With the constant rehearsals (unpaid) and touring there was very little time for company social gatherings. There were one or two wonderful Thanksgiving dinners that Pauline whipped up. These were given at Doris's old apartment on East 16th Street. Pauline was a gourmet cook, so we all starved ourselves the day before. Besides the usual turkey, there was mulled wine and cherries jubilee. We could forget the fatigue, the aches and pains. At these times there was a warm family feeling among the company members that was not always present otherwise.

In 1956 the Juilliard School was celebrating its thirtieth anniversary with a festival of American music. José and Doris were invited to present a dance series using six scores by American composers. Three of the scores were specially commissioned, as was the choreography for three of the dances. Doris created *Theatre Piece No. 2*, and José *Variations on a Theme*, which we now know as *There Is a Time*, to original music by Norman Dello Joio.

We started to work on this in the very early spring, as soon as we returned from the annual February tour. José chose *Ecclesiastes* as his theme, a source rich with the possibility for variety and contrast. To start with, we had only scraps of music. The dance opened and closed with a circle, our arms entwined in a circle of life, in which some thematic movement was introduced. Solo and duet sections were assigned. I was given "A Time to Heal," a duet with Harlan McCallum (one of the new company members); "A Time to Laugh," a minute-and-a-half solo; and "A Time to Embrace, A Time to Refrain from Embracing," a duet with José.

José had the music for "A Time to Laugh . . . A Time to Dance," but it was a very short segment, wonderfully bubbly music that was perfect for me. I suggested that, if Dello Joio agreed, I would like to plan my solo to that music; it could be repeated for the group dance. I discussed with José what he would like me to do and improvised a few patterns. Then I went off to play around with these ideas. Using Doris's theory on gesture as a point of departure, I sought every possibility of laughter—giggling rhythms transferred to the feet, head shakes, belly laughs, shoulder twists, and guffaws. After a few days I asked José to come and see what I had set. "That's just what I want," he said. "Don't change it."

José and I worked Sunday afternoons, when the company really wanted to be off, on the duet "To Embrace." He said, "I would like to see something like those Chagall floating-upside-down figures." By the end of the rehearsal we had developed a wonderfully unexpected upside-down lift, from which I then rested across his shoulder and, as he spun in place, spiraled to the floor. It was smooth, unusual, and very much Chagall.

This duet had a warm and delicate emotional quality, which I had rarely experienced with him in other works. I had always felt that for José, it was easier to dance heroic or tragic roles, given his hidden, brooding quality. Now there was a challenge—a dance on a man-woman relationship. This was the first time we needed to reach out to each other. In some ways José did extend himself, but it was an emotion within himself rather than toward me. I tried to break through the gossamer veil that was always between us. One or two moments it happened: at our entrance, when we met and I twined my leg about his thigh and gently framed his head with my arms (I could not help thinking of the "Song of Songs"); in "A Time to Refrain from Embracing," the simple gesture I made wanting to touch his face as I was pulled away by the group. Those moments were very real for him and for me. However, reaching the inner José on a one-to-one level was almost impossible.

The "Time to Heal" duet with Harlan was very short. I quickly worked out a few phrases for the two of us, as José made suggestions and approved.

There Is a Time had many sections, some of which I thought were outstanding. "A Time to Keep Silent and A Time to Speak" was a duet performed by Lavina in silence, and Lucas to the accompaniment of backstage rhythm claps. Lucas was superb in this. A surprise was to see the lyric Betty become a raging Fury in "A Time to Hate." I had never believed she could be that violent or that sharp.

The day before the dress rehearsal, my right Achilles'—the good one—was swollen and tender. I could not use my right foot. Of course, no understudy; I never had an understudy during the fifteen years I danced with José. I rushed to the orthopedist. The Achilles' was fine; it was the bursa that was inflamed. The doctor gave me a shot of cortisone and said it would take from one to three days to heal. I went home, rested, kept my fingers crossed, even said a little prayer. At dress rehearsal the next night, I whizzed through the solo (which was fast, with some very demanding leaps) as though nothing had happened. Over the years the bursa acted up occasionally, but the cortisone always cured it, although not always in twenty-four hours. The gods had listened that first time.

We presented *There Is a Time* on April 20, 1956, at Juilliard. Tharon Musser was still with us and did her usual sensitive, creative lighting. The work was an instant success. With this piece, which required five men in addition to the basic group, the company grew in size. We were now, not counting Letitia who appeared only occasionally, a company of four women and seven men, a stage manager, and Simon—thirteen or fourteen in all. The enlarged company may have been visually more flamboyant, but it was losing the jewel-like quality of our original small group. Doris's energies were now divided, since she also directed the Juilliard Dance Theatre. José was leaning more and more toward works for men.

It was about this time that I began to wonder what my next step should be, but decisions under strenuous work conditions are hard to make. My life was constantly pressured by time—time for Fritz, time for José, time for myself. What kept me involved was my interest in the new company works, and that my own works were sometimes included in our programs. *Cassandra, Interlude for Angelica,* and *Concertino* were used to give José a breather as well as to offer variety in style.

Touring, however, was becoming even more distasteful and unfulfilling. As travel expenses mounted, we went from overnight roomettes in the train and an occasional plane flight to small chartered buses. Morning departures were a trial; someone was always late. Long distances on the bus made us stiff, cramped. There were schedules to meet, and a late arrival was hectic. Yet we always managed to give a good performance. The senior members, especially José and I, were very aware that we had to set an example for the younger ones. We were always first at the theater. After making up, we spent our time warming up, until the last minute. I would get into my costume and try to imagine this was the first performance of the piece. Since we did not carry lighting or sound equipment, we were subject to whatever facilities were available, which were often pretty sparse. Some of our music was live piano accompaniment, so we were not totally at the mercy of mechanics.

Summer 1957 was traumatic for me. I had just arrived at New London for the annual teaching session when I got an urgent call from my brother. Dad had been taken to the hospital with a major stroke. I left Lucy Venable to take over my classes and rushed back to Manhattan. Mother and Marvin were at the hospital. Mom's face was drawn and her eyes tear-swollen. She and Marvin had been there since dawn and it was now early evening, so I sent them home and stayed on alone. At about 2 A.M. I decided to go home to shower and change, and I told the nurse I would be back soon. When I returned I was told things were critical; Dad had slipped into a coma. I stood in the corridor, tears streaming. It could not be happening. Dad was always the strong one of the family, the adviser, the guide, always helping others.

At this moment, someone tapped me on the shoulder. "Miss Koner, I am a surgeon on the Workmen's Circle staff, and I know your father very well. I have just looked in on him. The only way we can save him is to perform a tracheotomy. He cannot breathe. I will have to do it in his room. There is no time! Do you give me permission?"

Permission! Anything was better than just waiting.

"Yes. Yes, please go ahead. I take responsibility."

Three hours later, when Mom and Marvin returned, I told them what had happened, and Marv and I went into Dad's room. He opened his eyes. "Dad, we're here. Pauline, Marvin. Do you see us?" He blinked his eyes up and down, and we knew he had recognized us. Although he never fully recovered, he lived for nine more years. After a few days I returned to New London and blocked out the trauma by escaping into teaching, rehearsing, and preparing for the European tour.

Doris's new work, *Dance Overture*, had thirteen dancers, among them Lola Huth. Of the Limón dancers, she was closest to my quality of movement and I hoped could understudy me. For the European tour I cast her and Lucy in *Concertino*. Besides our original small company and Letitia, there were Vol Quitzow, Chester Wolenski, Michael Hollander, Ronald Chase, and Kenneth Bartmess.

During the week between New London and our departure, I managed to drive to the family's summer house to see Dad. Mom had brought him to this house, which he dearly loved, to help him recuperate as much as he could. When I arrived he was seated out of doors. His eyes lit up. He had come a long way from the last time I had seen him. He could speak haltingly, and he was thrilled about my trip. Seeing him so improved gave me strength against the fatigue and anxiety I felt about some of the programs. Compared to what Dad had gone through and survived, and the trials Mom would endure nursing him, my worries seemed insignificant.

With less than a week to pull ourselves together, it had been an inspiration to decide that we would travel to London on the *Queen Mary*. This gave us four days of good food and rest after the strenuous summer. How we needed this with twenty weeks of touring ahead.

We arrived in London on August 27, 1957, a little less haggard. The plan was for Simon to pick up an orchestra in London, which would then play for the entire tour. The morning after our arrival we heard that Lola had been taken to the hospital for an emergency appendectomy and would have to go home when she was well. We were upset for her, but this created an additional crisis for me. *Concertino* was scheduled for the third program in London. I was desperate until I remembered that Elizabeth Harris, from the original cast, was studying at the Wigman School in Germany. After much telephoning I located her, and she agreed to join us for the tour. Luck was with me.

We were to open at the Sadler's Wells Theatre on September 2. The advance publicity did not adequately describe our work and, having heard about Martha Graham's reception two years earlier, we were a little apprehensive. On opening day we had an orchestra rehearsal from 2 until 5 P.M., then a 7:30 curtain. The first program was *Dance Overture*, *Rítmo Jondo*, *There Is a Time*, and *The Moor's Pavane*. We were tired and nervous. The audience was small—the inadequate publicity and the concurrent Edinburgh Festival—and the reception was lukewarm. To most of the audience we must have seemed like some strange breed of dancer, with no pointe shoes, no tutus, no swans, no scenery, and a movement style they had not seen before. Some thought what we did was ugly, but there were strong supporters as well.

The press was condescending. In the reviews much was made of José's age (he was then forty-nine), but I was applauded as a fine artist and sensitive actress. There were complaints about program changes. Aside from a few perceptive critics, Doris's pieces were just disregarded. The works that made the most impact during the season were *The Emperor Jones*, *There Is a Time*, *La Malinche*, *Night Spell*, *The Moor's Pavane*, and strangely, *Concertino*—most likely because it was light, airy, feminine, and delicate. Clive Barnes and a few others like Cyril Beaumont were enthusiastic, but most reports were disastrous. London in 1957 was not ready for modern dance. By the second week, however, there was a decided change, with audience interest growing.

ANTA had engaged a European concert manager, Anatole Heller, to handle the bookings and expedite our travel. A charming, warm, sophisticated man married to an English dancer, he understood the dancer's need for moments of relaxation. Each time we traveled to a new locale, he chartered a plane (we were now more than fifty people, with orchestra and stagehands) that always had the finest food and all we wanted to drink (for me it was champagne). This would be our holiday—and we made the most of it.

Paris was a nightmare. We performed at the Marigny Theatre—small stage, little advance publicity, tiny, drafty dressing rooms. I was so cold that I dashed to the Galeries Lafayette to buy a warm robe (my size was in the children's department), a woolly royal blue affair that remained my theater robe for many years. The Parisians hated our dancing. They found the movement dull and ugly, the female dancers unattractive. Not much had changed in seven years.

Our first performance was September 17, and after it we could not wait to finish the engagement. Of course there was a small group of painters, actors, and dancers who appreciated what we did, and a beautiful reception was given for us by American ambassador Amory Houghton, but these were not enough to compensate for the callousness and chill of the general atmosphere.

Our next stop was West Berlin, to appear during the Berlin Festival. Here there was an audience, exposed to the expressionist dance of Mary Wigman, Harald Kreutzberg, and Gret Palucca, that had no problem understanding and appreciating our American dance. Our first performance was greeted with an ovation that healed our bruised egos. Although I was not happy to be in Germany, I could not help appreciating the artistic level of the German audience and critics.

After opening night there was a big reception, and I was happy to be seated at a table with Doris, José, Pauline, the president of the New York Chapter of ANTA, and especially the honored guest, Mary Wigman. Wigman was fascinating. She had lived through great trials during World War II in Germany, but now her school was functioning again. We talked dance, and I told her how much she had influenced me. She was enthusiastic about our work. It is truly the criticism of one's peers that counts.

During the week we played in Berlin, I learned from my dresser in the theater that there was still a very active Nazi underground. She was half Jewish, and somehow had survived. "Don't be fooled by what you see," she said. "It hasn't changed that much." This was brought home to me when we were taken on a bus tour. The tour guide, in his very crisp voice, kept saying when he showed us the bombed-out areas, "In the old times." By his sneer we knew that "old times" meant "good old Hitler times." Our English orchestra members, having lived through the London bombings, were ready to throttle him. I was furious, ready to say something nasty, then controlled myself. We were representing the United States. Most of the young members of our company were totally unaware of his insinuated "You Americans, this is what you did to us."

There were other incidents to confirm my discomfort at being in Germany. It was still all there, only covered with icing and whipped cream for public view. It was hard for me to forget what had been, perhaps because aside from Simon and Michael I was the only other

Jewish member of our company. Dance success notwithstanding, I looked forward to our departure for Poland.

We arrived in Poznan. The difference was shocking. Truly a postwar country, the clothes were dreary, the shop windows displayed a few tired canned goods, which I knew were rarely available in the store—I knew because Poland in 1957 reminded me of Russia in 1935. However, we were housed in a fine hotel and our plain but adequate meals were served in a private dining room. I am certain that this food was not easily available to the general public. This starkness was in direct contrast to the warmth of the people. In each city we played—Poznan, Wrocław, Katowici, Warsaw—the local cultural organization acted as our hosts. They provided transportation and arranged sightseeing tours.

At the end of our October 8 opening in Poznan, in spite of a fifteen-minute electrical failure during the performance, there was a standing ovation. A delegation of dancers from the opera came backstage afterward. They were emotionally overwhelmed, and said, "We have been waiting for this for a long time." Wherever we went we were besieged by dancers. They entertained us at parties, asked questions, were starved for information and dance stimulation.

Warsaw was our last city. In its center stood a tall white building, the Palace of Culture, a gift from the Soviet Union. This building had one of the largest auditoriums we had ever danced in. The stage was an enormous semicircular thrust affair, and no matter how close I danced to the front edge, I felt miles away from the audience. Every seat was sold; throughout Poland, the houses were sold out for all performances as soon as the box office opened.

Leon Woizikowski, a former Ballets Russes dancer, was director of the Warsaw opera ballet. He took us on a tour of the newly built opera house—opera houses were the first things to be rebuilt in Poland after the war. It was elegant in the old style, with marble staircases, luxurious decoration, and the most wonderful studios for the ballet school. We could not help comparing them to the small, dingy studios we worked in at home.

There were frequent press conferences and interviews, and as official representatives of the United States, we were honest, but tactful. Our last evening in Warsaw was made festive, if a bit teary, with a lively party given by the dancers' organization. Artists' acceptance of our dance and of us as people had been total and heartwarming.

Back in Germany we played Bonn, Düsseldorf, Munich, Stuttgart, and Essen. Although artistically satisfying, it left me with an emotional trauma: who had won the war? Here the shops were overflowing with luxuries, furs, jewels, elegant clothes. Foodstores were crammed with cheeses and salamis, and bakeshops with elaborate cakes and tortes piled with whipped cream. Coming from economically oppressed Poland, I could not condone what I saw in Germany. By the time we reached Essen, I thought that if I did not get out of this country I might create some sort of scandal. Just in time we left for Brussels.

Belgium was more open-minded than France had been. Brussels and Antwerp called us fine artists, while in Liège and Ghent we were again pioneering. The Théâtre de la Monnaie in Brussels had a very steeply raked stage. Going upstage was like trying to run up a steep hill, while moving downstage felt like "keep your foot on the brake."

From Belgium we went on to Holland, and here of course Lucas was featured. He was home, and the Dutch audience loved him. We played the resort town of Scheveningen, then Utrecht, The Hague, and Amsterdam as well as Enschede, Rotterdam, and Arnhem. In Amsterdam we performed at the famous Concertgebouw, a large, not too attractive hall. The stage was at one end and behind it rose tiers, amphitheater fashion. We had to run up and down these tiers to our dressing rooms. What tickled me were the bathroom fixtures of Delft porcelain —even the toilet, which looked more like a flower vase.

On our way to Yugoslavia Edouard, a stagehand, said, "Pauline, I know you from a long way back."

"How?" I said. "I've only met you on this tour."

"That's what you think," he answered. "Do you remember a performance at Le Pré Fleuri in Alexandria? Well, I helped build that outdoor stage."

We found that Yugoslavia, much more prosperous than Poland, was open-minded and warmhearted, and here we felt we were really ambassadors of good will. Our first performance was in Ljubljana, where the fog was so thick I could barely find my way to the theater. We were greeted with bravos—what a wonderful sound that is! The following morning, the mayor of the city invited the company to a reception. He commented on how much he had enjoyed the performance. "Oh, but you have not seen our most important work, *The Moor's Pavane*," I said. "I'm sure you would enjoy that even more. We are dancing it tonight."

"I would like to come," he said, "but it is sold out."

At José's table he expressed a wish to see our second program, and one of our USIS men offered up his box. The next day we learned that the mayor, an important Communist official, had been unapproachable to all Americans. Art had opened the door.

We danced in Rijeka, which had an opera house that was a jewelbox. Many of the theaters we performed in on our trip were old-world opera houses, with gold and velvet trim, crystal chandeliers, and an atmosphere of elegant warmth that very few contemporary opera houses can boast.

In Zagreb, we were invited to a special showing of Yugoslavian folk dance. The men's dances were among the most exciting and intricate I had ever seen, with elaborate, dynamic footwork, while the women glided smoothly and lyrically. If they came to America I was sure they would create a sensation. One of the men assigned to us from the Cultural Division was a Yugoslavian, Nuno Boric. He seemed to take a fancy to me, and told me that if I ever wanted to come back with my own company they would be delighted.

Yugoslavian dancers were as enthusiastic as the Polish had been. They followed us from Sarajevo to Belgrade, Subotoce to Novisad to see as many performances as possible. Our final stop was Skopje, close to the Greek border.

This small town was middle-eastern in flavor, the women in Turkish trousers, the men in embroidered vests and full trousers. The performance was sold out, and we heard that the pressure against the entrance doors to the opera house was so great, the glass broke. Every spot backstage was filled with faces peering at us from the wings, from light platforms. At the opening of *The Moor's Pavane*, I heard Lucas whisper, "Get a load of the prompter's box." I stole a glance and there were two heads looking straight at us. Even in this small city that had never seen modern dance, they would not stop applauding.

Greece had been canceled because it was the wrong season, so we went on to Portugal, our last stop. The San Carlos in Lisbon was an exquisite white and gold opera house, with an audience dressed in evening clothes. This luxury stimulated a very exhausted company of dancers. José was worried about how *The Traitor*, with its religious connotation, would be received, but it brought down the house and had to be presented on all four evenings. My problem was a stage raked even steeper than in Brussels. Lisbon was one of the few places I performed *Cassandra*, so I rehearsed like mad in a house studio that had a platform matching the stage. The performance must have gone well because the press was enthusiastic.

Our final performance was December 21 in Oporto. Here the theater was an ugly old movie house with practically no heat. I could barely feel my feet under me. We shivered in the wings, shivered on stage, and froze in the dressing room. Waiting in the wings, I noticed a young man in uniform arguing with a fire inspector. I asked what was wrong.

"I am a dancer, at present in the military service," the young man said. "I came here especially to see your performance. There are no tickets, so I came backstage. The inspector says it is against the fire law."

I spoke to the inspector, said I would take responsibility should he be questioned, and discreetly hid the young man in one of the wings. Unfortunately the cold and our fatigue made this performance hardly a grand finale, but at the end the young man came to me with tears in his eyes. "Thank you. You don't know what it has meant for me to see you," he said. Suddenly I felt very warm.

Until now we had hesitated to visit Spain (it was the height of the Franco regime), but we were told by embassy officials that it would be desirable, if only to show our standard of living! With Spain so close, José and Pauline took an extra week to vacation there. Lucy and I went along. We rented a car with a driver and had a lovely trip through Portugal, stopping in little inns and seeing small villages and well-kept olive groves. The moment we crossed the border from Portugal to Spain, within a span of fifty feet, there was a shocking change. Children begged as we passed, the olive groves were bedraggled, poverty was apparent in every line of people's haggard faces.

We arrived in Seville and went to the great cathedral on Christmas Eve. I expected an elaborate Mass, but it was very simple. Easter is the time when the cathedral is in all its glory. We wandered through the Alcazar, took buggy rides in the ancient part of the city, and watched flamenco dancing in the nightclub of Hotel Christina, where Lucy and I stayed. Then we were off to Madrid. I had expected "sunny Spain" to be warm. Instead, Madrid was as cold as New York, and the hotel not well heated. Seeing the Prado, with its wonderful paintings by Velasquez, Rubens, and Goya, and visiting the antique market did compensate for the disappointing weather. After three days we were thoroughly homesick and took the first available plane home.

As spring 1958 approached, there was the usual planning for the summer at New London. Doris, depressed and tired, was concentrating on her book. I worked at reevaluating my Helen Keller piece and making essential changes. José had two pieces in mind: a company work called *Dances*, to music of Chopin, which would not involve me; and *Serenata*, with music by Paul Bowles with a song text by Federico Garcia Lorca. They were not successful and were soon dropped.

I think José was very tired and Doris did not look well, although she did not complain. She taught classes and worked with a repertory group reviving *Life of the Bee*. The winter tour had taken its toll on all of us. We all felt a strange pall. We knew something was very wrong with Doris. She could no longer hide it from us, and no sooner was she back in New York than we heard she was in the hospital.

José had begun work on *Missa Brevis*. Since I was not cast in it, I was able to spend more time with Fritz, and whenever I was in New York Doris brought me up to date. José was using a large cast—his company supplemented by Juilliard students—and was carried away by the excitement of it. I instinctively realized that this would mean a great change for me. There would be fewer roles since I was not precisely a company member. I saw myself left with the old repertoire, and although I loved my roles, there would be no chance for further growth or challenge.

I was haunted by what the future might hold, knowing that soon I would have to cope without the security of Doris's guidance. Her death in December left me desolate. For a time I felt I was in a vacuum, suspended in midair, afraid to put my feet on the earth, afraid to rely on my own judgment. Yet I knew I had to challenge myself.

I began a work on the alienation of youth, based on the premise of John Donne's "No man is an island." Alexander Scourby narrated the text on tape. I used a collage of various kinds of music—Villa-Lobos, Jimmy Guiffre, and Harold Faberman—and had the dancers shout words. I cast myself as the Catalyst, a kind of abstract Mother Image. The work was *Tides*: *Islands of Loneliness, Façade of Loneliness, Pieta*, and *Rejoice with them that do Rejoice*. It premiered August 14, 1959, at the American Dance Festival. Although there were some excellent sections, the absence of Doris's final word to point out the weaknesses was frightening, and I dropped the work after its first performance.

The Limón company also seemed to me to be slipping in quality without Doris. Tempi and lighting faults were not corrected, the fine dynamic nuance—a trademark—became blurred. There was nothing I could say. I knew José, perhaps subconsciously, disliked my criticism. This was his domain. He did listen to Lucas, whom he felt was no threat, so I relayed my remarks to Lucas and he talked to José.

When José suggested doing a duet with me I was surprised and pleased. He was planning to do the characters Macbeth and Lady Macbeth, drawn as harpies more than people to symbolize the hunger for power and how it can destroy. I thought José's concept ingenious and was excited to begin work on it.

José chose a trio by Gunther Schuller, which we had on a very bad tape. It was sparse, aleatory music, difficult to work with. José devised a vivid opening. Capitalizing on our divergent heights, he had me stand directly behind him. My hands crept through his arms to his mouth and heart. He grabbed my hands, pushing them away, to insinuate the power of suggestion that Lady Macbeth had over him. We felt we were creatures, not people.

Since I was contributing a good part of the duet choreography as well as my own solo parts, I steeled myself and for the first time asked for credit as choreographic collaborator. There was dead silence from José when I brought this up. The piece was well on its way. He was tired, pressed, and often ran out of movement ideas. His face went blank, then surprise registered. "Why? How can you ask this?" He did not speak the words, but I could almost hear him ask the question aloud. It had never occurred to him that I might want a little acknowledgment for what I had created. True, dancing with the company had helped me grow and working with Doris had been a privilege, but now a new stage had begun. José was silent, then said, "Let me think about it." I sensed a hidden resentment, even anger. It was the beginning of the end, but there was no going back. Ultimately, an agreement was reached; the program credit read, "José Limón, Choreographer (In collaboration with Pauline Koner)."

I had some wonderful dramatic moments and a solo that I set to the percussion section of our tape. José had an enormous square of red velvet, which became the regal robes for both of us as we wrapped it about us. A red velvet panel hung center stage which, when it rose, revealed a ghastly apparition, a mask of China silk. This set did not work, and was discarded. Pauline could not solve the costume problem, although she tried several versions. The piece was somehow saturated with obstacles. Our final disaster was the rehearsal with live music. Everything sounded different. We came to my solo and it had a completely different percussion sound. I stopped dead on the Juilliard stage and said to Frederik Prausnitz, the conductor, "But this is not my music." He retorted, "The score reads percussion improvisation."

There was total silence. We had never known it was meant to be an improvisation. Impossible for me to redo my solo. José stood there, too polite to say, "The music generally sounds all wrong." We abandoned the rehearsal. When I got home I called Gunther Schuller and asked him please to come to the rehearsal the next day and straighten things out. I think José and Martha Hill, director of the Juilliard Dance Department, never forgave me. Neither of them had thought to contact Schuller, and I knew it was the only solution. He came, the matter was resolved, but there was an icy atmosphere.

The work was *Barren Sceptre*, based on the lines from *Macbeth*, "Stars, hide your fires; let not light see my black and deep desires." It premiered at the Juilliard School on April 11, 1960. This work had many interesting facets, but the ending, a solo by José, somehow seemed unable to lend final power. We performed it several times out of town, and uncostumed at an open rehearsal at Connecticut College on their summer lecture series, where it was filmed.

From behind-the-scenes repercussions, I knew that sooner or later it would be time for me to leave José. An exchange of letters pointed out how tense the situation had become, but I did not yet have the courage and put it off.

Another Cultural Presentations tour to South America was scheduled for the fall. We left New York immediately after the New London summer session, with no time to recover from the summer fatigue. This South American tour had the same lack of organization as our first. Some of the theaters were unequipped movie houses with makeshift dressing rooms; some were lovely opera houses. I often had to try three hotels to find one I thought I could tolerate. Everyone in the company seemed on edge. A sense of rivalry between company members percolated in a very disturbing way. I constantly felt an undercurrent of resentment toward me. Without Doris's magic touch, many fine details of performance were disappearing. I was still striving for that perfection I had learned from her and asked Lucas to make suggestions.

The tour started in Barranquilla, then on to Bogotá, Medellín, Quito, Guayaquil, Lima, and Santiago. My legs felt like rubber. It was hard to adjust to the constant changes of altitude, and for the first few performances I worried about maintaining my personal standards. In Quito, a quaint old city nestled in the heart of the mountains, I was told some singers had dropped to the floor because of the altitude. I asked to have an oxygen tank backstage. My solo in *There Is a Time* was short but taxing, and without the whiff of oxygen between the solo and the duet with José, I would have passed out. The second night, I barely made it. There were the usual parties and receptions given by embassy officials, which helped to alleviate the dreariness of constant packing, unpacking, rehearsing, performing, and on again.

At last I found my legs and my strength returned. *Concertino* and *There Is a Time* were particularly successful. We arrived in Santiago after a long, tiring trip. Our performances were at the Teatro Municipal. The opening night was attended by the president of Chile, with a party afterward at the American Embassy. We had a free day September 18, and performances on the nineteenth and twentieth.

All my procrastinating with the thought of curtailing activities with the company was solved for me on September 20, 1960. The program featured *There Is a Time* and *Concertino*. The day was long—rehearsal at 11 A.M. followed by a film, a half hour for rest, then back in the theater at five for a seven o'clock performance. During rehearsal the stage felt slick, so I used my ballet shoes with rubber soles. That night, toward the end of the third movement of *Concertino*, I landed from a jump and my left foot stuck in rosin. I heard a crunch. I kept going, faking, keeping the left foot flat on the floor covered by the long skirt. The audience never knew anything had happened. I assumed the injury was a slight twist, and even walked back to the hotel, knowing that sometimes exercise is better than allowing the foot to swell. I did not mention it to José. At the hotel I wrapped the foot in ice and spent a worrisome night.

The next morning the foot was badly swollen, painful. I could walk flat-footed, but it would be impossible to perform *Pavane* that night. All summer I had begged to have my roles understudied. No one had time for anything so trivial. Now I spent from 12 noon to 6 P.M. teaching my role to Lola Huth. That night, Lucas made a point of raving about Lola's performance.

We went on to Buenos Aires, and since José insisted that *There Is a Time* must be on the program, he asked me to teach Ruth my part. On September 23 I arrived at the theater to see several dancers from the local ballet company seated and ready to watch rehearsals. Ruth was nervous. I started to teach her "A Time to Heal," the duet with Harlan. This was comparatively simple. Then we started "A Time to Embrace," my duet with José. Ruth was not accustomed to lifts, and this dance had some very complicated ones. The more she tried, the worse it got. Finally I took José aside and asked if he would explain the situation to the guests so that we could work in a more private atmosphere. José, with his accustomed politeness and ability to block out surroundings, had not realized that Ruth was almost in tears. The dancers left and we finally got some semblance of the duet working.

It was now four o'clock. There was a performance at six, and it was time to prepare for it. At this point, José said, "And now, Pauline, teach Ruth your 'Time to Laugh.'" I could not believe my ears. This was a solo I had choreographed for my own personal style, fast, tricky, and effervescent. Several girls in the company had tried to learn it and had failed. I knew Ruth could not do it. Besides, she was near exhaustion. With my hurt foot I could not even demonstrate it. José refused to listen. Since I was walking, albeit flat-footed, he did not realize the seriousness of the injury. I myself did not know it.

"It's impossible, José. There is no time. I could not learn all this and perform it the same day. The music is a repeat; cut the solo and skip to "A Time to Dance" with the group. It's a perfect solution."

A change came over him. He was suddenly full of rage. "I know *you* couldn't, but Ruth is different from you. I will get down on my knees to thank her. I will never forget it my whole life. As for *you*, I've had enough!"

"Then you're not interested in my working with you any longer."

"As far as I'm concerned," he said, "you can go right now."

"Well, if that's how you feel about it . . ."

"Yes, that's how I feel about it. Get out. I never want to see you again. *Get out!*"

I walked out and slammed the door. My immediate anger carried me through. I gathered the costumes for my own works and my other personal belongings and stood there shaking. José asked the company manager to arrange my departure before I even had a chance to talk to him. I wired Gertrude Macy, who was in charge of the ANTA program, saying I was fired. She called and asked me not to leave until she spoke to José. "I have not made the decision," I told her. "It was made for me. But I'm willing to wait until I hear from you." On September 27, I received this cable: "José's attitude remains unchanged. Regret can do nothing. Macy."

I knew I might need confirmation for insurance purposes. Since Ruth had been the only one present, I called and asked her to verify what had happened. Her answer: "I'm sorry, Pauline, I can't remember a thing." I was bitter since all of this had been triggered by my desire to save her from what looked like near collapse. I did not know then that I had torn the muscles in my foot. It took one year to recover.

My reaction to the entire event: first anger, then dismay, then hurt. José was a man I had respected, to whom I had given time and energy, often at the sacrifice of Fritz's welfare. Still, I had always sensed that beneath the overly polite, seemingly controlled surface, there was a violent, dark side to José. The volcano had erupted. I had looked forward to easing up on touring, but remaining available for key performances; I certainly did not want a complete break.

Letter from Tom Skelton:

> Just a note before we leave to again tell you how terrible I feel about all this mess. The company, too, seems demoralized and stunned, but the pressure of getting through those last few performances has made it easier for them. Ruth wasn't ready for 'laugh' last night so we made several cuts. [Eventually, José rechoreographed "A Time to Laugh."] Lola filled in quite well in *Pavane* and faked what she didn't know with aplomb, but I sure wish you had more time with her. . . . I'm sorry for all of us that it has to end in this ugly way, and I hope the wound will heal quickly for you. You've given so many years and so much of yourself that I know it will heal slowly at best.

I came home in despair, sick at heart, sick physically. Fritz was there to comfort me. I tried to rationalize José's action: he was tired—he was desperate—he knew he had no understudies. Above all, he should not have had viewers at a crucial rehearsal. This had triggered the outburst.

For the sake of the remainder of the tour and to avoid the resulting gossip and scandal, a press release stated that I had decided to leave the company to pursue my own career. To be kicked out after years of dedicated work was hard to take.

Gradually I began to recognize that the break with José, traumatic as it had been, was perhaps the best thing that could have happened. After a year of silence, I made the first move toward a rapprochement —I wrote him a conciliatory letter in December 1961:

In our ledger of values how can fifteen years of good be outbalanced by one day of weakness, and would we be human beings of any depth and perception without our frailties? I am now firmly convinced that Fate took an important hand, for had it been otherwise, I would have danced once more—and then never again.

Now . . . I am dancing again and with deeper sources and more containment than ever before. I can only believe that though one may question events at the moment, there must be some overall purposeful pattern governing our lives.

There was no response.

One day in 1964, a call came from Alice Bingham, public relations assistant to Ben Sommers at Capezio. "Pauline, we haven't had an answer to your invitation for the Capezio Awards ceremony for José Limón."

"I never received an invitation, Alice. Nor do I think they would want me there."

"On the contrary. They specifically asked me to send it to you," she said.

"Well, I haven't received it, and if they want me to come I would want them to verify it by telling me so." The next morning I got a call from Pauline.

"I can't understand why the invitation didn't arrive. José specifically gave them your name."

"Yes," I said, "I'd be happy to attend. Thank you, Pauline."

When I arrived at the award party, José rushed up to me. "Pauline, my dear. I'm so happy you could come. You look marvelous."

It was hard for me to absorb. The greeting was as enthusiastic as in the earliest years, quite genuine. The last four years were washed away, blocked out for both of us. Undoubtedly José had heard about my activities and perhaps had also realized that mistakes should be accepted and forgotten. From that moment on, he went out of his way to make recommendations for very important assignments: to the Fulbright Committee that I be invited to Japan, to the North Carolina School of the Arts at its inception. José became one of my most ardent champions.

In 1967 the Limón company received an invitation from the Johnson White House to perform *The Moor's Pavane* at a state dinner honoring the King of Morocco. Much excitement. José wanted the original cast.

We had not danced together for seven years. Was it possible? My first thought was, Do they realize that Othello is hardly an admirable character? I even mentioned it, but we *did* want to dance at the White House. Our first rehearsal was a strange, touching homecoming. It was again a premiere—a premiere of four mature people tasting a seasoned work and discovering a freshness, a newness that astonished us. The *Pavane* was born again.

On February 19, when we arrived in the afternoon for orchestra rehearsal, the stage presented a problem: a raised platform at one end of the East Room, it had a crystal chandelier that hung over the center of the stage. Both men ran the risk of hitting it when they raised their arms or jumped. However it did make an elegant setting for this particular work.

We were told we would perform about 10 P.M., after dinner. As the late afternoon blended into evening we waited for someone to bring us some food. Nothing! Finally a message was sent that the dancers would need food. Sitting in my dressing room, knowing a lavish dinner would be served upstairs, I felt as if we were hired help, rather than performing guest artists. After some time a huge silver tray arrived, piled high with delicate little tea sandwiches of turkey and ham, the crusts of the bread meticulously trimmed. This was hardly the fare for two tall, hungry men and two women not so fragile as they looked. Solution—we discarded the postage-stamp bread, made layered sandwiches of turkey and ham, and washed it down with coffee. At least it would get us through the performance.

The performance went well. The king *seemed* pleased but the following morning, though the reviews of our performance were good, some did question the subject matter. Shortly thereafter, PBS videotaped the work because having the original cast was good publicity. We performed again on August 19, 1967, at the twentieth anniversary of the American Dance Festival. There were those in the audience who found it as thrilling as the premiere. *The Moor's Pavane* had lived on with the four of us, regardless of what had happened in the interim.

The last time I saw José was in New York. We met at a small Italian restaurant on 72nd Street. We sat and talked, and after his usual polite compliments—"Oh, Pauline you never looked better. You look simply ravishing"—the conversation hit a focal point. "Pauline, I've never spoken to anyone as I've spoken to you because we're both going through the same thing."

We were both involved with the tragedy of the human condition. Pauline was dying of cancer and José was deeply concerned. I was overwhelmed with the beauty of his feeling for her. Fritz had been ill for more than two years and I was facing the inevitability of his death. For the first time José and I were meeting in a realm where there was no competition. We were simply two people helping each other at a moment of great trial. I was grateful.

"It's funny," he said. "I'm the one who has had cancer, and now it is Pauline who is dying. The doctor says I am doing fine." It was winter 1971.

We hugged each other. "I'll see you soon," I said.

It never happened. José died December 2, 1972.

Alone Again

The Farewell/Solitary Song

When Doris Humphrey died, I felt numb and lost. She had given me new life. Now what? At the reception for the 1958 *Dance Magazine* Award, given to her posthumously, tears were streaming down my face during the moment of silent tribute. Later, Doris Hering asked, "Did Doris Humphrey really mean that much to you personally? Were the two of you really that close?" I answered, "I don't know. All I do know is that since her death she inhabits me. She is my dybbuk."

I kept recalling things I had heard in rehearsal: Learn containment — Go back to your original motivation — Think of your ending before you are half-finished — Look for new arm shapes, new body shapes — Asymmetry is challenge; symmetry is security — When finished, cut a dance by one third. Her voice was very real. As I worked alone, I felt her absent-presence, relied on it, and realized how much I had absorbed in those thirteen years. I wanted desperately to say, "Thank you, Doris, for rebirth, for helping me find myself, for guiding me to new discoveries." The only way I could do this was with dance, a tribute that might be worthy of her.

It was not until I had left the Limón company that I began seriously to think of a dance tribute. If anything helped recovery from my foot injury, it was the need to fulfill this desire. The big question was how; I needed a premise that would trigger my imagination. I knew I did not want to imitate or quote Doris's works. Her voice was in my ears, but I could not quite grasp the meaning.

Life, death, immortality. I brooded. Of life, we each find our own meaning, or at least struggle to do so; of death, no answer; but immortality? Doris was there with me, helping me. She was alive in the legacy of her spirit. That was immortality. I had found my seed of motivation.

One quiet evening in Hartford, Fritz and I were listening to Gustav Mahler's *Das Lied von der Erde*. The last movement is "Der Abschied," "The Farewell." I was listening closely to it, and the sound sang in my heart. I began to see images. The seed was growing. The songs are free translations from the Chinese poems of Li-Po. They deal with the "ephemeral beauty of the visible world, and the essential tragedy of human life, autumn following spring, old age, youth, and then the last farewell."*

I began to see a form for what I wanted to say. But could I use this sublime music? Could I live up to it? I turned to Fritz. "What do you think? Dare I use 'Der Abschied' for a solo dance? Will the orchestra be overpowering?"

"As a matter of fact," he said, "this last section is sparsely orchestrated. It is very transparent. With your musical sensitivity, I'm sure you can do something wonderful." He always encouraged me, but he was honest. Had he felt the music were wrong, he would have said so.

I listened again. The words of the poem were signals suggesting metaphoric images of my own life. The poem's lines, "The sun sinks behind the mountain / Evening falls in the valley,"* became in my own image, The sun is setting on my life / The shadows of my life enfold me. The work began to take form: a sequence of four dances—"To the Earth," "To Youth," "To Love," "The Last Farewell"—linked by two symbols—a white rope ringing the stage in a semicircular pattern, the memory line; a white elastic band, cutting diagonally across the stage, the lifeline.

I tried to strip away consciousness of externals and dig for essentials. What do we take with us in death? Only our deeply personal memories.

*From the note by Martin Cooper for the London Records recording.

What is left? Only what others may know or remember, only what we have illumined or inspired, great or small. I distilled these thoughts into two lines for my program note: Our shimmering memories we take with us, / The luminous self we leave to others.

When I create I must find a series of inner images that suggest fresh movement. I call it my "Inner Song." In performance it keeps me aware of why I am moving. A single phrase or a word from the original poetry suggested many images.

The first part was a ritual of nature. I am a woman in the autumn of life, sensing with ultimate awareness the beauty, the splendor of the earth. My image:

> I open the curtain of my withinness
> And see the earth anew for the first time.
> I touch the air, I embrace the air.
> The flowers grow, bloom bright
> Then close their petals in the twilight.

From this I found emotional color, a design in space, touching, embracing the air. From the shape of flowers growing, their curved roots, to opening buds and closing petals, I created twining movement for arms and legs, hands searching up into air, fingers bursting open and then circling space, a closing into myself. I discovered movement and shapes that were a revelation.

The words "Oh, beauty, oh life, oh intoxicated world" were the key to the second part. I knew the movement had to be light, airy, joyous, fast. I also knew that as a mature woman it was ridiculous to imitate youth. I had to find what I thought was its essence:

> Youth full of wonder
> and carefree delight,
> Sparkling joy, surprises
> dreaming, explorations.

The dynamics had to be sharp, quick changes of direction (youth changes its mind easily); moments of ecstasy, clapping gestures of joy, running patterns using space. The music was very slow, so working fast against it was the answer. This was also important for contrast in the piece as a whole. My first attempt was a disaster—I was trying too hard to be young by being too busy, too frenetic.

Then it came to me: You must not be young, but remember the feel of youth. I stripped the work down, doing a movement only once that in the earlier version I had repeated three times. By breathing with ease to sense lightness, rather than striving for a jump, I found movement that became youth. Instead of dreading its demands, as I had at the beginning, this movement became a joy. At the end of the dance I gathered up a section of the rope, a symbol of my memory of youth, and placed it on the lifeline.

What could I do with the third part, also a flashback? I cringed at the thought of sensuous, passionate, sexy dances I had seen. Definitely, no! Two lines from the "East Coker" section of T. S. Eliot's *Four Quartets* were the solution: "Love is most nearly itself / When here and now cease to matter." I patterned the body design, the space design, on roundness. It became a gentle dance, devoid of the pain of the here and now. My Inner Song was The ripeness, the fullness / The beauty, the warmth / My arms are round with / The renewal of life. At the end, I gathered the remaining segment of the memory line and carried it offstage, held high. I recognized that I, the woman must go / And I know that never again / Shall I feel, or have, or be.

The final section was an elegy of parting, my personal farewell To all the life lived and unlived / All the tears wept and unwept / All the dreams dreamt and undreamt. Each time I have performed it I have lived through these moments of finality: The desire to go back / The wish to go on / The anguish of the now / The burden of life is too great / And yet at this moment so trembling light / I weep to leave all that is left undone. In some mystic way I seemed to identify these feelings of my own mortality with those of Doris's. The elastic band across the stage, my lifeline, was a symbol of tears and burden, and I was caught in its meshes.

Toward the end I consciously paraphrased two movements from Doris's works: a *bourrée* José did in *Night Spell*, which I did with the lifeline in my hands; and a slow turn on a small platform that José did at the end of *Lament for Ignacio Sánchez Mejías*. I turned under the elastic, holding it high, then slowly walked toward the exit still holding it high as two people in the wings raised the ends to arm's-length. As I disappeared I let go. The lifeline snapped back to center stage, trembling, luminous in the empty space.

When the work was completed, I needed an objective opinion. The subject matter was sensitive, and I was apprehensive lest I had not lived up to it. Marcia B. Marks had written perceptively about my Elements course for *Dance Magazine*. She came, and afterward nodded her head. "It's beautiful," she said. "This is a very touching tribute to Doris. You must show it." Marcia was rarely given to superlatives. I took a deep breath. Then I allowed Mom to see it. At the end she was almost in tears. "Pauline, it's wonderful." Coming from Mom, who was my severest critic, I felt it must be true. Finally, when my lighting designer Nick Cernovich also agreed, I began to believe I had a meaningful work. Every time I rehearsed, I felt I had lived and died. Living a lifetime daily was nerve-wracking, but also revealing. It allowed me to discover nuances and greater depths.

The costumes suggested themselves as I worked. "Earth" was in autumn colors of orange and brown, a pleated skirt falling from the bodice, with an image of a bent tree from the back of the skirt over one shoulder, its branches spreading out on the bodice in front. For "Youth," chiffon, light pink shading in panels to an intense deep pink, flying loose, peignoir-style, in back. For "Love," red chiffon, draped bodice, one shoulder free, and yards and yards of skirt. For "Last Farewell" I reproduced the first costume, but in black, with a shaft of red rising from the back of the skirt ending at the heart.

For the three costume changes, I allowed intervals of music during which there were "gobos" (light projections, designed by Nick) on the cyclorama. Each introduced the mood of the piece to follow. Since I would not permit the music to be stopped, I had to rehearse the changes—thirty to forty seconds—with a stopwatch to be sure I could make my next entrance on cue. The changes were more demanding than the performance.

I called Ted Shawn. "I have a new work, Ted, a tribute to Doris. It's a half hour long and could fit into one of your programs. Are you interested in its first performance?" He definitely was, and requested further that I give a two-week Elements of Performing course. I accepted, anxious to try *The Farewell* on stage. Then an old back injury flared up—impossible to perform. Bitterly disappointed, I had to substitute a lecture on the Elements of Performing, which turned out to be very successful. I promised Ted a performance of *The Farewell* the following summer. Perhaps it was fateful. The delay allowed the work to mature and gave me time to look at it objectively. I was able to improve it before the first public performance.

In order to perform *The Farewell*, I now had to get dancers for *Concertino* and *The Shining Dark* to fill a program. The company was actually a trio: Deborah Jowitt and Carol Wallace, both quite tall dancers, and me. Before appearing in New York, we had to have an out-of-town tryout. That opportunity came at the Fourth Annual College Dance Festival in Richmond, Virginia. We had one performance on February 9, 1962, which constituted a preview of *The Farewell*. Fritz thought it would be wonderful if I could do it on one of his Hartford Symphony programs, so on February 28 I gave the official premiere of *The Farewell* with the Hartford Symphony Orchestra and mezzo-soprano Maria Kova from the New York City Opera. With my husband conducting, I knew the music would be perfect, and it was. There is no greater thrill for modern dancers, who rarely get to dance to a live orchestra, than to hear the music vibrantly welling up from the orchestra pit, filling the theater with true sound. With *Concertino* also on the program, the evening was a great success.

Now I was ready to face New York. I booked the 92nd Street YMHA for April 30, 1962. I arrived the day before for a space and light rehearsal, and found the floor like glass. Even the rubber on my ballet shoes had no traction. Nothing could be done that day. I demanded that the next morning the floor be scrubbed to remove the wax.

I spent a sleepless night worrying. At the theater the next morning, the stage surface was improved. I was in all three dances. There was no time for rest. I had to pull myself together while I put on makeup and try to forget the disturbance around me, digging deep into myself to find the life I had to live in *The Farewell*. I was nervous and bone-tired. *Concertino* went well, the adrenalin was working. The theater was full —this helped. When I started the last movement of *The Farewell*, I suddenly felt my thighs alternately go into spasm, then the calves. I was doing a crawl and was afraid I would not be able to stand up.

This had never happened before. My legs felt leaden and the pain almost unbearable. Panic-stricken, I reached the end of the dance with a sense of, Now I am finished. When I exited, there was dead silence. Then the applause started, weakly, and grew and grew. Later, backstage, I was told that most of the audience had been in tears, especially the many who had known Doris Humphrey. Somehow I had not expected this reception. John Martin wrote in the Sunday *New York Times* of May 13:

> She could not have expressed her gratitude [to Doris Humphrey] in a more substantial way. . . . Not emotional gratitude alone . . . but

tangible appreciation in terms of the work itself, for its composition, its texture, its substance bear eloquent testimony to Miss Humphrey's influence on the development and maturity of an admirable artist. . . . Through all the variants of her theme . . . she has been eloquent and intuitive. Instead of yielding subjectively to Mahler's profoundly moving song, she has rather drawn its substance to an edge, it is perhaps too deep to be called tender, but too elevated to be merely mournful. The closing *ewig—ewig* publishes not only finality, but also timelessness.

It was clear from the weakness I had suffered during the performance that a full program of dancing was now unwise. I developed a format for solo appearances: the first half a lecture, either The Creation of a Dance or The Elements of Performing; the second, a complete presentation of *The Farewell*. I was not afraid of doing an entire evening. What was difficult was the switch from speaking, an effort of the mind, to dancing a work from the heart. However, there were demands for this approach and I knew it was the only solution. I presented this solo evening at the University of Colorado, where I taught for the summer. Then I kept my promise to Ted Shawn and in mid-August performed *The Farewell* at Jacob's Pillow. The work remained in my performing repertoire for a decade and was filmed for the archive by New York Public Library's Dance Collection in 1971.

At the end of summer 1962 New York, where one still had to appear at least once a year, loomed. The lecture format would be impossible. I needed a program with a company, a company I could maintain for the future. I asked Norman Walker if he would be guest artist for a concert at the YMHA, and persuaded his partner Cora Cahan to dance with him. Deborah Jowitt and Carol Wallace agreed to join me again. Voilà! a company.

I wanted a bright, dancey work for the group to offset my serious pieces. I chose Aaron Copland's *Dance Symphony*, a fairly unknown composition. Named after the music, the dance was in three movements, "In Celebration of—Being—Discovering—Merrymaking." I made the first and last movements a quartet, the middle a duet for Norman and Cora.

To fill the program I started work on another solo, which was easier than always worrying about rehearsal schedules. In Fritz's record library I had found a wonderful piece of music by a Norwegian composer,

Fartein Valen, called *Cemetery by the Sea*. It had the lost, bleak character of much Scandinavian music. I began to improvise to it. The ambiance was one of isolation. I felt removed. Fritz was in Hartford most of the time.

I stood in the empty studio. My image was that of a lone bare tree, swaying in a cold and barren landscape. Sometimes I walked in mist; sometimes I became a leaf, wind-tossed from a concentric circle to a still center. I froze—a long icicle. For a moment, a wild cry, beating out against this aloneness, and then a realization. I was not lonely, I was alone. I must find my own true depth in that aloneness—a quiet acceptance swaying in the wind.

This had been the leitmotif of my life. Even with others, I had always felt apart. Aloneness need not be isolation, but a search for its various facets. For me it was the most difficult dance I ever had to do. To find the exact quality took an impossible kind of concentration, almost self-hypnosis. The movement phrases were long, extended, slow, minimal. This solo was the beginning of a series of works I created between 1962 and 1975 that I called *Solitary Songs: Opus I, II, III, IV.*

On November 30, 1963, I gave the planned performance at the 92nd Street Y. It was the only time I performed that first solitary solo in New York. Walter Sorell, writing for the December 8 *Providence Sunday Journal*, said: "*Solitary Song* . . . is a memorable solo of dramatically heightened feeling of aloneness. A swinging wide circular pattern was filled with movement phrases in which the recurrence of the tilted head framed by closed arms recreated a withdrawn image. The intensity, the dynamic power . . . has not led accumulatively to a climactic point in this dance, but seemed evenly distributed and consciously restrained in order to stress isolation."

Though the concert was well received and a few engagements followed, it was obvious that keeping the company together was impossible. The only answer was to function alone, to teach, lecture, dance whenever possible, and create—my deepest motivation for living. Accustomed to the discipline of daily working alone in a studio, I felt driven to carry on. The year 1964 was difficult. Fritz had left Hartford and we now lived in our New York apartment. Neither of us knew what the future would hold. Although we tried to maintain a cheerful façade, both of us had moments of desolation.

What buoyed my spirits and gave me courage was being named one of three to receive the 1964 *Dance Magazine* Award. The citation read:

"To Pauline Koner: She offers a unique sense of perfection to the art of performing, and her most recent works add an inspiring new dimension to the medium of solo dance." John Martin, in his presentation speech, made note of my "two works that I think are probably her loveliest. One is *The Farewell* . . . a very deeply moving and fine piece of work. And last winter she did it again with another piece called *Solitary Song*, which has some of the most remarkable phrasing that I have ever seen."

In the studio I delved farther into my sense of aloneness and apartness. There were times I needed it and enjoyed it, even found in it a moment of inner peace from my anxieties. I heard a piece of music, "When the Bells Justle," from Lukas Foss's *Time Cycle*. It was a sparkling, luminous work for voice and orchestra, with some striking dissonances. The text was by A. E. Housman: "When the bells justle in the tower . . . The taste is sour."

The music was in sharp contrast to the first *Solitary Song*. This, I thought, would add a new dimension—wonder, a zany laughter at self, anxiety banished for a moment, and at the end acceptance of aloneness as the core of living. The second of my *Solitary Songs* became "Wondrous Moment."

I never had the opportunity to perform it in New York, but did present it at Jacob's Pillow in July 1966. To the original, simple, pearl-gray costume of the first *Song*, I added a diaphanous, flowing gray-pink robe. At the end of the dance, I dropped the robe and returned to the final music and movement of *Solitary Song: Opus I*.

I now had *Solitary Songs: Opus I and II* and, just as composers often use and re-use themes to develop a basic concept, I returned to these pieces as a source. In 1973 I was conducting a technique workshop in Manila, when I was unexpectedly asked for a choreographic work as well. I had used Luciano Berio's four-movement *Sinfonia* in improvisation classes, and the music had taken hold of me. The Samuel Beckett words as well as improvised words in the score grew meaningful. Unconsciously, I had been relating them to *Solitary Songs*. Here again was the theme of isolation; deep within all of us the nucleus is there. We are born a lone being, we die a lone being, and most of us spend the time between trying to overcome our innate loneliness. Luckily, I had this music with me and could use some of the thematic material from my earlier solos as a springboard for another *Solitary Song*, this time for a group of four girls and three boys. As I worked, new material evolved. I created characteristic themes for one who feels boxed in, for one who searches, for one who is angry, for one who screams in lost-ness, like Edvard Munch's *The Cry*. It fascinated me.

I had blocked the first movement when I received the news of Fritz's death and flew home. Returning to Manila, I worked out material for the second movement on Evelyn Shepard, whom I had brought along as an assistant. The words of the vocal line were very simple: "Martin Luther King." We worked in our apartment and the movement poured out of me, not a lament, a homage. I taught it to the company. The first two movements began to look good.

I started the third and was stymied. Nothing worked. Time was draw-ing short and rehearsal time was always problematical. I decided that these two movements were complete. The second was so simple, so mysteriously ecstatic, that it seemed I could not top it. This was *Solitary Song: Opus III*. They never performed it, preferring *Concertino* instead, but it was videotaped.

Back once more at the North Carolina School of the Arts, I was more apart than ever, following my own path, not belonging when new staff joined. I was haunted by the Berio work and decided to stage it for a student performance. The response from the dancers and the audi-ence was unexpected: "Please complete this work, you must—you can."

I was not at all sure, but if ever I would, I felt this would be the time. After two unsuccessful tries, some of Beckett's words grew insistent: "Keep going. Where going? Why going?" Many times I had watched people in crowded areas, rushing in all directions, yet each alone. I saw the third movement. I saw people always passing, never meeting, never caring, crazy laughter turning sour. Momentary reaching for contact and then apart. Individuals, nations, the world falling apart. Everyone fading away to nothingness. The fourth movement of the music, segueing from the third, was perhaps a distant hope, a wish-fulfillment. Somehow we must learn compassion in order to care for each other, to break the isolation, to feel the need for communication. I bound the dancers in a linked circle, breathing together as one. The third and fourth movements became *Opus IV*.

Solitary Songs was complete, drawing from time past and time future into the now. It is still my leitmotif: I follow my own direction, I search for compassion, I search for communication.

In fall 1964, I received a letter from the Fulbright-Hayes Commission saying that Japan had requested an American modern dancer to conduct a workshop in technique and choreography and asking if I would be interested in going for a year. This was the first time a dance grant was being offered. I had few plans and felt as if Fate had stepped in. I responded that much as I would love to spend a year in Japan, I had other obligations, but would consider six months.

My early association with Japanese dancers and intrinsic love of the Orient made Japan irresistible. A call from Washington, D.C.: the Japanese sponsors had accepted my proposal. I was so excited, I was sure I had not heard correctly, and asked them to repeat it. "Yes," they said, "you will begin in mid-January." Documents were signed, and it became a reality. I busied myself gathering books, music, teaching notes. I also took my *Farewell* costumes and props.

There was a fascinating three-day briefing session in Washington for all the scholars. We were told about Japanese customs and warned what to do and what not to do. To say I was slightly terrified is to put it mildly. Fritz gave me names of people who had been helpful to him when he was in Tokyo conducting the Japan Philharmonic. I had no idea of the state of modern dance in Japan, no idea of the living and working conditions.

I arrived in Tokyo on January 18, 1965, and was met at the airport by a Fulbright representative. We immediately hit a snag: my visa was in the wrong category, good for three years rather than one, and three-year visas needed a Ministry of Justice certificate. The entire immigration staff ran around; no one would or could make a decision. I felt as though I were in the midst of a crazy operetta.

After an hour I was given a temporary permit, and finally arrived at International House at 2 A.M., Tokyo time, 7 A.M., U.S. time. I was exhausted and already homesick. How was I ever going to get anything done in this strange, unknown environment with a language barrier? The following day, without much rest, I was taken to the United States Educational Commission to meet their executives. One of them, Mrs. Maki, became a trusted friend and adviser.

Then I was taken to the Tokyo-American Cultural Center to see the hall where classes would be held. There I met Sumio Kam'bayashi, whose specialty was aesthetics, with a particular interest in dance. Assigned to work with me and translate for classes, he took it upon himself to brief me on Japanese culture. We hit it off immediately, and suddenly the future looked brighter.

From there we went on to the Embassy to meet the personnel of the United States Information Service (USIS), then on to the International Artists Center to see the director, Mr. Kimura. There were 200 applications for the workshops; we would have to audition for classes. I was so tired I began to lose track of time. After dinner at the Officers Club, I reached home at 10 P.M., completely spent after my first day in Tokyo.

The following day I had at last a few moments to settle in. International House, a hotel for visiting scholars, had been an old Mitsubishi estate. My room was simple. A beautiful *shoji* screen opened onto a balcony that looked out on a Japanese garden. It was built on several levels, with lanterns lining the paths, hidden stone benches, and little ponds. Just to open the screen and see the garden was a calming experience, and many times a twilight stroll in the garden eased the weariness of the first days. Not at all calming was an earth tremor that hit at 4 A.M. I did not know what to do. Did one stay in, or run out? I soon learned that this could be an almost daily occurrence. During class we would all freeze for a few seconds and then go on. It felt like standing on Jello. If the tremor was sideways, there was no danger; if it was up and down, then it was serious. It gave me a strange sense of excitement.

Tokyo was not a beautiful city. There were tall modern buildings jutting out above tiny little Japanese houses and small open shops. The kimonos hanging to dry on bamboo rods looked almost like a stage set. I soon learned the marvelously organized subway system. It was in a subway car that I realized everyone's hair was as dark as mine. There was a startling unity of appearance.

Modern dance was in its early stages. A few dancers had been to the United States and studied with Martha Graham, and one of the leading schools was that of Takaya Eguchi, who had studied with Mary Wigman. I was invited to observe a class. The weather was cold, so I wore woolen socks, two sweaters, a winter coat, a wool hat, and *froze* as I sat watching the students—barefoot, no sweaters, no leg warmers, some in low-cut sleeveless leotards.

Eguchi gave a very interesting class. His method was to develop from one movement a constant series of variations. One exercise started with a bouncing movement of the feet, then went into various leg and body movements, always linked by the bouncing ground base. There was no sharpness or punctuation; everything was sustained. But this was evidently the problem for that day. The trick for staying warm was never to stop. There were some marvelous girls, all of whom had extremely limber backs and high extensions.

I also observed a class by Midori Ishii, a disciple of Baku Ishii. The class was a mixture of styles—ballet barre, ending in acrobatic splits and roll-overs, then combinations influenced by Graham, Limón, and ballet, all out of context.

At the cultural center we established a plan for my workshops: advanced technique (thirty-five students), intermediate technique (thirty), and choreography (forty-one to forty-five). The more advanced group could show assignments once a month to the others. I also scheduled time for myself to practice daily. The schedule was demanding, but the enthusiasm buoyed me up.

Word travels fast, and it soon spread that what I was giving was not competitive, but illuminating. Directors of dance schools, teachers, and dancers who had already made reputations and had schools and companies of their own came as students or observers. Distracting as visitors were, with the feeling that I was always on stage, I had to be polite and bear with it because the point of my visit was to reach as many in the dance world as possible.

Saeko Ichinohe was a devoted student and took her first choreography class in my workshop. Mariko Sanjo never missed a class. Bonjin Atsuge occasionally attended. I knew that the influence of the classes had taken hold when I saw performances by these dancers and recognized the change. My main theme, however, was "Please do not try to imitate me. I do not want you to take what I give you as an absolute. I want you to apply the principles of my movement, of my theories, and then use your Japanese roots. Use your heritage, but expand in new directions. Don't be imitation American dancers."

In addition to all the teaching, meetings, and group discussions, I was besieged by press and photographers. I had to be very careful about what I said—just like everywhere else, internal politics played a part in the Japanese dance scene. I always thought through in advance not only the material, but the manner in which I should express it. At one major press conference I was asked about American modern dance and had to be very cautious not to appear biased.

The pleasantest activity was being taken to see every dance performance possible. Modern dance performances were slightly naïve, sentimental—characterized by the costuming, which tended to be fancy leotards with wispy ways of draping a bit of fabric. Very few concerts had choreographic interest, although there were many excellent dancers.

My first visit to the Kabuki Theatre was enlightened by Kam'bayashi-san. He translated for me and expounded on the various traditional styles. The theater was enormous. A ramp, called *hanamichi*, ran from the back of the left side of the audience to the stage. The important characters made their entrance on this ramp, and some of the action took place on it as well. A chanter and samisen player sat high up on stage left, while percussion players sat on a red cloth stage right. The visual beauty of the actors' costumes in elaborate silks and brocades, the sliding platforms, elevators and stage mechanics, were a challenge to absorb.

Most interesting was the dexterity of the stagehands dressed in black, with head and faces masked, who worked on stage in full view. I found that what they did with such speed and precision was fascinating choreography. All was done so calmly that they blended into the theatrical concept. Still more impressive was the actor's power of concentration during long pauses. The thread of continuity was never lost, this in spite of the fact that the house was always dimly lit.

The audience was, for me, part of the show. They came with lunch boxes, chopsticks, bottles of soya, bags of tangerines, and ate throughout the performance and intermission. A play could last four or five hours. This was completely new in my experience, and it took me time to be able to concentrate on the stage. For the actors, such behavior evidently was not even noticed or was part of the theater experience.

Noh was an ancient theater tradition that demanded patience and understanding from the viewer, who in turn was rewarded with a purity and stylization of drama. Almost a ritual, Noh gave one a sense of timelessness—the bare stage, with a pine tree painted on the background, the bridgelike ramp along which the actors made their entrance with a slow gliding walk on a satiny, polished wood floor. I was told one must study for years simply to achieve that walk. The costumes were heavy, medieval, brocade robes. Female characters wore their hair hanging long in back and wound with ribbon both below the neck and farther down. The masks denoted the characters. All the action was extremely slow, so that every moment of movement was visible.

The beauty and power of Noh also lay in the concentration. Noh was even more intense than Kabuki, more hypnotic in its minimal slow-motion. The detail and subtlety of single isolated movements lent it power. Here I learned that less is more.

It was incredible to hear that many of my students had never seen a Noh play or watched Kabuki drama. American films and rock music interested them instead. Coffee houses played records at peak level, while the young people sipped coffee and drank in the music with their ears.

Folk dancing was very popular in Japan. I watched a group of dancers rehearsing for a tour. A carpenter from Nagasaki was teaching them a marvelous dragon dance, the dragon made like an accordion, so that it could stretch, contract, and coil into unusual shapes.

Since I was particularly interested in Japanese classical dance, I was invited to see a rehearsal conducted by Kabuki-actor Kinosuki Hanayagi. He was training a group of geisha for a special performance. The rehearsal was in an old part of Tokyo. The studio had a stage and a large *tatami* floor. The girls, in cotton rehearsal kimonos and no makeup, were very unattractive. Probably with the stylized makeup and wigs they looked better. The dance was in unison, with the typical pigeon-toed foot movement and very interesting fan manipulation.

Then a geisha dressed me up: an underkimono, two or three undersashes, a small pillow in the back of the *obi* sash, with all sorts of strings (there are no buttons) so that the middle of the body feels rigid. The kimono was wrapped so tightly about the legs and knees that the feet had to take tiny steps. No wonder the toes turned in. I thought it would be fun to learn some of the movement, but found the kimono so confining it was impossible to bend. I could not even put on my *tabi* (socks). Help in dressing was a necessity.

Soon after my arrival, I was approached by NHK Educational Television to work on a program to be filmed April 18, 1965. From five minutes it grew to thirty, which meant a great deal of preparation. I had been rehearsing my *Solitary Songs* solos and wanted to have them filmed; they wanted a lecture-demonstration. We reached an agreement to film both while we were in the studio. Those films in practice clothes are the only record, and were of tremendous help in later years.

March 2–5 was devoted to a Fulbright conference held outside of Tokyo at a *ryokan*, a Japanese-style inn. A decision was made that I would teach until May 16, take a month to prepare for a performance in Tokyo about the middle of June, then do two weeks of lecture demonstrations in the "Kansai" area. This meant requesting a longer stay in Japan, and by now I had become so enamored of it that I hated the thought of leaving. From time to time, I had moments of homesickness for family, but these were quickly dispelled by all the attention I was getting from students, friends, and the press. I justified my acceptance with, I may never have this opportunity again. I must grasp and use every minute of my stay.

Kam'bayashi-san brought to one of my rehearsals a dance critic, Natsuya Mitsuyoshi, whom I dubbed the John Martin of Tokyo. He had an index-card file on dancers, subscribed to all the dance publications, and had material on me that I myself had forgotten. He spoke perfectly understandable English, but always apologized. He was also a photography critic, and endeared himself to me when he said that my brother was a big name in Japan. Mitsuyoshi took me to festivals and showed me wonderful pageantry, old shrines, and the double-blossom cherry trees in the famous Shinjuku gardens.

I had the good fortune to attend a performance of the ancient court Bugaku, given only twice a year, outdoors at Meiji shrine. The stage was a square raised platform in the courtyard, black lacquer floor, red lacquer railing, and the central dancing space covered with green velvet carpeting. The costumes were magnificent. They also used spears and shields. The dances were slow, majestic, the arms usually fully extended to make a design of the huge sleeves. Head movement was sparse and sharp, the hands were rarely used; most of the movement was in the feet and knees. Since this was theater in the round, the dancers did the movement in all directions. Again I found the concentration hypnotic.

I also became an aficionado of Bunraku. The puppets' infinitely detailed movement took over and became lifelike. Mitsuyoshi-san also took me to see a Japanese striptease, which was delicate and charming. "You know," he said, "I took Ted Shawn to see this."

My workshops were making great progress. The technique classes created a range of movement new for the students, and the choreography classes began to show studies that were original and provocative. Open classes on April 20 and 22 had about forty observers, among whom I noticed quite a few professional dancers and choreographers. Mr. Takeachi, who was choreographer for Ballet Moderne Bleu, said all Tokyo would be talking. The choreographer for the Takarazuka Theatre in Osaka also came.

Since this was the first project in dance for Fulbright, it carried with it extra responsibility. It was up to me to make the workshops a success. All these months I had felt the pressure, the challenge. Now I could relax a little; I was told they intended to continue the program.

Of the few modern dance performances I saw, I was impressed by only two works, one of them by a student of mine, Tanagashima. The work was a requiem for a lover and a duet. The second piece was by a girl, Kamizaka. It was a Japanese primitive performed to sound effects of wind, water, natural sounds, and strange inarticulate vocal sounds, like an effort toward language. Both these works intrigued me with their unusual vocabulary and feeling of Japanese heritage.

At the last day of classes everyone was enthusiastic. I had asked the students to bring questions for a final discussion to round out the course. Having heard that Japanese students rarely asked questions, I expected just a few. To my astonishment they prepared enough questions for a two-week seminar. Some brought costumes for criticism. I answered as many questions as possible, and hoped we could continue in July.

The final question was, "Koner-san, when will you perform?" I told them the performance had been canceled for fear of a lack of audience.

Mr. Kimura, director of the cultural center, resented the fact that my lecture tour would be supervised by the USIS. He felt that it compromised his prestige. Furthermore, since the classes had been profitable, stopping them to do a performance might mean financial loss. Kimura even stated (never having seen me perform) that I was not as good a performer as I was a teacher. Learning how negative he was, I was furious, but simply said, "I'd rather not give a performance."

The students rallied to my cause. Not only did they write to the Embassy, but one of the dancers delivered the letter personally. Mitsuyoshi-san, who was present and witnessed all this, contacted the All-Japan Art Dance Association, which agreed to sponsor the performance, but only if Kimura was out. My supporters and I met, set a budget, and outlined a flyer. Yes, there *would* be a performance.

I was touched by the enthusiasm of the dancers in taking batches of tickets to sell. I also met a most intelligent lighting designer and discussed the light cues. The next day he came with a fantastic layout of the stage. The colors! It was a work of art.

I set to work on a script for the lecture part, which had a specific rhythm. Kam'bayashi-san translated and maintained this rhythm. There seemed to be endless detail for this one appearance, but everyone was so eager to help, I was sure it would all pull together. I trained two girls, one of them Saeko, to help with the costume changes for *The Farewell.* On June 14, when I arrived at the theater for light rehearsal, everyone was eating lunch. I had to rehearse with the music and costume changes in work light. I was terribly worried. At a point like this, I always say, "I will never do this again." On June 15, I arrived at the theater at 1 P.M. Nothing was ready and I was panicky. At two o'clock I had a run-through with lights. It was working out. I also was told that the tickets were sold out.

I was moved when I saw how the girls who were helping me had made the dressing room into a place of comfort and rest. They had placed two tea roses on the table and had brought coffee and vegetables. A tatami mat was ready in a corner, in case I had time to rest. Some of the dressing tables were set for our dinner. This was their way of making work more like play, life more pleasant.

The lecture went like a dream. My brain was clear and vibrant. I could feel the excitement of the audience. Kam'bayashi-san was following through with translations in great style. After intermission, I performed *The Farewell*. At the end, the audience applauded loud and long, a rare occurrence in Japan.

Several of my students, dressed in their finest kimonos, came on stage with bouquets of flowers. I was presented with an exquisite Noh mask made by the most famous maskmaker in Nara. When I thanked them I broke into tears at this demonstration of appreciation from the students and the Japanese people. The thought came to me: Here I am, thirty-six years after dancing with Michio Ito, finally appearing in Tokyo and being accepted on my own terms.

After two intensive weeks on the USIS tour, lecturing in Fukuoka, Osaka, Kyoto, Nara, and Nagoya, I was happy to get back to Tokyo. I was exhausted, but delighted to hear that I had a reservation on a brand new United States Line freighter for the return home.

Now when I attended a modern dance performance, I found several of my students participating. Their dances had better form and greater originality, particularly in arm shapes and foot use. It was rewarding to see that all my hard work had been worthwhile. I resumed teaching in Tokyo on July 15, eager to see small compositions that many of my students had prepared.

One was rarely invited to the home of a Japanese—usually the invitation was to a restaurant—so I was pleased when Mariko invited Kam'bayashi-san and me to dinner at her parents' home. Another welcome invitation was from Akeo Watanabe, the conductor of the Japan Philharmonic. Learning that I was very interested in Noh drama, he and his wife invited Kotoku Yamaguchi, a Noh actor from the Kanze school, to teach me a few elements. I was particularly interested in the slow, gliding steps of the ceremonial walk. The woman raises the foot halfway with the heel still touching the floor and steps forward only the length of her foot. The man takes a longer step and raises the toe higher. A ghost starts with longer steps. Turning is done with both feet on the floor.

Determined to take some lessons in Japanese classical dance, I was on the lookout for possibilities. I had passed a house with a small sign, "O Han San." It seemed mysterious. Intrigued, I inquired, and was told that it was a very exclusive restaurant, only for private guests, owned by Takehara Han. She was one of the outstanding classical dancers of the juta-mai style of Kyoto. She had been one of the most exclusive geisha of her time; according to custom the geisha's sponsor provided for her future. I had seen Takehara Han perform; she was subtle and understated and her concentration and focus were without peer. I asked Mitsuyoshi-san if I might have lessons with her. He thought it would be difficult. When I was told, "Yes!" I trembled with excitement. At last I would try the authentic movement.

A high wooden wall enclosed a garden. Taking off my shoes, I entered another world. The house was the finest Japanese architecture, beautiful rooms of wood varying from neutral tans to browns, with variations in texture. The studio was small—juta-mai is done in minimal space. One wall was mirrored. The wood floor was polished to a satinlike finish. Takehara Han was fragile, small-boned, delicate, not pretty—beautiful. I had brought along a *yukata* (summer kimono) and *tabi*. Kam'bayashi-san came along to translate.

Takehara Han had an assistant. They did not teach by analysis, but by imitation, even placing the body. For me this was a totally new sensation. I was given a fan to work with. The use of the fan and the long hanging kimono sleeves were very important and complicated. The feet were comparatively simple. The style was mainly the nuance of the head and use of the eye. Emphasis on upper-body movement defined mai. Watching the Japanese dancers' delicacy, I felt terribly awkward.

Two days later I had my second lesson and was taught a dance called "Black Hair." Since I am accustomed to learning intellectually, I found it difficult to learn by having my arms and hands placed into position. The continuity of movements was not clear to me. After the lesson, O Han-san's sister took me to the upper part of the house, which was the living quarters, and performed the tea ceremony for me. It was a very special courtesy. O Han-san came in with a little note in English, "I am giving a party tonight for my friends. Will you please join us?"

It was a birthday party. Among the guests were leading intellectuals and artists. A row of teakwood tables was set along the center of the room, and we sat on purple velvet cushions. Each dish was presented on a masterpiece of pottery, with food laid out for color and design almost like a painting. The pièce de résistance was a large basket of molded ice filled with tofu.

Takehara Han did not eat with us. Her sister served the food with helpers. One of the movable studio walls facing the salon had been opened. Silver screens were drawn to shield the mirrors. The studio was now a stage, with a small garden dividing salon and stage. Between courses Takehara performed two dances, which for me were the ultimate of classical dance.

The guests then insisted I show them what I had learned. I was terribly embarrassed, but it would have been an insult to refuse. I could not remember a thing. The assistant sat in a corner and cued me in the "Black Hair." I thought I was terrible, but everyone, being polite, said it was amazing how I had absorbed the Japanese style.

My duties were still not over. I still had to face a repeat of my lecture-performance for the Japanese Classical Dance Society on August 3. I would have to surmount all their previous resistance to modern dance. I made a concentrated effort and worked hard in advance to make this a special event. The stage was small, so I had to hold back, but everything went perfectly. The house was full. The lecture was recorded by a stenographer and filmed. Afterward there were questions, much bowing and thanking. I was presented with a most beautiful fan by Mitsugoro Bando, one of the leading Kabuki actors. He said I had pointed out many things he had been stressing. Then my assistants, the stage help, and I were served lunch in the dressing room—a lovely Japanese custom.

As a final duty I judged with Mitsuyoshi-san and Eguchi at the Fulbright auditions for grants to Japanese modern dancers to come to America. Bonjin Atsugi, Mariko Sanjo, and Kyoko Kudo auditioned. I also recommended Saeko Ichinohe and Mitsui Maeda for travel grants; Saeko has made a fine career for herself.

Finally, I was ready to leave Japan. The boat was leaving from Yokohama, and of course all my friends and students wanted to see me off on August 13. I did not know that I should have had refreshments available, and when I tried to buy some on the boat I was told it was impossible until we left port. I apologized for my ignorance, and was able to serve small snacks from the gifts I had received. The leavetaking was very emotional.

The boat sailed around 7:30 P.M. The tugs towing the ship from the dock heaved and pulled as the ship moved slowly away, and the lights from the harbor dimmed slowly as we passed the blinking buoys and pushed into an opaque darkness. I had a strange, sinking feeling as the lights faded. After an intense experience of seven months, I was in a vacuum, wondering where life would take me. Torn between a desire to remain and a wish to return home, I took with me a new perspective of sensitivity, tolerance, and patience.

North Carolina School of the Arts

When I received the invitation to teach at the North Carolina School of the Arts, I hardly had time to adjust from Japan to New York before I whizzed down to Winston-Salem. It was early September 1965. I met Robert Lindgren to discuss plans and was disarmed when he said, "Look at me, a high school dropout, and now I'm Dean of Dance." With his professional background in the Ballet Russe de Monte Carlo and the New York City Ballet, I knew the emphasis would be on ballet. Modern dance? Since José and Agnes de Mille were on the advisory board, modern dance was at least included in the curriculum. Bobby admitted he would leave it to me and Duncan Noble to follow our own paths.

The ballet department consisted of Lindgren and his wife Sonja Tyven (Taanila), a charming and perceptive person. Duncan taught both ballet and modern dance. I was to teach technique, composition, and Elements of Performing. With New York and performing still an important part of my career, it was agreed that I would come down each week for three days, and Duncan would take over when I was away.

Commuting like this seemed a little wild, but I could not resist the promise of the school's potential.

No sooner had I begun this new schedule than I received a call from Anna Sokolow: "A national Jewish organization is planning a gala devoted to Jewish composers and performers. They have asked me to choreograph William Schuman's *Judith*. I wonder if you would be interested in dancing it?" I was quite surprised. I had seen and admired Anna's work, but we had evolved from very different styles of movement. I had always intended to choreograph *Judith* myself, but it would be an interesting and challenging experience to work with Anna. There was honesty and sincerity in her work that I felt I could meet.

From mid-September we spent weekends working. Anna had an idea, I followed through with movement that stemmed from her motivation, but that suited my body. We worked very well together. The performance, to be played by the Oakland Symphony, was to take place at the War Memorial Opera House in San Francisco. Anna kept telling me not to worry because the stage would be extended to accommodate dance, a good lighting designer had been engaged, and the costume would be made in New York. She promised that she would come to California to supervise the performance. For me that was important; the strain of a new teaching project, the commuting, and the rehearsing were wearying.

I arrived in San Francisco to find that nothing had been done about extending the apron of the stage, so there was absolutely no space to dance in front of the orchestra. The lighting was nil. The costume, a woolen affair, refused to follow my body lines. I got in touch with a local costume designer, and every free moment was spent trying —unsuccessfully—to refit the dress. They finally did extend the stage and bring in a few spots, but at this point it was best just to get it over with. The next day the papers called *Judith* the highlight of the evening. Anna, unable to come, never did see it.

The North Carolina School of the Arts was the dream of the writer John Ehle, who was Governor Terry Sanford's special assistant for new projects. He had persuaded the governor, who was cultivated and interested in the arts, to support legislation for a state-sponsored school of the performing arts, the first of its kind in this country. In 1963, legislation was passed with the help of composer Vittorio Giannini, who was appointed president. Some called it the "Tippy-toe Bill," but one strongly pro legislator concluded, "If there is going to be toe-dancing,

I want to be there," and he probably was. Open to statewide bidding for a location, Winston-Salem set up an impromptu phone bank and in forty-eight hours of calling, spearheaded by R. Philip Hanes of the Hanes Knitting Mills, 1,000,000 dollars was raised. The city contributed an abandoned high school, and the Ford Foundation contributed 1,500,000 dollars. The school was launched.

At the outset, there was just the one old building with three dance studios (including the old gym), an auditorium, some classrooms, a cafeteria, and practice rooms for the musicians as its center. An old field house became the drama building, with studios and a small performing space. What we lacked in facilities, we compensated for with hope and a vision of what we were striving for and how we would grow. Because this school was a new and exciting challenge, the spirit of both the student body and faculty was at a high pitch. My own personal dream of doing works that used all the component resources—music, drama, dance, design, and production—could flourish.

That first year there were only 250 students, 45 in dance, of whom 12 were modern dance majors. Since the school offered academics —junior high through college—schedules varied, so that trying to create a dance curriculum was a major problem. The modern dance was given what we called "the dungeon," a studio on the basement level. It was damp, with a difficult floor, but no one complained. In modern, all levels were in one class. Students were approved by audition; a few with inadequate ballet training were advised to take modern. Modern dance was tolerated, rather than accepted. Slowly I could see a change in the dancers. Some, who had had no previous modern training, began to blossom and discover new ways of moving.

This was the first time I could look forward to a continuous teaching schedule and begin to devise a method of basic movement principles that would unfold as time went on. I found that most students lacked rhythmic training. Exercises are usually given in 4/4 or 3/4, so I tried to plot exercises using 5's, 7's, syncopations, and alternating symmetric and asymmetric rhythms. This changed the quality of a movement as well as stimulated the mind. Then there was position: ballet stressed turnout, modern a more natural stance. The well-trained body needed to be trained for both, so I devised exercises based on rotation. Movement that was usually done in the turned-out position I turned in as well, and vice versa. I developed a series of short dance études for the various stretches. I applied to technical exercises the use of one's own voice, which created a new dimension of intensity. I tried to instill the concentration that made oriental dance so powerful. Some unusual movement grew out of all this new technique. That could happen only in a school where there were no transient students.

Midway in the first school year I gave an enthusiastically received lecture-demonstration, which included a performance of *The Farewell*. Not having my costumes with me, I was fortunate to have Christina Giannini of the costume department design accessories to superimpose on my lecture dress (she did wonderful costumes for some of my later works). The local reviewer wrote that more such programs would greatly increase the audience for modern dance throughout the country.

For the end of the 1965–66 year I planned a technique demonstration, based on the principles of my approach, as an incentive for the students. This was a school of *performing* arts; it was important to expose the dancers to this very vital element. Within their still-limited capacities, I put together a choreographed class and talked about basic movement principles. I had music composed by Evelyn Lohoefer, whom I knew from New London days. The continuity of material was paced dynamically for constant interest. We performed on May 25, 1966—it was a real sleeper! No one had expected anything so professional from a year-old modern dance department. Agnes de Mille was there, and afterward she said, "This is one of the most terrific demos I have ever seen. You ought to copyright it immediately."

In spring 1968, to give the unfledged dancers more performing experience and spur their technical study, we undertook a two-week tour, giving performances in North Carolina high schools. I arranged a program that would be accessible to young people, most of whom had never seen live dance before. The tour became a staple of the curriculum, eventually including my *Concertino* and *Poème* and, after he joined the faculty, Job Sander's *Screenplay* (all in full costume), and always a section of student compositions.

We did two performances a day, in different schools, the first at 9 A.M., the second at 2 P.M. We carried our own lights and sound and the dance students helped as stage technicians. There were no dressing rooms, so we had to get ready beforehand. The 6 A.M. scene: Georgiana Holmes (who went on to dance with Louis Falco, Jennifer Muller, Pilobolus, and my own company) perched on top of the dresser, peering into the mirror to make up; my niece Pamela on the bed, struggling to secure the chignon and multicolored ribbons for *Concertino*; talented

Alana Holloway stretching in a split on the floor—then off to the school by 8:30. There was never time to pace the stage; the dancers had to assess the space visually.

Sometimes the audiences were difficult. Despite much talk of desegregation, we found most schools mainly all black or all white. I forestalled the older tough guys from sneering at boys in tights or whistling at the girls by telling them that the leotard was originated by a male circus trapeze artist named Léo Tard. I equated male movement to sports and explained each work as the program progressed. For me the challenge was to create a sympathetic atmosphere in a sometimes hostile environment, to develop an awareness and response to art. At the end there was usually a standing ovation.

After the first school year, finding that weekly commuting was self-destructive, I expanded my stays to two weeks, then finally arranged to be in residence for three five-week periods each year. Guest teachers were invited for the alternate periods, among them Valerie Bettis. As enrollment and the department grew, Nelle Fisher and Richard Kuch were added to the faculty and Richard Gain became my permanent alternate.

My appetite for the East was satisfied once more by a State Department-sponsored swing through India and Southeast Asia: New Delhi, Bombay, Calcutta, Bangkok, Singapore, and Seoul. Through March and April 1967 I was to present lecture-demonstrations, seminars, technique workshops, and portions of my choreography to dancers and teachers starved for new stimulation. In turn, I had the chance to absorb all their indigenous dance forms and to meet many of the artists. Dance activity was boiling, especially in India, but there was an undercurrent of competitiveness and, as in Japan, I had to tread carefully.

In New Delhi I stayed at the Ashoka Hotel, where I spent half the first night trying to get my room operating. The bathroom electric plug and the hot water were not functioning. When someone came, after my frantic calls, the door lock jammed—I was locked in. I finally got it open to find two porters ready to move me to another room, but I had already unpacked. By this time a mechanic had shown up and at last got everything working. I fell into bed at 1:30 A.M., feeling as if I had participated in a Marx Brothers movie.

My main stint in New Delhi was a two-day seminar on choreography at the Sangeet Natak Akademie. Question and discussion sessions were included and produced a lively repartée. Dancers here were ripe for change, but did not know how to break with age-old tradition to create a new form.

In Calcutta, I was conducted around by a rather concerned Sigmund Cohen, assistant cultural attaché, who admitted that he did not know what a dance symposium should be. He need not have worried; dancers from all over the subcontinent convened, in spite of a fierce Hindu-Sikh uprising the day before. Sig and I had gotten caught in the middle of it—Sikhs advancing toward us brandishing swords, sticks, and bottles; Hindus closing in behind. We managed to extricate ourselves. No deaths were reported, but that evening there was a curfew.

A second symposium was held at Visva-Bharati, Rabindranath Tagore's university at Shantiniketan. The place gave me a strange feeling, as if it were a retreat removed from this world, consecrated as it was to the life of the great poet and philosopher. The session took place in Tagore's own home, in the studio where he had rehearsed his dance dramas. It was exquisite. The walls were lined with bookcases that housed his works and all his memorabilia. There was a center area of black marble with wooden columns in four corners, and an old German upright piano. The audience sat in alcoves formed by the pillars. Behind me there were black-curtained windows to screen the afternoon sun. I was honored to be the first foreign dancer to appear there and to have opened Shantiniketan to American representatives. Pictures of the symposium became part of the museum.

Before I left Calcutta, I visited the school of Amala Shankar, Uday Shankar's wife. Amala was energetic and eager to develop. I offered my help to get her a grant to Connecticut College.

An unexpected success took place in Singapore. I did a lecture-demonstration on gesture and performed bits of *Cassandra* and *Concertino* for videotape—without any advance preparation! The result was even better than the film I had made in Japan.

My two weeks of teaching in Seoul were gratifying, but it was freezing cold. A few nostalgic days spent in Toyko on my way home warmed me up.

Upon my return to North Carolina, I found a new addition to the staff. The year before, a young dancer touring with a Hungarian dance ensemble had decided to remain in the United States. The school offered him a position to teach character dance in spring 1967. Gyula Pandi was a find. He had excellent ballet technique as well as the zest, facility, and dramatic ability that character dance develops. His dark hair, sparkling eyes, high cheekbones, and a striking personality, backed by a quick, intelligent mind and an outstanding stage presence eventually stimulated my desire to choreograph a work for him.

I remembered the duet I had done for Norman Walker and Cora Cahan, the second section of *Dance Symphony*. It had some extraordinary lifts. Georgiana would be Gyula's partner in this duet. Geordi was a natural. She could do anything, her tiny, pliable body adapting to all kinds of movement.

I believe people have auras. Our bodies emanate electricity. One can sometimes sense a person at a distance without even looking. This was my motivation for the dance. I used a long coral-colored veil attached to the girl's waist, covering her face and trailing high off stage, as a symbolic aura. A young man enters and the first part of the dance is his response to her visualized vibrations. Every time he touches the veil, she responds. They meet. He removes the veil and they face each other for the first time. What follows is a love duet that I wanted to be sensitive, understated, tender yet provocative, rather than overtly sexy. It was influenced by Chagall, whose women, when transported emotionally, fly in the air or soar upside down. I called this work *Poème*, and set it to the second movement of Samuel Barber's Piano Concerto.

We worked whenever we three could get together. *Poème* had its first performance on April 2, 1968. Its romanticism seemed to appeal to the young and the mature. Eventually Geordi's role was taken by Gina Vidal, a blond with a cameo face and long limbs quite the opposite of Geordi's. Before meeting and marrying Gyula, she had been with American Ballet Theatre. The duet was perfect for them.

The choreography fellowship from the three-year-old National Endowment for the Arts I received in December 1968 gave me the chance to use Stravinsky's Concerto for Piano and Wind Orchestra. For thirteen dancers at the school I created a piece, in three separate sequences to match the music's isolated movements, called *Fragments: The Celebration, The Dreamer,* and *Comic Strip*. The last part was a sardonic comment on the Vietnam War, but since the music for this section had a carnival sound, I changed it to a circus milieu and called it *Arena*—the arena of life and the characters we play in our fantasies.

As my teaching progressed I was able to develop Elements of Performing and the composition course. These I enjoyed more than the technique classes. When not concentrating on mechanics, the students revealed themselves as individuals. I called it peeling the banana to find the real thing. Talent was uncovered in the creative and performing areas that often was not visible in the technique. However, the composition class presented a constant problem. Each year new students were admitted, and since there was only one class for high school and college, students with no background and those with a year or two behind them were in the same class. During my eleven years at the school this problem was never solved. What I did find very stimulating was the chance to work on Elements with the ballet students. They loved it, and some achieved remarkable results.

By 1970 the school had acquired a Commons building with a large dance studio and a cafeteria. Dormitories were also added. With the experience of school tours and fall and spring festivals, a nucleus of excellent young performers was developing. Modern dance was gradually accepted, rather than tolerated.

By now the school's activities were a focus of tremendous interest throughout the country. The Southern Newspaper Publishers' Association held a seminar there, and for two-and-a-half days, lectures and demonstrations by all the departments generated a lively response. These newspaper people wanted to learn more about the school and about arts criticism. Another event of the 1970–71 season was a Copland Festival to celebrate the composer's seventieth birthday. I challenged myself to teach *Cassandra* to two students. The solo was technically and dramatically demanding, and the dancers had to learn the complicated music note for note. It was intriguing to see two very different personalities handle the role—Lynn Keeton, wiry, with an inner burning and Evelyn Shepard, with strength and weight in the movements.

In such propitious circumstances I began to think of a professional company as an adjunct. In early spring 1970 I had written to John Christian, assistant to Ted Shawn at Jacob's Pillow, suggesting that he engage our young company. The answer I received said, "Yes, we're interested. Send more details." Programs were drawn up and we opened the season with a two-week engagement. The reviews fulfilled my belief in the possibility of establishing a permanent company at the school.

I savored the vision of at last having available a company without the personal responsibility of studio rental, costumes, and even to a degree fund raising. A plan for a grant had been submitted to the Rockefeller Foundation, but there had not been much response. I knew Norman

Lloyd, now director of the Arts and Humanities Division of the Foundation, and wrote to him that I thought we had the possibility for an interesting company. In reply he suggested that we submit a proposal. I spoke to school president Robert Ward, who called together Bobby Lindgren, Duncan Noble, Job Sanders, and me.

My idea was to form a company with a nucleus of classical ballet dancers, of modern dancers, and of dancers who could do both. This would enable us to give three kinds of programs. Lindgren was named producer; Sanders, Noble, and Koner, artistic directors. When Job Sanders left the school, Duncan and I were left as artistic directors. The proposal was sent off, and we waited.

The Rockefeller Foundation, considering our new proposal, expressed interest in viewing the dance company. A small amount of token money was contributed to help with production. It so happened that Edward de Soto, who danced with José, had taught some classes at the school and was invited to join our company. Ed had performed in *La Malinche*, and it occurred to me that there was a potential cast for a revival. Gyula would make an excellent El Indio, Ed had danced the Conquistador, and both Lynn Keeton and Sharon Filone were capable of doing my role. I called José to ask for permission. "Pauline, if you say you have a cast, you can have the piece. All I ask is that Daniel Lewis come down to stage it, and that you pay him 500 dollars."

I had not seen *La Malinche* since my break with the company in 1960. The original had never been filmed, so when Danny showed me a working film he had brought I was aghast: José had completely rechoreographed my solo and changed some of the final duet. Neither José nor Lucas appeared, and the work had lost its impact. The starkness had gone. It was just another dance.

When Danny played the music, without thinking I got up and did the original versions of my solo and the duet. The body remembered. Danny looked at it. "It's terrific," he said. "I wonder why he changed it?"

I called José again: "José, if I can revive the original version, would you mind?"

"Why, no. Go right ahead."

"But why did you change my solo?"

"Who could do it but you?" he replied.

"Well, I have two girls who I think can."

Danny taught the men, and Gyula was enthusiastic about his part. In order to remember, I got up and danced with Danny standing in for

José. Lynn and Sharon learned my role. Suddenly, *La Malinche* came alive again. I stressed the dynamics, the characters. Danny was enthusiastic.

A special showcase performance was scheduled for the Rockefeller representatives. On the program with *La Malinche* (it was decided that for this performance I would dance) were my *Concertino* and *Poème* and Agnes de Mille's *A Rose for Miss Emily* (Gemze de Lappe and David Evans appeared as guests) and *The Cherry Tree Carol*. In fact there was not one classical work on this sample program.

Norman Lloyd was not expected to attend, although his assistant Howard Klein certainly would. I wanted Norman to be there, so I let him know about the performance, that I would be dancing, and that I had revived the original version. I got an immediate answer: not only would he come, but his wife Ruth, who had played for Doris, would come along.

The performance took place on February 19, 1971, to a packed house. There was a large reception afterward. Agnes came to me and said graciously, "There is no doubt that this was your evening." I was embarrassed because her work had been on the program too, but Agnes did not mind. Her forthright honesty was disarming. A warm, congratulatory letter from José followed.

When word came shortly thereafter that the Rockefeller Foundation had awarded us a 250,000-dollar matching grant for the creation of a professional company, I was euphoric. This was what I had hoped for, worked for, and dreamed about. Bobby called a meeting with Duncan and me to discuss organization. When it came to repertoire, I reminded them of our agreement at the time the proposal was submitted that repertoire would be decided by a three-way vote. "No, it won't be that way," Bobby said. "I've changed my mind. I will have the final decision."

"But you're the producer, we're the artistic directors."

"This is how it's going to be," he said with finality.

I saw my dream evaporating. I was sure that the company would be ballet-oriented, with an occasional semi-modern dance inserted. All I had worked toward would slip away. "In that case," I replied, "I'm afraid I can't go along with you. But to give you the benefit of the doubt, I'll try to stay on for three months and then make a decision."

At the end of three months, I sent a letter of resignation to the company. Bobby asked if he could meet me for a talk. He was forthright, almost naïvely honest, saying that he had always wanted a company of his own and admitting his ambitions. He was sorry it had worked out this way. Rather bitterly, I wished him luck and said I would like to stay on and teach (I needed the job).

During this period, Bill Hanna, director of the Television Department at the University of North Carolina at Chapel Hill, asked to film my works for broadcast on the educational station. I agreed since in return I would have copies, a precious record worth any effort. We did *Cassandra*, *Poème*, *La Malinche* (the only film of the original version), and *The Farewell*. These were shown repeatedly, even after I left.

In summer 1971 I accepted an invitation to teach at the International Ballet Seminar in Copenhagen and from there went to Oslo to work on modern dance technique with the ballet company. In 1972 there was a repeat invitation to Copenhagen.

That fall closed another cycle in my life. On October 12–14, I presented *The Farewell* for the City Center American Dance Marathon at the ANTA Theatre. I performed it well, still having the strength to survive the grueling physical demands, but as I sat quietly in my dressing room between a matinee and evening performance I thought, This must be my farewell to performing. I do not want to be seen at less than my peak. This is the same theater that used to be the Guild, where I made my solo debut. It is an omen.

When I returned to the school for the 1973–74 year, after a summer of teaching in Manila, I had completed two movements of *Solitary Song, Opus III*. It was presented at an informal student showing in the spring, and everyone badgered me to complete it. Frankly, I was afraid to try. By the next season I had moved to the new New York apartment, after thirty-three years in the one I had shared with Fritz. New surroundings helped relieve some of my personal anxieties. My mind seemed fresh again. Ideas for completing the work were germinating, and the need to create was again becoming a primary force. We were nearing Easter break, so I asked the cast if they would agree to stay; I would pay for their food and the school would house them. They agreed. Fresh ideas came almost faster than I could manage, and there it was—Opus IV— complete. After its first showing on April 25, 1975, the Winston-Salem newspaper review called *Solitary Songs: Opus III and IV* an incandescent statement.

Now I knew that I had a good work. To get it seen in a professional milieu I offered it to Charles Reinhart, director of the American Dance

Solitary Song I (1963). Photo © Peter Basch.

Above: "The Last
Farewell" from *The
Farewell* (1962).
Photo © Peter
Basch. Below:
"Farewell to the
Earth" from *The
Farewell* (1962).
Photo © Peter
Basch.

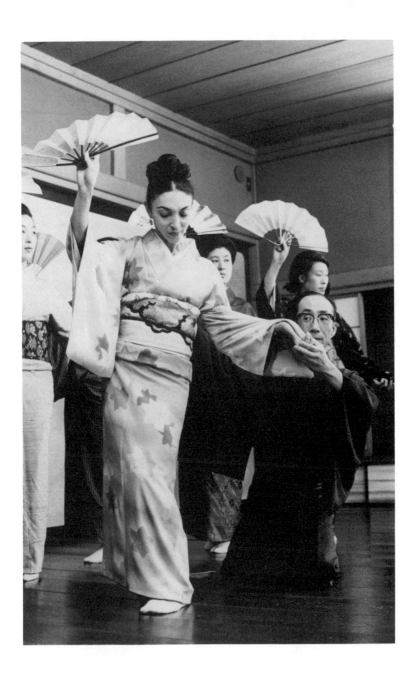

Opposite: Receiving lesson from Kinosuke Hanayagi at a rehearsal of geishas, Japan, 1965. This page, top: With Tokyo Workshop Group in class, Japan, 1965. Photo, Osamu Énomoto (USIS Photo, Tokyo). Bottom: With students in Rabindranath Tagore's studio, Shantiniketan, India, 1967.

Opposite: Pauline Koner Dance Consort in *Solitary Song (Move 11)—Homage to Fritz Mahler* (1973). Photo, John H. Fell. This page, top: Pauline Koner Dance Consort in "On a Summer Midnight" from *A Time of Crickets* (1976). Photo, Marvin Koner. Bottom: Georgiana Holmes and Gyula Pandi, North Carolina School of the Arts, in *Poème* (1968). Photo, Frank Jones.

Festival at Connecticut College. He was interested, but it had to be on a professional company. I told him it was the Pauline Koner Dance Company. He also wanted me to teach technique and Elements of Performing at the college, to which I agreed. Anything to get the performance at the festival. Unfortunately, it was too late to put us in his budget, but he could offer housing. This presented a problem, which I took to the North Carolina School of the Arts Foundation. They were kind enough to give me money to cover expenses. The performance was a tremendous success, and being back where I had spent so many summers was exhilarating—the place was a beehive of creativity.

Heady with the experience, I began again to formulate a project for a professional company, this time a modern dance company affiliated with the school, but based in New York. It could offer the modern dance students some prospect for a future performing outlet. This was my primary reason. A secondary reason was the unpleasant atmosphere developing in the modern dance department.

In 1972 Richard Kuch, a fine dancer who had been with many companies, including Graham's, was engaged as full-time faculty member. He admired my Elements course and even sat in on some classes, but insisted on having Graham technique as the principal departmental approach. He was also a stern and watchful disciplinarian. My way to achieve student rapport was different. Cliques began to form, and students were disturbed. Inevitably all this led to conflict, especially in the evaluation of students. I was interested in their artistic potential. Technique can always be learned, provided the instrument is there; presence, inner electricity, the mind, these interested me more.

These tensions grew so uncomfortable that I felt concentration on a company with supplementary teaching would be better for me. Early in 1976 I presented my idea for the formation of a company to Chancellor Robert Suderberg, and he was quite enthusiastic. The school Foundation agreed to offer some help. I was encouraged to make plans. There was almost a complete program ready, but it needed one more work. Having just done a serious dramatic piece, I wanted a lyric, pastoral work that was fresh and young, with contrasting sequences from full company to duets, quartets, and solos.

For music I contacted Michael Colina, a composition graduate of the school. Michael's poetic and kinesthetic responsiveness was stimulating, and ideas flew back and forth. He brought a poem about crickets, which gave us an idea. I started choreographing without the music, and as I showed Michael what I had done he would send me bits and pieces of music, even real cricket sounds, on tape.

Once again I turned to Eliot's *Four Quartets* as a source of imagery. I found individual phrases that inspired me, from which emerged a love duet and a peasant harvest dance. The line from "Burnt Norton," "At the still point of the turning world . . . there the dance is," was a solo for a girl, who then disappeared. When Michael saw it he said, "It seems odd that the girl never reappears. I wish she could be there from the beginning." He was absolutely right. In the final version, she opened the piece, wove through the company, did the solo, and ended the work. Eliot also inspired the theme of *A Time for Crickets*: the cycle of a day or of a lifetime.

I was now ready to show a company. The chancellor suggested that I talk to the drama department and get a date for the de Mille Theatre. We were all excited at the prospect—spirits were effervescent, a whole new beginning, young dancers with a future. Then Bobby Lindgren called me into his office. He looked uncomfortable. "I know you're planning your performances for May, the same week my Dance Theatre is performing in Winston-Salem at the Community Center." With his straightforward honesty, he added, "You can't have your performances open to the public because if you do, you'll get all the press." I thought this was a backhanded compliment. "I'm happy to let you have the services of the costume department [Evelyn Miller, who ran it, was a gem], all the program printing, and the time slot at the de Mille Theatre."

I could not change my date; it was the only available time in the theatre. I had not been told about the Dance Theatre engagement. The fear of intradepartmental competition, I think, cooled Dr. Suderberg and the Foundation on my entire future project. My answer to Bobby was, "All right. I will not go public, but I *will* give the performance—by invitation only." I drew up a list, had elegant programs designed, and planned a reception at my own expense. We gave three beautiful performances of *Concertino*, *Cassandra*, *Solitary Songs*, and *A Time for Crickets*. No press, but the audience was enthusiastic. I felt it was time to move on, so immediately afterward, I resigned from the North Carolina School of the Arts.

Oddly enough, it was the best thing that could have happened. I was ready for new adventure and needed only the push. When I realized this, I felt rather grateful to Lindgren. Bobby and I have remained good friends and greet each other with enthusiasm when we meet.

The Dance Consort

A frightening time. Could I start again, alone, at this late date? Did I have the stamina? Why did I persist? I knew why: dance was life, the need to grow, to explore, to pursue my own vision, to enter a new stage of development. I could choreograph for many bodies, not just my own. I wanted to give to young dancers everything I knew about dance, about performing. I had a company, a complete program, but no financial backing. Aware of the risk, but with no idea of the immensity of the task, I plunged in.

What was needed was to follow the May 1976 performance with one that would give us prestige and establish us as a professional company. The American Dance Festival! I offered Charles Reinhart the first professional performance of *A Time for Crickets* if he would include us on the series. He came to the rescue, but the fee covered only expenses. The dancers agreed. They knew that such an appearance meant starting at the top. It was the difference between giving up or going ahead. He gave us a house for two weeks, where we could live as a collective, and rehearsal space. The program contained two works originally premiered at the festival, *Concertino* and *Cassandra*. With the first performances of *Crickets* on July 2 and 3, 1976, my work here spanned twenty-three years.

Shortly after I was told that North Carolina School of the Arts would not sponsor the company, Ellen Parker, a young former dancer who had been a student at the School, called me. "You have to have a company," she said. "I'll help you as much as possible." At the same time, two young managers, Neil Fleckman and Bruce Michael, were starting a management bureau and were interested in representing the company. Ellen put me in touch with C. C. Conner, a lawyer and arts enthusiast. "I'll be happy to contribute time and help you when I can as a business manager," he said. Unbelievable! We decided on a name: "Pauline Koner Dance Consort." A foundation was formed. I was initiated into the intricacies of running a company.

Our performances at the festival were most successful; the press excellent. Doris Hering wrote in the September 1976 *Dance Magazine*: "It was not the ensemble of 'everybody doing the same step the same way.' Something more subtle was going on. They all shared the same energy flow. . . . Koner has also made her dancers conscious of detail, the many ways in which the hands can articulate at the wrists, how freely the head can bend without seeming merely restless. . . . It takes time to discover these nuances, or it takes the guidance of a wise artistic director. . . ."

In training the company, I tried to instill some of the qualities that give modern dance substance: the style of weight, the suspension in hanging on a breath, the dynamic phrasing that lends subtle color, and the energy of sharpness and attack. These gave the Consort a distinct image. I revelled in the artistic growth of each dancer as these qualities were absorbed. I demanded much from them and it was taxing, but they developed from good dancers into fine artists.

Since the original company stemmed from the school, the undergraduates had to return after the summer vacation, but I still had a good nucleus of four women and two men trained in my personal style. They were a core that kept that style intact, even when I engaged new men as replacements. This first company—Deborah Pratt, Martha Curtis, Karen Shields, Georgiana Holmes, Tamara Gross, Michael Freed, and George White, Jr.,—changed and evolved into a permanent unit. Paco Garcia joined and remained. Martha Curtis and Karen Shields stayed and were also assistants; Patricia Casey, Evelyn Shepard, and Valerie Farias were added. I felt these young women were my children since I had taught some of them through high school and college. The men—Paco, Keith Sabado, Zane Rankin, and Jim Clinton —helped to make a company that was a finely honed instrument. They were a small family, caring for each other, helping each other, with no sense of competition or jealousy. Everyone was interested, contributing to the choreography for the good of the whole.

Working with such a company was stimulating. Being able to see what I was creating was a new experience. The potential in using space and making it come alive, taking a simple movement and developing it, moving many bodies opened a whole new vision of emotional relationships and subject matter.

I am a romantic—concerned with the human condition, not involved with tricky trends that come and go. The cycle is such that true values always return. Friends said, "You're insane to start a company now," but it was essential to prove the value of my belief in dance that had form and meaning.

One of the small miracles that occurred was meeting Robert Lear, who had come to New London specifically to see the company. He was executive director of the just-completed Minskoff Cultural Center and was interested in developing dance activity there. In return for setting up dance classes for children and adults, I was offered a residency and a place to rehearse. This was vital. I had no studio of my own. Here we had two to four hours daily in a new gymnasium (but with a cement floor). Although Lear left the center, we remained through winter 1977. With a permanent place to rehearse, my mind was free to concentrate on choreography.

Well, not so free. The need for financial help was obvious. Some came from small grants and a trickle from personal friends, but I was not very good at raising money. To survive in the company, the dancers had to find supplemental work. Our appearance at the American Dance Festival had been important, but for future touring purposes a New York appearance was essential. I also needed someone who could devote full time to the business management so I could direct all my energies toward artistic goals.

When C. C. Conner announced he was resigning from his job at a brokerage firm in order to devote full time to the company, I was astonished. Although by profession a lawyer, he is intrinsically an artist—a fine flutist, versed in dance, with an uncanny sensitivity, and a superb critical eye. I call him a true Renaissance man. Eventually he became associate director and ran the company on all levels—lighting (John McKernon was our designer), sound, rehearsal, residencies—a troubleshooter. I could never have continued without his support, and all this for no salary except an occasional pittance. He arranged for our first New York appearance at Brooklyn College and a spring season at the Henry Street Playhouse. Anna Kisselgoff reviewed us in the *New York Times* of October 6, 1976: "Much of [the] program harked back unabashed and proudly to a view of dance that is now conveniently called classic modern dance. It is Miss Koner's triumph that her brand of dance now seems not old-fashioned but refreshing. . . . Essentially she is a romantic, but she is also dramatic. . . . Her group compositions are brilliant. She is a master at counterpoint and contrast. . . . Miss Koner's works need to be seen more often."

This was the kind of encouragement I needed. I felt compelled, as I had in my earliest days of dance, to go on. Group choreography was fascinating, and for the first time in my life I welcomed it. My goal was not a large company; rather, I thought of it in terms of a chamber ensemble of distinct individuals, each with a specific personality that could blend or emerge.

To broaden the repertoire, my first thought was to drop *Concertino* and replace it with a new opening piece. For the sake of program contrast, baroque music was essential and I chose Bach's *Italian Concerto*. The piece was called *Mosaic*, with three sections: "Of Greeting," "Of Dreaming," and "Of Merrymaking." When I choreograph, certain phrases of movement, once used but now dormant, remain in my mind. These often inspire development of new material that complements, expands, and enhances the original.

For the first section of *Mosaic* I deliberately chose some key material from my older work, *Fragments*. This was integrated with new movement drawn from gestures of greeting. What resulted was much better than the original. I added a few measures of bells as an introduction and the dancers continued in silence. Then the piano tones sang out. The *Italian Concerto* began.

The second section of *Fragments*, a trio, I transferred intact. It was fascinating to see how the choreography, originally set to Stravinsky music, was perfect for the Bach with only slight changes in timing. The motivation: there is no ideal person, no one person who has all the essentials we look for. A woman sees in her dreams two men as the composite of her ideal. Her relationship to the two is vague, nebulous, and very often they blend into one—a wish fulfillment. In the third section young people enjoy being together, even being a little zany. *Mosaic* turned out to be a good program opener—colorfully costumed, bright, and dancey. It was a challenge for the company since technically and stylistically it was quite demanding.

Slowly the company was gathering impetus. John Goldman, a devoted member of our board, induced an artist, David Fradin, to design striking brochures. C. C. was busy trying to book us; we were now accepted on the touring program of the National Endowment for the Arts. Engagements were sparse, but the success of our performances held the company together, with some inevitable cast changes. Whatever funds we received went to the company in salaries and production costs; C. C. and I worked for next to nothing. Dance was a luxury, and after fifty years I was still paying for the privilege of being involved. The small tours helped cover some expenses, but mostly gave the dancers what they needed artistically, the opportunity to perform. Residencies in schools, teaching, lecture-demonstrations helped. Although I personally had had enough of touring, I loved the school performances, especially for young children. Their fascinated response to our dances was a joy.

The seed for a new work began to germinate. Terrorists, murders, wars, illness, and accidents appeared daily in the news. Life at times seemed like a wilderness. Returning home from rehearsals—people shoving, pushing in all directions as I mounted the subway staircase—I was certain I would be trampled if I fell, and no one would even turn to glance. We were all vulnerable to violence and lack of compassion. It reminded me of medieval times.

The piece became a reflection on time, then and now, and the uncertainty of life. *Then* was the many faces of death, the plague, the brutality, and the crumbling of morality; *today* was the wilderness of society, with its outbreaks of violence, fear, and random death. Early in 1978, I began to visualize the form of this work, a sort of masque consisting of medieval dances (not authentic, but with that flavor) alternating with episodes that were timeless. Each episode ended with a sudden death. I did research and sought out prints of the *Dance of Death* to create the atmosphere I wanted.

The more I delved into this idea, the more challenging and exciting it became. I made a music collage using excerpts of the medieval *Cantigas de Santa Maria* and selections from George Crumb's *Madri-*

gals. The old and the new sound somehow blended perfectly. I called the work *Cantigas (A Medieval Masque).* It opened with a processional for the company, then Episode One, "Love Song." This started as a duet for a boy and girl. A second woman entered, who at the final moment was revealed as Death, as she carried off the young girl. "Interlude," a medieval dance, followed. Episode Two, "Tipplers," was set for three drunkards, a jester, and a bawd. At a moment when the jester was held aloft by the boys, he pulled a black cloth over his face, again the surprise figure of Death, and took the three drunkards with him. Another medieval "Interlude," then Episode Three, "Lullaby." A mother and child at play were joined by another woman. The child suddenly fell limp in her arms as Death carried her off. The lone figure, the mother, was left on stage. In Episode Four, "Wilderness," the entire company joined in wild, disjointed movement, which ended with all the dancers prostrate. My source for this section was the St. Vitus Dance, hysterical movement that was thought to help prevent or cure the plague. All the episodes were timeless in the sense of mingling time then and now.

The episodes were in unitards; the interludes in caftans of varying tones of gold outside with black and turquoise inside, which varied the shapes and colors for the medieval dances. After "Wilderness," a dancer entered carrying the caftans, and as she draped them over the figures they slowly rose. With the black panel visible to the audience, they walked upstage and blended into the black drapes. Then, turning slowly, the turquoise emerged and they walked downstage as though a new dawn, a resurrection, had begun. They started to whirl, and as the speed increased they flipped the costumes, so that the stage burst forth in the sunny golden colors to end in a final processional.

It took months of searching for movement that was new, learning to work on dramatic or breath phrasing (never counts) to the Crumb music, and especially acquiring facility for the complicated manipulation of the caftans. I was demanding much of the company. Knowing this was valuable experience, they worked with enthusiasm. By spring I had a strong dance that I thought was an important step forward. Now I was faced with the problem of scheduling a first performance that could do it justice. Inspiration! This was the year the American Dance Festival was relocating to Duke University in Durham, North Carolina. My association with the festival was strong, so once again I turned to Charles Reinhart. Once again the familiar, "I can give you an appearance on our festival if you will agree to teach your Elements of Performing." "Yes," I said, "if Martha Curtis can be my assistant, and the company can be in residence two weeks before the performance."

It was beastly hot as we sweated through rehearsals every evening. I polished the new work until it shone. The caftans were a problem, but we made them work. My old friend and a respected dance teacher from Utah, Virginia Tanner, watched a rehearsal. When she said, with tears in her eyes, "This is a great work," I felt compensated for all the struggle that creating and producing something new demands — a long, often difficult gestation and birthing. Without the help of C. C. Conner and John McKernon and the dedication of the company, it would have been impossible. An added incentive was that I was celebrating my fiftieth year in professional dance.

Page Auditorium at Duke was an enormous theater, with a large stage of excellent proportions, especially the high proscenium. In the last row of the auditorium I waited apprehensively. This July 1 premiere was one of the most important of my life — my first major serious work for the company. At the end, the applause was thunderous. There were bravos and finally a standing ovation. I sat in my seat, overcome, shaking. *Cantigas* had true impact. Coming totally fresh and new, it gripped the audience, taking them by surprise. The reviews were equally extolling. It was one of those rare times when all the elements combined for a special moment.

Cantigas had its New York premiere on February 8, 1979, as part of the Riverside Dance Festival. The historian Barbara Tuchman came at my invitation. I had discovered in the foreword to her book *A Distant Mirror* the same premise I had used for the dance. Clive Barnes wrote in the *New York Post* on February 9, 1979: "This is a very special troupe. Koner has gathered together some fine dancers, but she has also put together some very interesting choreography . . . it is [her] choreography and her dancers that give the work its shape and image. . . . Koner listens to music with the kind of scruples that Humphrey herself applied to her choreographic ear. But Koner in a work such as this *Cantigas* has more pure power."

We could not always present the work on tour; it needed a stage atmosphere like that of Page Auditorium. I did set it on the Bat-Sheva company in Israel later in the year. It was interesting to see the differences when another company performed the work.

Also on the Riverside program was *The Farewell*. The girls had begged to learn it. "Please let us try. It will help us to grow. It's a challenge," they insisted. "Okay," I said, "but it's a difficult dance. Don't be disappointed if it doesn't work." I was interested to see what might happen, and wanted the piece to stay alive.

As we worked I saw that as yet no one was ready to do the complete solo, but each girl seemed able to find the quality of an individual section. I took a radical step and decided to revive *The Farewell* by dividing the sections. Evelyn Shepard did the first section, "To the Earth," and the last section, "The Last Farewell"; Karen Shields and Valerie Farias alternated in "To Youth"; and Martha Curtis had "To Love." Since time for costume changes was no longer necessary, I prolonged the final moment of each section by altering timing slightly and adding one additional phrase to the first section.

Though the effect was not as strong as the original solo, I still felt it was valid, and was amazed at the sensitivity and artistry that each of the girls achieved. Evelyn Shepard even did what I would have thought impossible; she insisted on learning the entire four sections, despite the fact that I was not convinced she could handle it. When she finally showed it to me, I was in tears. I worked with her then to polish the dance to its finest detail.

The most beneficial result of the concert was the interest David Manion, artistic director of the Riverside Dance Festival, took in the company. He gave us a permanent place to rehearse and the prospect of being resident company for the 1980–81 season. His generosity and moral support helped us survive.

With a strong dramatic work in the repertoire I now needed something light, flowing, and if possible humorous. Humor had been one of my strong points as a soloist, but it is a very personal thing; trying to transfer it to others would be an exploration. I never wanted to do a new work unless it meant inner growth.

I heard Joaquin Rodrigo's Concert Serenade for harp and orchestra. The first movement sparkles with a sweeping sense of flow and sudden surprising dissonances; the second is a slow intermezzo that sounds like an ancient tune; the third is a bright, rather wild Spanish fiesta. How could I make a coherent work out of such divergent styles? I searched for other music, but this piece kept creeping back into my consciousness. One day I saw kites flying. That was it; it suited the first movement perfectly. The images came fast. I borrowed a film and studied the soaring, the spiraling tails, the swooping and unexpected drops of kites.

What about the second and third movements? Late one night, in that moment when the mind hovers between conscious and unconscious thought, the word "flight" came to me. Flight would be my overall theme. The first movement was "Kite-Flight"; the second, "Heavenly Flight," a gambol for Renaissance angels, senior and junior angels. The seniors have had enough of heaven and go on an unexpected small binge. The third movement, "Flight of Fancy," was a takeoff on Spanish dance, with the dancers upstaging each other. A shawl grew in size from a neck scarf, to a shoulder shawl, to a parachute painted like a Spanish shawl, engulfing all the dancers. I invited Matteo, the ethnic dance expert, to coach the company in Spanish style, and drew on my own Spanish background for material. Since I saw each section as a complete dance, I needed three costume designs.

The work was planned as a closing piece that would leave the audience with a giggle or guffaw after a heavy dramatic dance. Could I do it again?

"Kite-Flight" went well. The company took off as kites, often creating phrases that were striking. I stimulated their imaginations and allowed their bodies to come forth with movement that was theirs. From this I structured what I wanted, phrasing the music and the space design. At the same time I was constantly suggesting or improving.

The second movement was troublesome. Very contained and serene, it had to get slightly zany. Sharp timing was essential, and these young dancers still had much to learn in this area, but finally the humor began to gel.

Of course they loved the last movement, which they could ham up a little, within bounds. Dancers sometimes need this release. If we have a good time, we hope the audience will too. So we decided to let loose and spoof—very healthy, indeed!

Flight had its premiere October 25, 1979, during a week's residency at the University of Southern Mississippi, and was then performed at a concert in Cleveland. From the review by Wilma Salisbury in the November 11, 1979, *Cleveland Plain Dealer*: "This spoof is a winner. In the first movement . . . the dancers captured the feeling of flying. . . . 'Heavenly Flight' . . . became a parody with well-aimed stabs at classical ballet . . . 'Flight of Fancy' was a witty satire on Spanish dance. . . . The sharp performance by [the] company brought down the house."

Being director of a company had many meanings. I felt responsible for these young dancers, not only as dancers, but as human beings. They had come to New York from places far away. On minimum income, even with supplemental work, life was difficult. Housing, food, carfares were expensive; yogurt was a diet mainstay. I worried about them. If they were sick, I found a doctor; if they were depressed, I listened to their problems and tried to help. And then there was always the occupational hazard of accidents, last-minute changes. Worry. Worry. Worry. All of this was draining, but when I watched the performances it, was worth it—even when they were plagued by last-minute crises.

C. C. took over more and more of the responsibilities, trying to save me from growing nervous strain. He even insisted that I need not be present at all performances. He knew how upset I was when I could not obtain the perfection I always aimed at. We needed every possible engagement to survive, no matter what the conditions. The company never complained, always gave their best, and enjoyed the free moments, eating together, visiting, partying. Touring was always an adventure for them. Often, traveling in a large van, they sang and told anecdotes.

I thought it would be a new experience for them to perform *La Malinche*. My restaging of the original version had not been seen in New York, and the Mexican characters, the style of movement, would be a challenge. We chose two casts. Daniel Lewis coached the men and I coached the women. They quickly absorbed the texture, the mood, and the particular naïve quality that was the essence of the work. Bobby Lindgren gave me the set of costumes we had used in 1971. I had to laugh when both girls, very blonde, at first resisted wearing a wig of black braids.

In a two-week season at the Riverside Dance Festival in January 1981 we presented three programs, including *La Malinche* and Loyce Houlton's *Wingborne*, which had just been staged for the company. I felt that although the company had reached a peak artistically, the future looked economically precarious.

One program, "The Beginnings," was a daring departure from the usual format. It was suggested that since I had survived fifty-three years in the dance world, why not open a program by talking about my creative experience, with personal demonstrations. I chose *The Farewell* and the thirteen-year genesis of *Solitary Songs*.

I was terrified. It was daring to expose myself in movement after nearly a decade absence from the New York stage. Speaking without notes made timing the introduction difficult. The first night I got carried away, and it was much too long. It was actually my dress rehearsal. I cut and tightened the material, so that the two following evenings were just right. I never thought I would survive, but I did. People who came backstage said I had opened for them a whole new understanding of dance. My former dancer, Deborah Jowitt, described it in the February 4, 1981, *Village Voice*:

> She spoke about the precepts of her mentor Doris Humphrey and demonstrated her own ideas about gesture and choreographic motivation. . . . Then her body started to get wonderfully busy amplifying what her voice was saying . . . She understands all the gradations of attack, how to shade a gesture into quietness, how to let it get weak at midpoint and bloom again at the end without any noticeable break in flow. She has a sense of just how much weight a gesture needs, how much illusory space it should fill. The texture keeps modulating before your eyes.

Deep within I knew that this appearance on stage was my performing swan song.

After six years of struggle to develop a very special group of people, I now had to face the fact that this would be the end. The National Endowment for the Arts budget was cut, and small companies were the first to feel the blow, mine among them. The Endowment's dance touring program, beset by rising costs, was phased out. By fall 1982 I knew I would have to abandon my dream. Even C. C., dedicated as he was, was forced to go back to law practice. Aside from a residency in the New Rochelle school system, there were no bookings in the offing. I tried to get teaching jobs for as many of the company as possible. The men, who were excellent, had no trouble getting into other companies. The polished jewel I had so painstakingly created was fragmented.

I was left with a repertoire of works, a storage room of costumes, and a mass of clippings and photos. The only positive value of the company's end was that I was released from the constant pressure and worry of choreographing new works, released from the fear of running out of ideas. Although the company was disbanded, our attachment remains. We keep in contact with each other; I help whenever possible with recommendations for new positions. Some of the girls are now mothers. My family has grown, and I have "grandchildren."

From time to time I give master classes and lectures. I teach at the Juilliard School. I have staged some of the works on other companies. This keeps them alive.

Dance is ephemeral, dependent on visual immediacy. Films and videotapes often diminish the impact of a performer, and restaging of a work often weakens the heart of the choreography. Music suffers in the same way, but painting, sculpture, and the written word remain intact. Recognizing this, I made a decision: I would have to write.

Index

Choreographers' names (in parentheses) follow titles of choreographed works.

Joio, 218; Harold Faberman, 228; Lukas Foss, 150, 247; David Freed, 41; George Gershwin, 114, 141, 145; Vincente Gomez, 175; Jimmy Guiffre, 228; George Frideric Handel, 176; Jerome Kern, 145; Leon Kirchner, 183; Lev Knipper, 111; Franz Liszt, 30, 211; Pietro Locatelli, 179; Otto Luening, 181; Gustav Mahler, 123, 130, 240, 245; Freda Miller, 164; Claudio Monteverdi, 201; Carlos Montoya, 175; Wolfgang Amadeus Mozart, 78, 129, 165–66, 211; Nikolai Myaskovsky, 111; Lionel Nowak, 153; Giovanni Pergolesi, 178; Norman Peterkin, 41; Genevieve Pitot, 197; Sergei Prokofiev, 43, 49, 105–6, 147; Henry Purcell, 201; Nikolai Rimsky-Korsakov, 19; Joaquin Rodrigo, 284; Anton Rubinstein, 12; Camille Saint-Saëns, 76; Pablo de Sarasate, 33; Arnold Schoenberg, 122, 201, 206–7, 210; Gunther Schuller, 229–30; William Schuman, 214, 264; Robert Schumann, 12, 28, 30; Alexander Scriabin, 28, 34; Andrés Segovia, 175; Dmitri Shostakovich, 107, 127, 149; Antonio Soler, 209; Richard Strauss, 147; Igor Stravinsky, 269, 280; Carlos Surinach, 167; Piotr Ilyich Tchaikovsky, 12, 126; Fartein Valen, 246; Antonio Vivaldi, 192; Yamada, 28
Concentration, 25, 27, 30, 252–53, 255, 258, 266
Concert (Limón), 206
Concertino in A Major (Koner), 131, 178–79, 183, 220, 221, 222, 231, 243, 244, 248, 266, 268, 272, 275, 277, 280
Concerto in D (Koner), 159–60, 161
Connecticut College Dance Festival.

See American Dance Festival
Conner, C. C., 278, 279–80, 281, 283, 286, 287
Contracts, 73, 80, 92, 97, 109, 140, 144, 249
Le Coq d'Or (Fokine), 19–20
Cornish, Nellie, 33–34
Corvino, Alfredo, 141
Corybantic (Humphrey), 157–58, 168, 200
Cosmic Poems (Koner-Nimura), 41, 52. See also *Chaos, Beginning, Primeval*
Costumes, 18, 28–29, 30, 33, 41, 45, 47–48, 51, 66, 78–79, 91, 114, 115, 126, 140, 146, 152, 164–66, 172, 175, 176, 185, 198, 203–4, 206, 207, 209, 211, 215, 217, 229, 243, 247, 252, 253, 254, 264, 266, 282, 286
Covarrubias, Miguel, 208–9
Covarrubias, Rosa, 209
The Cry, 248
Currier, Ruth, 160–61, 162, 166, 167, 169, 170, 179, 181–82, 188, 201, 206, 207, 215, 216, 217, 221, 231–33
Curtis, Martha, 278, 283, 284
Cycle of the Masses (Koner), 789
Czaja, Michael, 153
Czarny, Charles, 167, 169

Dalcroze eurhythmics, 24
Dance Consort, 266, 277–87; disbandment, 287; formation, 278; repertoire, 280, 281–82, 283–85, 286; style, 278; tours and residencies, 281, 285–86, 287
Dance Guild. *See* American Dance Association
Dance Magazine Award, 118, 204, 239, 246–47
Dance of Death, 281
Dance of Longing (Koner), 78, 91, 94
Dance Overture (Humphrey), 186, 221, 222

Library of Congress Cataloging-in-Publication Data
Koner, Pauline.
Solitary song / Pauline Koner.
p.   cm.
Bibliography: p.
Includes index.
ISBN 0-8223-0878-9 (alk. paper)
  1. Koner, Pauline.   2. Dancers—United States—Biography.
3. Modern dance—United States.   I. Title.
GV1785.K596A3   1989
793.3'2'0924—dc19
[B] 89-1546